(De)Mobilizing the Entrepreneurship Discourse

(De)Mobilizing the Entrepreneurship Discourse

Exploring Entrepreneurial Thinking and Action

Edited by

Frederic Bill

Björn Bjerke

Anders W. Johansson

Linnaeus University, Sweden

Edward Elgar

Cheltenham, UK • Northampton, MA, USA

Published by
Edward Elgar Publishing Limited
The Lypiatts
15 Lansdown Road
Cheltenham
Glos GL50 2JA
UK

Edward Elgar Publishing, Inc.
William Pratt House
9 Dewey Court
Northampton
Massachusetts 01060
USA

A catalogue record for this book
is available from the British Library

Library of Congress Control Number: 2009941283

Mixed Sources
Product group from well-managed
forests and other controlled sources
www.fsc.org Cert no. SA-COC-1565
© 1996 Forest Stewardship Council
FSC

ISBN 978 1 84980 145 4

Printed and bound by MPG Books Group, UK

Contents

Figures and tables

FIGURES

TABLES

Contributors

Karin Berglund, Senior Lecturer at Mälardalen University, Västerås, Sweden.

Frederic Bill, Senior Lecturer at Linnaeus University, Växjö, Sweden.

Björn Bjerke, Professor of Entrepreneurship and Small Business at Stockholm University and Visiting Professor of Entrepreneurship at Linnaeus University, Kalmar, Sweden.

Daniel Ericsson, Associate Professor at Linnaeus University, Växjö, Sweden and Visiting Researcher at Stockholm School of Economics, Stockholm, Sweden.

Johan Gaddefors, Associate Professor at the Swedish University of Agricultural Sciences, Uppsala, Sweden.

Henrik Hultman, PhD candidate (sociology) at Linnaeus University, Växjö, Sweden.

Andreas Jansson, Senior Lecturer at Linnaeus University, Växjö, Sweden.

Bengt Johannisson, Professor of Entrepreneurship at Linnaeus University, Växjö and at Jönköping International Business School, Sweden.

Anders W. Johansson, Professor of Entrepreneurship at Linnaeus University, Växjö and Visiting Professor at Mälardalen University, Västerås, Sweden.

Shelley Lin, entrepreneur and PhD candidate at National Sun Yat-Sen University, Kaohsiung, Taiwan.

Katja Lindqvist, Research Fellow at Linnaeus University, Växjö, Sweden.

Pernilla Nilsson, PhD candidate at Umeå University, Sweden.

Lena Olaison, PhD candidate at Copenhagen Business School, Denmark.

Erik Rosell, Lecturer and PhD candidate at Linnaeus University, Växjö, Sweden.

Foreword

Daniel Hjorth and Chris Steyaert

When we set out in 2001 to initiate a new movement in entrepreneurship studies, we hoped to prevent the field from settling into an already established discipline. Indeed, 'the field' is still somewhat of an awkward metaphor, and we noted back then that: 'Some suggest that it is only through movement that a space – or a field – can be described or identified. The field of entrepreneurship, indeed, is a number of movements, and this is how we relate to it here' (Steyaert and Hjorth, 2003, p. 11). What we sensed around the turn of the millennium was precisely the gradual loss of movement, of energy, of intensity. The 'Movements' book series (Steyaert and Hjorth, 2003; Hjorth and Steyaert, 2004; Steyaert and Hjorth, 2006; Hjorth and Steyaert, 2007) became our response to this – our response to the potential loss of movement.

This endeavour for 'powering up the field', for infusing colleagues, journals, books, conferences with the energy and urge to move, was sketched along some line of thinking that we still find pertinent. In order to move from the past and to counter stabilization, we saw it as crucial:

1. to keep open a space for reflecting, that is, what we would now describe as reflexivity;
2. to stress the need to multiply entrepreneurship;
3. to intensify and connect entrepreneurship (develop communities);
4. to experiment, radicalize and move entrepreneurship.

This, we imagined, would result in a number of possible movements:

1. to remove obstacles and to move into new directions;
2. we would become moved, in the sense of passion and play;
3. we would need to create movements, in the sense of organizing collectives;
4. and we would place emphasis on the momentum of the process, embrace the processual, and start asking what entrepreneurship could become.

This was and remains a highly ambitious programme, if we can call the 'Movements' series such. As for its main qualities, we would like to manifest principles and parameters of entrepreneurship studies to come.

It strikes us now that the book you hold in your hands could well be described as being responsive to our call to look at the movements and to enable new manifestations of these movements. We do not write this in the manner of the strategist who seeks to appropriate a space of their own – movements of entrepreneurship have indeed to be considered as the result of very open and collective efforts – but rather as colleagues engaged in a movement, affected by its latest contribution, we are enjoying to see how the movements alter and take surprising shapes. As first readers, we can tell future readers that this book is worthwhile plunging into to find out how it changes what we imagine the entrepreneurship discourse can create and what it cannot do.

In this sense, we still believe it is correct to describe our collective effort as one of resisting the majority (Hjorth and Steyaert, 2009). Our project was, from the start, one of the minority's: we wanted to create a series of books that:

> should perhaps be described as a transformative insinuation, a tactical move, trying to make use of the dominant strategy of the field at the time: to locate its boundaries, define its concepts, appropriate a place in the world of business schools. The book series was thought of as one contribution to remedy this tendency to strategize a place by trying to argue for keeping the adolescence of entrepreneurship, for staying with its child-like curiosity and playfulness, keeping the language of minoritarians, staying on the move. (Hjorth and Steyaert, 2009, p. 1)

If we maintain that we are operating in a minority of entrepreneurship studies – which is not a reference to the number of people that constitutes 'us' in this case, but rather describes the mode of engagement with entrepreneurship as discourse (to speak with this book) – the question vis-à-vis this book is how it changes the minority by its publication. We may ask like the poet what is made possible, what is opened up; or, what kind of people to come is imagined in this book? We may inquire into its political possibilities: What does it interfere with? What does it try to alter? What ethics does it propose?

We acknowledge that we might inevitably come across as possessive as we implicitly limit this present book to a function in a minority discourse that we see energized by the 'Movements' book series. Obviously this is not the whole story. Even as we, for reasons of limited space, focus on our own contributions, it is obvious, as Steyaert has shown (2007) and we have also indicated elsewhere (Hjorth et al., 2008; Hjorth, 2008), that several forces have operated to move the field of entrepreneurship, including process thinking, qualitative methodology, and an emphasis on creative and contextual approaches in entrepreneurship. Furthermore, the critical position inscribed in the 'Movements' book series can be positioned in a much broader and emerging community of critical scholars that destabilizes what can be called entrepreneurship studies. As a consequence, critical, feminist, poststructuralist and postcolonial theory has moved into and will continue to interrupt theoretical analyses of entrepreneurship, which becomes questioned, critiqued and unmasked. There is thus a critical-affirmative force that interferes with the proliferation of the entrepreneurship discourse as a grand narrative (Weiskopf and Steyaert, 2009).

The present book – *(De)Mobilizing the Entrepreneurship Discourse* – carries a clear reference to the politics of moving the field of entrepreneurship studies by taking a critical stance on how entrepreneurship discourse has been mobilized, as well as by investing in other versions of framing entrepreneurship practices. Although the book is explicitly related to the 'Movements' series, what we wish its readers is to grasp is how its multiplication of entrepreneurship demobilizes many taken-for-granted assumptions of the entrepreneurship discourse, and mobilizes entrepreneurship in novel ways.

1. Demobilizing or mobilizing the entrepreneurship discourse: something else or none of it?

Frederic Bill, Björn Bjerke and Anders W. Johansson

Data never speak for themselves. Words say more than just a constellation of letters do. When communicating a language we try to transfer meaning by employing systems of culturally determined arbitrary labels (Saussure, 1916/1977). The mechanics of meaning has been approached in different ways. Derrida (1976/1998) has argued that meaning arises from the position of a word within the confinements of a system of words, thereby creating endless chains of deferred textual meaning. Since words are defined from their differences vis-à-vis one another, meaning becomes effectively elusive. Others have argued that meaning resides not in the difference between words, but rather in the nature and design of a system in which a certain word is included (Lévi-Strauss, 1945). Thus meaning stems from positions within a structural system rather than from any qualities inherent to a word or phenomenon. However, no matter how the words of a language are loaded with content, when confronting them we are lured into a specific mode of thinking. Regardless of whether this is intentional from the sender's point of view, thinking in a specific way makes us prone to act in a particular way. Thus, words and the meaning we ascribe to them affect the way we perceive and act within our everyday world.

We can make a distinction between everyday language and scientific language (and phenomenologists, in particular, make such a distinction). They are used in different contexts. However, they are both related to thinking and action, even if for different purposes. And all languages are part of what is referred to as discourses, that is, different praxis in communication, governed by (often implicit) rules. However, in general, discourses deliver not only a style of communication, but also a way of thinking – and, in extension, of action – in our everyday life as well as in our scientific endeavours, implying, to use the words of Fairclough, that:

1

'specific discursive events vary in their structural determination according to the particular social domain or institutional framework in which they are generated' (1992, p. 64). Thus, as we insert the ideas of mobilization and demobilization into a discursive framework, we also discursively frame the meaning to be allocated to the words and actions of (de)mobilization (cf. Foucault, 1969/1977).

Using an artistic discourse, we are supposed to think and act artistically. Using an economic discourse, we are supposed to think and act economically. The economic discourse is a strong discourse – it has heavily influenced society. Even if the role of the entrepreneur has not always been a self-evident part of economic theory (Adam Smith thought the principal role of the economy was performed by the capitalist, while he was silent about the entrepreneur), he (the entrepreneur used to appear as a man) was recognized by classical economists (for example, Jean Baptiste Say). In modern times, the economist Joseph Schumpeter (1883–1950) attributed to the entrepreneur what is often seen as the most important of all roles in connection with economic development. While the entrepreneur, according to Schumpeter, brought disequilibrium to the market and thereby changed the economy at a macro level, the same creature has after Schumpeter come to be equated with new, small and growing firms. The latter idea has been adopted to the extent that policy-makers design governmental initiatives to 'pick the winners', which means the promotion of very fast-growing firms ('gazelles'). Not only policy-makers, but also private companies use the strategy to elect the 'entrepreneur of the year'. Thus we witness a very strong alliance between the economic discourse and the entrepreneurship discourse. However, in recent years the signs of exaggerations or a lost balance are at hand. A very illustrative case is provided in this book (Chapter 9) of an 'Entrepreneur of the Year' who turned out to be a complete 'bluff'.

The example of Schumpeter (1934/2000) is somewhat illustrative, since what we are trying to do with this book is to revisit an idea that has basically been forgotten in entrepreneurship research. Due to the semantic principles described by Saussure (1916/1977), Derrida (1976/1998) and Lévi-Strauss (1945/1963), we are so accustomed to thinking in terms of differences and dichotomies that we tend to be blind to the interplay between seeming opposites. Through the strong connection to the economic discourse, our general understanding of entrepreneurship has been tilted to an angle that hides its dual nature as both creator and destructor from our view. To mobilize entrepreneurship is seldom questioned and prizes are instituted to celebrate the mobilizer (Bill, 2006) but the force of demobilization instituted as creative destruction by Schumpeter (1934/2000) is more seldom publicly appreciated. It is, rather, considered a serious problem when industries and big companies falter and are pushed to the verge of eradication.

However, even if the entrepreneurship discourse has been and still is dominated by its coalition with the economic discourse, in recent years we have witnessed its broadening. In this book (Chapter 6) this is referred to as different situations where entrepreneurship takes place and occupies space. It is situated in business and markets but also in institutions and public places outside the market. This book therefore follows in the footsteps of the Movements of Entrepreneurship series of books edited by Chris Steyaert and Daniel Hjorth (Steyaert and Hjorth, 2003; Hjorth and Steyaert, 2004; Steyaert and Hjorth, 2006; Hjorth and Steyaert, 2007) and responds to the call made by Steyaert and Katz (2004, p. 192) to reclaim the space of entrepreneurship to include the many new variations of entrepreneurship (social, cultural, civic, ecological, and so on) that have been included in the entrepreneurship discourse in recent years.

Furthermore, this broadening of entrepreneurship research has also opened up possibilities to challenge the one-sidedness and explore the interplay between mobilization and demobilization. Beyes (2006), for instance, in exploring the use of old Eastern bloc monumental buildings by contemporary artists, offers one way of perceiving how demobilizing is often simultaneously an act of mobilizing. By reinterpreting the building and changing its use, the former character of the building is slowly eradicated. As something is brought into existence, something else is brought out of existence. As words and concepts are moved along their lines of flight (cf. Deleuze and Guattari, 1988), they bump into one another, leaving marks and scratches that will subsequently follow them into the future. In this volume the focus is to highlight a number of such scratches that we believe will bear witness to numerous past bumps as well as some lingering interconnections.

Those who have contributed to this book (all, with one exception, from Sweden) have specific opinions about the entrepreneurship discourse, what it is and what it should be, opinions which have been honed mainly from doing research on entrepreneurs and entrepreneurship and their environments in European settings. The title of the book, therefore, calls for an initial declaration of what we mean by the term 'mobilizing' as well as 'demobilizing'. The initial call for contributions to the book contained the following paragraph:

> The proposed anthology 'Mobilizing the Entrepreneurship Discourse' takes as point of departure the assumption that all human beings have an inherent entrepreneurial potential. This entrepreneurial potential is naturally released in the interplay between individuals if it is not prevented. Therefore entrepreneurial

behaviour can be seen when children are playing. That is unless the rules of the game prevent entrepreneurial potential from being exercised and released.

This formulation caused a quite intensive debate among the potential contributors in relation to two issues. The first was about the term 'mobilizing'. For some, mobilizing was a metaphor for war (notice Chapter 10 and the references to the 'war machine'), while for others mobilizing referred to a more common meaning of getting something to move. These discussions brought to the surface the ambiguous implications of the entrepreneurship discourse: whether entrepreneurship implies something good or something bad for society. We argue that the entrepreneurship discourse, by and large, is dominated by the idea that entrepreneurship is inherently good, and this assumption is therefore usually not questioned and discussed. In this book you will find different nuances among the contributors about this issue. In doubtful cases the tendency is rather to divert interest to other phenomena. Bankrupt companies are seldom seen as the consequence of entrepreneurial mobilization somewhere else. Instead, individual scapegoats and systemic problems are sought for. Maybe this is because the consequences of creative destruction through demobilization are too painful to celebrate, or maybe because our hero according to the discursive script ought not to cause unemployment and insecurity. It might even be that the predominant and taken-for-granted discourses have caused us to believe that entrepreneurs should develop and improve our world rather than actually change it. In this book you will find different nuances among the contributors about this issue. The following eight chapters do not take for granted that entrepreneurship is either good or bad but hold that potentially it can be both. However, regardless of whether we think that entrepreneurship ought to be promoted or demoted, the need for understanding the character of its multifaceted discourse will not diminish. In the various parts of the book, the centre of attention shifts to some extent.

Chapters 2–5 come under the part title 'Demobilizing the entrepreneurship discourse'. These chapters have in common that they account for processes that on the surface appear to promote entrepreneurship as a phenomenon and/or are in line with the ruling entrepreneurship discourse. What appear initially as successful or praiseworthy initiatives are shown to lead to failure or could on other grounds be questioned as to where they lead or what they were meant to lead to. Two of the chapters are concerned with the direct promotion of entrepreneurship in the sense of starting and developing new firms and/or encouraging individuals to enter the role of an enterpriser alone or together with others. As is illustrated in these two chapters there seems to be an inherent contradiction between the role of helping the (potential) entrepreneur and the role of the entrepreneur, as the latter is expected to enact entrepreneurship on his or her own terms.

The two other chapters in this group illustrate the enactment of entrepreneurship which appears as successful. In one the initial success is however turned into failure. This failure is related to the structures of society which appear not to be able to bear or benefit from innovative and creative individuals. The second chapter is, by comparison, an ongoing success story about a woman entrepreneur. Still, the ambiguities of dressing oneself in the suit of the entrepreneur are made visible as an open process, a process where the clothes of the traditional profit-seeking business appear as too tight.

Chapters 2–5 thus have in common that they illustrate that the entrepreneurship discourse does not work as it is. The entrepreneurship discourse is in that sense demobilized; on good grounds it can be questioned whether it promotes change in society in the sense of opening new locations for entrepreneurship to take place, at least not before it is altered or modified. From here Chapters 6–9 follow on. These four chapters are united by arguing for a modification of the entrepreneurial discourse. The awareness of space and place has been lost in the entrepreneurship discourse and need to be reconquered (Chapter 6).The inevitable and dynamic relation between imitation and creativity for innovation to take place needs to be revalued in order to mobilize entrepreneurship as a potential among all men and women (Chapter 7). Resistance to change is not something that hinders entrepreneurship but is rather an inherent part of the entrepreneurial process, which means that resistance to change is necessary for structures to be changed (Chapter 8). The spectacular aspect of entrepreneurship, which today seems to be the most visible, needs to be balanced by the mundane side (Chapter 9).

Together Chapters 6–9 argue for modifications of the entrepreneurship discourse if this discourse is to mobilize entrepreneurship in order to change society. The underlying assumption is that the entrepreneurship discourse as it stands today works as a conservative power rather than a power that works for renewal. The critique of the entrepreneurship discourse as conservative has already been made explicit elsewhere (Ogbor, 2000), while these chapters take steps to modify the discourse.

The book could have ended with Chapter 9, but it does not. In Chapter 10 it is argued that the entrepreneurship discourse acts as a war machine colonizing all that stands in its way. The right question to ask therefore is whether it is possible to find a place (or space) of peace outside this discourse, where individuals can avoid being classified as entrepreneurs or non-entrepreneurs, as either good or bad for the society. A case is provided – Aquarian Nation – which is argued not (yet) to be part of the entrepreneurship discourse. This means a place not for conflict but for 'constellations of another other'. This place might of course appear as Utopia, given that we accept that the entrepreneurship discourse is so strong that we are all consumed by it (cf. Foucault's ideas about the discourse of sexuality; Foucault, 1990). However, even if we here are approaching Utopia, the chapter balances other chapters of this book by looking for a position outside the entrepreneurship discourse. If this position is utopian, then the question is surely legitimate to ask.

Further, the book could have ended with Chapter 10, but it does not. The author of Chapter 11 argues frankly that whether to mobilize or demobilize entrepreneurship discourse is the wrong question. Looking at the behaviour of children, the conclusion is that by nature they are entrepreneurs. Here we touch upon the second issue that caused initial discussions among the potential contributors to this book, as to whether we should idealize the behaviour of (innocent) children or not. It is therefore interesting to notice that while the other chapters in this book build their arguments mostly on single cases, this chapter provides qualitative as well as quantitative research as a basis for the argumentation. Further, while the power of discourse is put in the front seat in the first ten chapters, this last chapter recognizes socio-biological forces to have a stronger impact than discursive forces on human beings as entrepreneurial selves. By these means the last chapter of this book provides a healthy counterbalance to the preceding chapters while still relating to entrepreneurial enactment in the broad sense, which means to recognize the entrepreneurial potential of all individuals to appear as entrepreneurs in numerous locations within society.

In a multitude of ways this book also asks again and again the rather unsettling question: What if there are no soaring entrepreneurs above us? What if it is up to us?

PART I: DEMOBILIZING THE ENTREPRENEURSHIP DISCOURSE, . . .

Chapter 2, 'Constructing P(e)ace-makers for Women's Enterprise', by Pernilla Nilsson

This chapter is about 'Ambassadors for Women's Enterprise', initiated nationwide by one Swedish government agency. The ambition is to interpret critically the entrepreneurship discourse among government officials in Sweden. The conclusion is that the signifiers 'woman', 'entrepreneur' and 'ambassador' will evoke quite different meanings, due to the way 'subject' is understood. The identities of the Ambassadors in question are discussed in three metaphors: (1) the embassy – an ace-maker? (2) the embassy – a pace-maker; and (3) the embassy – a peace-maker?

Chapter 3, 'Creating the Collective Hero: Stories of Cooperative Development', by Erik Rosell and Henrik Hultman

This chapter uses actor-network theory. It discusses a number of cases where a Swedish public agency, called Coompanion, aims at supporting the cooperation between small and medium-sized enterprises (SMEs). This frame of reference is used in order to elaborate on a perspective that emphasizes the collective effort of alliances of actors when objectives are acted upon. The purpose is to write a contrasting story to the one that is still argued to be tainted by a heroic view of the individual actors involved in development processes. The contribution of the support service organization in relation to the objectives of those they set out to support is interpreted based on this collective perspective. The conclusion is that we can understand it in terms of the creation of a collective hero.

Chapter 4, 'Seeds Germinate in Nature, Humans Gleam in Cities: An Exploring Expedition of Incorporating "City Management" Knowledge', by Shelley Lin and Anders W. Johansson

This chapter is about the identity of a Taiwanese PhD candidate when becoming an entrepreneur in her own country as provider of development training programmes to her city, which aims at acquiring better international affairs skills. In interaction with others in Taiwanese academies she set up a Southern Cultural Innovation Salon. She looks at herself as a good coordinator and integrator, but felt that her spontaneity did not fit with the ruling entrepreneurship discourse, nor with her role as a women in that context.

Chapter 5, 'Entrepreneurial Successes and Failures in the Arts', by Katja Lindqvist

This chapter is about the problem of applying the entrepreneurship discourse in the field of the arts: in general, the difficult relationship between entrepreneurship and the arts. Entrepreneurs (in the field of the arts) may encounter difficulties with their own success as their enterprises go from an initial phase to an established phase, and pressures to manage in the longer term begin to be felt by both management and the board of the studied organization. Visionary leadership as part of the entrepreneurship discourse can sometimes be seen as contrary to management of an enterprise.

This may express itself as a tension between the principal actors, in particular when long-term financing, stability, priorities and orientation of activities are concerned. The discussion of the chapter is based on three cases from the arts venture arena.

PART II: . . . MOBILIZING THE ENTREPRENEURSHIP DISCOURSE, . . .

Chapter 6, 'Entrepreneurship, Space and Place', by Björn Bjerke

This chapter contains a discussion of entrepreneurship in three different types of situations in the society of today, that is, market situations, common situations and social situations, in terms of space and place (where 'situation' can be interpreted as space, place or both). Market situations are seen as mainly space-based, social situations as mainly place-based, and common situations as space-based as well as place-based. Furthermore, in the same terminology of space and place, two phenomena related to entrepreneurship, that is, networking and social capital, and urban and regional development, are discussed as well. The general conclusion is that the entrepreneurship discourse would gain from being equipped with the conceptual pair of space and place.

Chapter 7, 'Innovation, Creativity and Imitation', by Anders W. Johansson

This chapter starts from the prevalent assumption in society that innovations and creativity are valued higher than imitation. However, this is a questionable constructive assumption. The entrepreneurship discourse has, by and large, incorporated ideas that go against the potential of every man and woman as an innovator. However, by discussing a number of cases, looking at innovation as an everyday phenomenon, the chapter suggests: (1) permitting and encouraging the creativity capacity which exists in every human being without focusing creativity (or innovation); (2) encouraging the followers, not only the innovators. They are both crucial in the entrepreneurial processes.

Chapter 8, 'Entrepreneurship Requires Resistance to be Mobilized', by Karin Berglund and Johan Gaddefors

This chapter aims at discussing the fact that resistance is not normally included in the entrepreneurship discourse. The basic question is: What role does resistance play in entrepreneurial processes? The discussion circles around one major case in the text. The authors assert that by adding more of the notion of resistance and power (in the Foucault sense of it), new questions could be raised about what it means to do entrepreneurship in everyday life. By adding these terms to the entrepreneurship discourse, new understanding of entrepreneurship will follow not only in theory, but also in practice.

Chapter 9, 'The Spectacle of Entrepreneurship: A Duality of Flamboyance and Activity', by Frederic Bill, Andreas Jansson and Lena Olaison

This chapter starts from two different, seemingly unrelated events; that is, first, the European Commission's announcement that one ambition should be to create a Europe that is competitive and creative; and second, a well published case of a huge entrepreneurial fake. One may ask: What has spectacle to do with entrepreneurship? The spectacular side of entrepreneurship does not seem to have much connection to the mundane everydayness of entrepreneurial activity. On the contrary, this chapter claims that the belief in entrepreneurship as both spectacular (entrepreneurship-as-spectacle) and mundane (entrepreneurship-as-function) will mobilize entrepreneurship.

PART III: . . . SOMETHING ELSE . . .

Chapter 10, 'Constellations of Another Other: The Case of Aquarian Nation', by Daniel Ericsson

This chapter uses the theories of the 'philosopher of difference' and the remorselessly 'horizontal thinker', Gilles Deleuze. For him there is always another 'and'. It discusses his 'war machine' in order to come up with alternative constellations of entrepreneurship; that is, to demobilize existing entrepreneurship discourse deconstructively and present alternative constellations of entrepreneurship. The presented Aquarian Nation could be conceptualized as 'something else'.

PART IV: . . . OR NONE OF IT?

Chapter 11 'In the Beginning was Entrepreneuring', by Bengt Johannisson

This chapter focuses 'entrepreneurship' not so much in thinking as in action, that is, starting from the basic fact that human beings are by nature entrepreneurial. This is seen, above all, among children. To ask about 'Mobilizing or demobilizing the entrepreneurship discourse' is with such a focus the wrong question, because that would be about mobilizing or demobilizing life itself. According to this chapter, children are, 'by nature', entrepreneuring. The important issue is therefore how we can prevent ourselves from stopping them remaining so, in particular through our formal school system. The chapter is a reflection upon the findings of two empirical studies of child creativity. The basic question is whether the compulsory schooling encourages, remains indifferent to or even counteracts the entrepreneurial force that children obviously accommodate.

DEMOBILIZING AND MOBILIZING ASPECTS OF THE ENTREPRENEURSHIP DISCOURSE IN THE BOOK

Demobilizing aspects of the entrepreneurship discourse in the book include:

- Forget the idea that there is one single type of entrepreneur, one single entrepreneurial personality and one single best way of entrepreneuring.
- Do not take for granted that entrepreneurship always is a positive thing.
- Entrepreneurship is not only a matter of economic growth.
- Do not keep entrepreneurship as a predominantly male-gender issue.
- It is not to be taken for granted that government officials have an exclusive, or an entirely correct, opinion of what entrepreneurship is and could be. The same goes for consultants.
- Entrepreneurship is very much a matter of metaphorical thinking. Be careful about which metaphors to use when trying to think and act entrepreneurially.
- Demolish the hero focus on entrepreneurs.
- Entrepreneurs often feel they do not fit into the existing entrepreneurship discourse.
- Actors around entrepreneurs may sometimes be more important for entrepreneurial success than the entrepreneurs themselves.
- There is a distinct difference between the entrepreneurship discourse and the management discourse.

Mobilizing aspects of the entrepreneurship discourse in the book include:

- Entrepreneurship belongs to the whole society, not only to its economy.
- Several entrepreneurship discourses are needed.
- Entrepreneurs function as role models for other entrepreneurs in a very intricate way.
- Artifacts can be important parts of the entrepreneurial life.
- Entrepreneurial narratives play many different roles, not just telling a story.
- The cultural aspects of entrepreneurship should not be forgotten.
- Entrepreneurial success may be an obstacle to future development of the entrepreneur(s) involved.
- Resistance may be an important aspect in order to understand entrepreneurs themselves as well as their success and failures.
- Entrepreneurship is very much a mundane activity, not just a spectacle.
- Entrepreneurship is as much about imitation as about creativity.
- Space and place can be an interesting conceptual pair with which to discuss entrepreneurship.

More general aspects of the entrepreneurship discourse in the book include:

- There are different ways of demobilizing and mobilizing the entrepreneurship discourse, some more oriented to genuine differences than others.
- Entrepreneurship is not only a discourse in words; it is also a way of life in action.

PART I

Demobilizing the Entrepreneurship
Discourse, . . .

2. Constructing p(e)ace-makers for women's enterprise

Pernilla Nilsson

Go out in the world, but you can start with Sweden. Spread your experience, your joy, and your knowledge. We will see to it that many women are mentioned when women enterprisers are asked for, and not just a few. Thanks for taking part in this! (Maud Olofsson, the Swedish Minister of Enterprise and Energy, speech at the inauguration of the Embassy for Women's Enterprise, 23 May 2008, in Stockholm)

The Foucauldian in me says there is no one site from which to struggle effectively. There have to be many, and they don't need to be reconciled with one another. (Judith Butler interviewed by Peter Osborne in A Critical Sense: Interviews with Intellectuals (1996, p. 123)

INTRODUCTION

With an Embassy we can widen our involvement and achieve synergies when it comes to politics, assistance, defense and culture, et cetera. There is a lot to do and we are very enthusiastic about the task, while at the same time we have great respect for it.

The quote comes from Svante Kilander, the Swedish Ambassador in Afghanistan, commenting upon the inauguration of the Swedish Embassy in Kabul, 31 October 2008. Due to the political circumstances in this region, the inauguration was not officially announced. The fact that Carl Bildt, the Swedish Minister of Foreign Affairs, was on his way to Kabul to take part in the event, was kept a 'top secret' until his arrival (Swedish Ministry of Foreign Affairs, 2008).[1]

At the time when I read about the inauguration in Kabul, I was involved in writing about quite another embassy; initially, an embassy very different from the one presented in a vocabulary of 'top secrecy', 'international peace support and humanitarian operations', which is used by the Swedish Ministry of Foreign Affairs.[2]

Embassy for Women's Enterprise

The embassy that caught my interest was a governmental measure with the overall purpose of inspiring women's enterprise. In 2007 the Swedish government allocated SEK300 million to promote such enterprise[3] over a period of three years. Alongside the measure a two-year project of 880 so-called 'Ambassadors for Women's Enterprise' was initiated in 2008 by the Swedish Agency for Economic and Regional Growth (NUTEK).

In the press release, the Minister of Enterprise, Energy and Communication, Maud Olofsson, stated that: 'The Ambassadors come from all parts of Sweden and represent a wide variety of branches. The Ambassadors' role is to inspire women by sharing their stories and experiences as entrepreneurs. Each Ambassador is encouraged to at least four times a year speak in schools, universities, different networks and so on.'[4]

The Ambassadors got some publicity during the selection process, and the inauguration of the Embassy held in May 2008 was mentioned in the Swedish media (Jacobsson, 2008). Selected Ambassadors were presented in the local press (for example, Smålandsposten, 2008b). Thus, there was no sign of secrecy about the Embassy for Women's Enterprise. And it does not seem to require much in the way of security operations, or careful management of dangerous liaisons, although a widened involvement to create synergies when it comes to 'politics', 'assistance', 'defense' and 'culture', as expressed by Kilander in the earlier quote in this chapter, would indeed appeal to the field of women's enterprise as well.

On the one hand, it could be stated that this measure fits very well within a discourse insisting on entrepreneurship and enterprise as unquestionable means of organizational (as well as societal) reform (du Gay et al., 1996; du Gay, 2004; Perren and Jennings, 2005). It is widely held to be important in the discussion on regional development and economic growth, and it is no exaggeration to state that the 'entrepreneurship discourse' is prospering (for example, Ogbor, 2000; Perren and Jennings, 2005). At this time of early recession, the expectations of its vitality are spelled out more than ever before.

As an initiative within the realm of governmental policies on entrepreneurship and enterprise, there have been more than fifteen years of 'promotion' of regional development programmes, employment programmes and business support programmes, programmes focusing on women and entrepreneurship, most of them run particularly by NUTEK together with regional agencies like Almi, and Coompanion (for example, chapter 3 by Rosell and Hultman in this book) as well as networks and coordinators (for example, Nilsson, 1997; Johansson, 2008a).

On the other hand, many years of studies focusing on the gendered aspects of entrepreneurship, starting up a firm, running and developing the business (Holmquist and Sundin, 1989), counselling services according to these processes (Nilsson, 1997) and the stereotypes that constitute (and are constituted by) the entrepreneurship discourse (for example, Ahl, 2002; Pettersson, 2002; Berglund, 2007), still demand that we be cautious about the taken-for-granted views on entrepreneurship. Thus, the task of promoting women's entrepreneurship, and challenging the gendered notions of it, is by no means a new one, neither in a Swedish public policy context, nor in research. But there still seem to be reasons to continue the work.

The Embassy: Yet Another Measure?

In inspiring the interlocutors with their views on entrepreneurship in general, and by sharing the narratives of their own experiences in business specifically, the Embassy and its Ambassadors can be seen as yet another measure supporting women's entrepreneurship. But as such, it is not only cherished within the entrepreneurship discourse. Although responses to measures directed to women by participants involved in the projects have been positive in many ways (for example, Nilsson, 1997; NUTEK, 1996, 1998a, 1998b), critique has been raised too. One of the recent examples that claim the end of 'inspiration campaigns' is offered by Renstig et al., 2008: 'Year after year inspiration campaigns have covered the lack of concrete measures. Of one hundred women inspired to start a business only two start. It isn't better than ten or twenty years ago.'

Not only is the result of the measures questioned, but the messenger is also scrutinized. Perren and Jennings (2005, p. 177) refer to websites of agencies for small businesses in six countries,[5] stating that: 'The Government is portrayed as having the right to impose its wishes and desires upon others, irrespective of the freedom of others to pursue, or at least to prioritize, their personal aspirations.' This is a critique that often comes together with statements concerning the one-sided, causal relation between governmental support and entrepreneurs' potential to achieve their goals, where the 'pragmatic/normative' view of business advice, as articulated by Anders W. Johansson (1997), dominates the governmental support (see also Hjalmarsson and Johansson, 2003). Thus the advisor, presented as an expert, relates to the client as in need of advice, whether he or she actually asks for it or not. Consequently, it is not seldom argued that it is important to call attention to the governments' discourses on entrepreneurship as well as on the targeted clients' dependencies constituted by policy programmes. In this regard, Perren and Jennings's study is no exception, claiming that the 'voice of small business' is a discourse of (un)representation that subjugates entrepreneurs so they become voice-less and are treated as dependents that must be spoken for like the worse portrayal of children' (ibid., p. 180).

Although governmental policies on entrepreneurship have been widely studied, the interest has been focused on scrutinizing the issue of working 'more effectively within their shared paradigm' (Perren and Jennings, 2005, p. 174), rather than to critically interpreting the entrepreneurship discourse constituting the services. Thus, the overall purpose of this chapter is to elaborate critically upon the (de)mobilizing potential of a governmental measure within the prevailing entrepreneurship discourse, highlighting the metaphorical signifiers of the measure at hand: the Embassy, the Ambassadors and the diplomatic relations.

I do not intend to analyse what the Ambassadors actually do, or to evaluate whether their conduct is relevant or misdirected according to the set goal of inspiring female enterprising. My interest rather concerns the Embassy as an overall metaphor for governmental measures directed to such enterprising. Interpreting what the signifiers according to the Embassy could contribute, within conversations on the entrepreneurship discourse, is a central task.

In the first section to follow, an intertextual reading is presented, relat-ing the Embassy for Women's Enterprise to its constituted counterpart, the Swedish embassies and the ambassadors regulated according to the Vienna Convention on Diplomatic Relations. There are certain similari-ties, although the Embassy for Women's Enterprise seems to be inaugu-rated with less of the most explicit symbol of traditional ambassadors' work, its signifying prestige. Then, the measure is presented in more detail. NUTEK's newsletter *New Tempo Special*, presenting the inauguration of the Embassy and the prerequisites for the Ambassadors' commission, is used as the material to be interpreted. Viewing subjection as a simultane-ous process of subjugation and recognition, the Embassy for Women's Enterprise is then critically interpreted according its possibilities to (de)mobilize the entrepreneurship discourse. The discussion is concluded by a metaphorical playing with words, interpretations of governmental interpellation of the Ambassadors.

SIMILES OF COMMISSION

One could firstly maintain that the approximately 100 Swedish embas-sies around the world could hardly refer to any one single model for comparison with the one promoting women's enterprising. Embassies are characterized by different conditions, according to practical key issues like bilateral relations between Sweden and other states, and European Union (EU) membership conditioning the relations between EU countries. Also, prerequisites regarding how Sweden could both contribute to and benefit from these different kinds of relations differ, due to the very idea of 'developing friendly relations among nations' according to the Vienna Convention on Diplomatic Relations from 1964.[6]

On the other hand, the commission of an embassy is highly institutionalized, and regulated according to the Conventions. Besides the many articles defining the 'rules of the game' of diplomatic missions that occur 'by mutual consent',[7] privileges connected to the 'head of mission' and the staff are also regulated. In Article 41 it is stated that: 'Without prejudice to their privileges and immunities, it is the duty of all persons enjoying such privileges and immunities to respect the laws and regulations of the receiving State. They also have a duty not to interfere in the internal affairs of the State.' Hence, one could conclude from the Vienna Convention on Diplomatic Relations that an embassy's relations with the receiving state are built upon mutual sovereignty. The Ambassador is accepted, as long as he or she does not mess with institutionalized ideas, or in other ways try to interfere with circumstances regulated by the receiving state.

At first sight, it might seem quite odd to relate an 'embassy' aiming to support women's enterprise in Sweden, an overall domestic issue, to any role-model embassy and its work, which is to a great extent accomplished abroad. So, where could the triggering links, temporarily, manifest themselves between foreign affairs in fragile states of democracy, such as Afghanistan, and the 'state' of the entrepreneurship discourse in the Swedish counties?

One could point to the Ambassadors' high status in society. They are seen as prestigious agents (for example, Due Billing and Alvesson, 1994[8]) sent to a variety of foreign states, privileged with personal and material immunity. Their enterprising counterpart constitutes a wide range of women enterprisers, traditionally not prestigious subjects, if seen as subjects at all. For many years women enterprisers have been in a quest for legitimacy and recognition (for example, Holmquist and Sundin, 1989; Nilsson 1997). Now they are sent on a mission to work with a common 'state' in their home counties, to conquer the supposed tepid interest in entrepreneurship among women. And even if this statement can be refuted (for example, Hedfeldt, 2008), also according to the huge response from women enterprisers wishing to join the commission,[9] the tepid interest is usually referred to the lower percentage of women enterprisers compared with men (and this is also a main argument for initiating measures).

But not everybody has to be convinced that starting up a firm of her own is a good idea – not even when the Ambassador rhetorically asks:

'Isn't that what everybody wants?' (*Smålandsposten*, 2008a).[10] Immunity is also guaranteed for the interlocutors. So, what are the significant constituencies of this specific measure? How are the Ambassadors said to accomplish the main purpose of the Embassy, working in and through 'diplomatic relations'? In the next section, I turn to the documentation of the inauguration of the Embassy for Women's Enterprise, to introduce the governmental measure.

INAUGURATION OF AN EMBASSY FOR WOMEN'S ENTERPRISE

To present the Embassy and the Ambassadors' commissions, a special edition of NUTEK's newsletter on the Web, the *New Tempo Special*, was dedicated to the inauguration of the Embassy held in Stockholm 23 May, 2008.[11] In this newsletter there are many details suitable for interpretation, although some of them seem to be more interesting according to the aim of my study than others. I could legitimize these according to their stated novelty as compared with earlier measures, or turn in the opposite direction, maintaining that this is what is often presented when initiating a governmental measure of this size. Here I draw somewhat more on the latter. In a broad sense, the stated reasons for this measure, that is, how the Embassy, the Ambassadors and the diplomatic relations are articulated in the newsletter, are focused upon here.

The Task

The Embassy's overall purpose is to inspire more women to consider enterprising and to contribute to the knowledge about what enterprising means in practice. In the newsletter the *New Tempo Special*, the Ambassadors' ability to accomplish this is applied directly to the enterpriser: 'In your role as an Ambassador you personify the enterprising, making it possible for more women to identify with an enterpriser. You turn into a role model.'

The 880 Ambassadors are expected to 'do' the Embassy, to paraphrase West and Zimmerman (1987), by personifying the enterprising, and by working on a regional basis. The counties thus turn out to be the counterparts of 'the receiving states' in the language of foreign affairs. In order to communicate their services to the public, the contacts between Ambassadors and their interlocutors are administrated by certain coordinators associated to the activities in the counties. Their task is to facilitate the appointments made with the Ambassadors, and book the meetings, as well to be mediators between NUTEK and the Ambassadors.

The Ambassadors are supposed to work voluntarily on invitations by organizations interested in enterprising (for example, schools, universities, voluntary organizations, networks), or by prompting the occasions of 'inspiring' themselves. They may get requests from the website 'The Embassy', from the coordinators in the regions or from their own networks. The purpose of conducting the task on a voluntary basis is declared in the newsletter by the comparison with a mentor's role: 'A mentor contributes without any expenses on his or her part, with his or her experiences and knowledge, for someone else's development. Correspondingly, an Ambassador wants to contribute to societal progress that makes it evident that both women and men are enterprisers.'

Generally, it is said that the Ambassadors decide themselves what assignments they will accept, but it should be noted that: 'The inquiries will probably be sent to many Ambassadors at the same time; thus it will be the first one who has time, and had announced her interest, who will get the assignment.' It is also stated that 'The ambassadors' assignments are not allowed to warp the competition on the consultancy market'. Although the enterpriser is free to choose any assignment or commission she wants outside the Embassy and its expected six assignments, as well as getting paid for these, the Ambassadors' commission is on a voluntary basis.

A Comment by the Minister

Although the whole newsletter may, in a wider sense, be regarded as 'the voice of the government', or at least its unchallenged prolongation (no critique or serious tensions regarding the task or the ways to conduct it are hinted at in the newsletter), some notes should also be mentioned coming from the Minister of Enterprising, Energy and Communications herself.

Her presence is staged, also in the newsletter. Thus when referring to her entering the conference hall, it is noted that she gets 'the warmest and longest applause' of the day. Markedly touched by the welcome, she says: 'I hadn't thought that you would be so many, and that it would be this mighty to enter this hall'. While wiping away a tear, she says: 'The Swedish people are used to the fact that I do shed some tears sometimes, and I do that when I meet people who, altruistically, spend their time on supporting others. I am so happy that so many of you are doing this.'

The minister underlines the importance of women role models, claiming that: 'diversity is better than stupidity, and that the more who participate in creating wealth, the better. What we do together matters, more people will have the courage to throw themselves out in the lianas!'

The Embassy on the Net

The Embassy is also a digital website, www.nutek.se/ambassaden, where the Ambassadors can communicate on different matters, and where contact can also be made by the public. The forum has two main functions, a blog for each and every Ambassador who wants to communicate her work in this way, and 'wiki-pages' (organized like www.wikipedia.com), where they can put different kinds of material to be stored, supplemented, edited and re-edited, in ways that turn out to be fruitful for the Ambassadors' task.

According to the Chief Executive Officer (CEO) of the company that created the website, www.nutek.se/ambassaden is not an ordinary one. Usually, websites offer a front and a back stage. On the front you can read and follow the information edited by others. But to change the information communicated, a certain password is required. According to the CEO, this site has only a front, making it possible for all users to comment upon it, change it or whatever. This, he says, 'develops the content continually, which makes it better and better'. And it also makes it seem like 'a common white-board, where certain things can be worked out together'.

In conclusion, he states that: 'From the perspective of a public authority, the Embassy is a minor revolution, the way communication occurs . . . What was earlier governed from the top is now replaced by dialogue and co-construction.'

In Need of Rhetoric

One of the speeches at the inauguration of the Embassy deals with rhetoric. The consultant (also an actor) recommends the Ambassadors not to fall into the teacher's role, when entering the classroom in the schools. As a guest in that setting it is a risk to 'put oneself behind the desk, talking, and writing on the blackboard. But the youth is rather tired of that; instead it is more effective to meet them on their part of the ground, and to ask what they want to do.'

The consultant also notices 'a remarkable potential among the youth, not taken care of in the right way today. That is really sad!' he says, and continues: 'The nice thing about being out in the schools, is that it often needs so little to make a great difference. A couple of hours can make the pupils burn again, and the teachers to get the positive spirit back.'

According to the consultant, role models are very important. These are seen as a key to get more women enterprisers. He claims:

Always going on about the fact that there are few women enterprisers may have an opposite effect than what is intended. The very presence of a woman enterpriser in the classroom is saying so much more than a lot of statistics on how few women there are starting business in Sweden – especially as 100 per cent of enterprisers in the classroom are women.

Artefacts for Diplomatic Relations

Some comments should also be made regarding two (gendered) artefacts mentioned in the *New Tempo Special*: the Ambassador's brooch and the Ambassador's briefcase. The brooch was designed by a student at the University College of Arts, Crafts and Design in Stockholm. In the newsletter she says that she started to search for symbols well suited for the Ambassadors' task, ending up with the handshake, symbolizing 'the business settlement', as well as 'the helping hand' according to the service.

To help the Ambassadors pursuing their task, an 'Ambassadors' briefcase' was delivered to them, shortly after the inauguration. The briefcase may not serve as a gendered eye-catcher the way the brooch supposedly can. But it was presented to the Ambassadors in order to 'equip' or to 'arm' them.[12]

The briefcase was said to contain information on the commission, information on the focused target groups, checklists regarding the assignments, and advice on how to relate to the media. It also contained a DVD called '*Fourteen Women, Eleven Businesses*', to be used as good examples in the dialogues with the target groups.

Ambassadors in Enterprise

Finally, some comments in the newsletter refer to the enterprisers themselves, as inaugurated Ambassadors at the Embassy of Women's Enterprise. Their comments are wedged into the text in side columns on the pages of the newsletter, and constitute answers to questions put under headings like: Why did you want to be an Ambassador? Who has been your role model? What do you want to achieve, as an Ambassador? What good is being an enterpriser?[13]

Giving an account of the variety of Ambassadors shown in the newsletter, there are women running their businesses in different regions. They run businesses of different kinds. Also company size seems to differ. The regional selection is, however, somewhat warped in representation. Six presentations out of 14 come from the western part of Sweden, four come from Stockholm. None at all refer to the northern part of Sweden or explicitly rural areas of the country.

Role models that are mentioned include family members, and professional forerunners. Well-known entrepreneurs (for example, Ingvar Kamprad, IKEA) are mentioned, as well as politicians (and among these the Minister of Enterprise, Energy and Communications herself).

Answers to the question why these enterprisers wanted to be an Ambassador are often spelled out in terms of 'giving back' to society, as well as 'giving back' to individual women, inspiring and encouraging them to 'dare' to start a firm of their own. Running a firm is thus said to be fun, and rewarding. Other answers concerning what is good about being an enterpriser refer to the possibility to make your own decisions, and to 'have control over the whole chain', as one enterpriser put it. Another said that '[a]ll that I sow, I can harvest myself',[14] continuing with: 'I also get a direct receipt on whether that which I have decided or started was good or bad'. Being quite tired of previous work, and the hindrances to advancement connected to it, were also reasons mentioned for starting a firm of one's own. All in all, these answers have stood quite firm over the years. To make your own decisions, for good or bad, is often mentioned to be an important reason (for example, Holmquist and Sundin, 1989).

Three presentations in the newsletter stand out. They seem to present the main directions of entrepreneurship measures today: (1) increased focus on entrepreneurship in schools, and the target of 'the troublesome pupils'; (2) 'the immigrant' entrepreneur, exploring diversity and ethnic prejudices; and (3) the 'disabled person' and the support according to problems in this regard. The first mentioned example refers to the Ambassador who explicitly wants to address her work to teachers, claiming that: 'Many pupils that are troublesome in school would in fact be good entrepreneurs'; and she refers to the 'insufficient knowledge about enterprising among teachers today'.

The second example presents the immigrant enterpriser in a suburban district in Stockholm, who wants to get more women immigrants to be enterprisers. She was asked the question: Did you have any role models of your own when starting the firm?[15] The answer was no. Starting a firm was the only way for her to get a job. But she says: 'I knew the industry and that there was a need for the services, so I never hesitated.' It is mentioned that 700 employees obtain their wages from this translator's firm.

The third example is the disabled woman (and her assistance dog). She says:

> I am the only one here who is disabled and who receives personal assistance. I want to promote more disabled women. Unemployment in this group has reached 70%. All cannot be enterprisers but many more can. You can turn a misfortune into prosperity. The limits are often situated in the brain, not in the physical handicap.

This presentation also shows the number of employees. At the time the newsletter was published, her business had 360 employees in five districts.

SUBJECTION OF THE EMBASSY

Theoretically there are many ways to make sense of a phenomenon like the Embassy and its metaphorical signifiers elaborated upon here. 'Ambassadors for Women's Enterprise' will indeed mean different things, due to the theoretical perspectives chosen. Metaphors, as well as the meaning of metaphors chosen, will supposedly change accordingly.

Here I will take a theoretical stance in reflecting on the concept of subjection, as first articulated by Louis Althusser[16] in 'Ideology and ideological state apparatuses' (1970/1971), and then taken up most notably by Judith Butler in *The Psychic Life of Power* (1997a) and *Excitable Speech* (1997b).

Although Butler, as mentioned by Janet Borgerson (2005, p. 66), seldom theorizes organizational life or business as such – she once noted that 'a critique of the market economy is not found in these pages' – this does not mean that a Butlerian reading of issues concerning organizing or entrepreneurship could not be fruitful. Rather it offers a possibility to explore the taken-for-granted views of the neoliberal subject in the conversations on the entrepreneurship discourse. Thus signifiers such as 'woman', 'entrepreneur', and 'ambassador' will evoke quite different meanings, due to the way 'subject' (and subjection) is understood.

I start with the 'voices' expressed by the Ambassadors, and reflections on the 'naïve subject'.

Transforming the Naive Subject

Ambassadors are sent out on a mission, with the focus on their home counties. They are out there crossing borders, but at the same time one could argue that they are 'domesticated' by entrepreneurship ideas, already established in the economy by the Ministry of Enterprise, Energy and Communication, agencies like NUTEK, and thus the entrepreneurship discourse generally (Ogbor, 2000; Perren and Jennings, 2005). One could state that the Ambassadors are going 'home' pleading for something they more or less take for granted; residing in an entrepreneurship-driven 'comfort zone'. When referring to the interest in their commission, the services are mentioned by a coordinator to be 'enormously longed for' (*Smålandsposten* (SMP), 2008b). Thus, they do not have to ask for legitimacy, do they?

Earlier gender studies in entrepreneurship, focusing upon Swedish conditions and the myths around the character (for example, Dareblom, 2005; Javefors Grauers, 2002; as well as my own studies, Nilsson, 1997, 2002), present stories of exclusion, marginality and the lack of legitimacy according to how women's enterprise is understood and treated. And for that matter, how resistance against marginalizing activities might occur (Kurvinen, 2009). At the same time, women entrepreneurs eagerly embrace the idea of 'doing it yourself'. They talk about the opportunities of making their own decisions, and the possibilities to choose 'freedom' instead of 'glass ceilings' connected to hindered advancement in employment, when they are asked to reflect on the conditions of enterprising. In this regard, comments made by the enterprisers acting as Ambassadors for Women's Enterprise reiterate these statements. Neither these nor the governmental presentation of the Embassy challenge the autonomous subject in their expressions. The example mentioned by one of the Ambassadors puts it clearly: 'All that I sow, I can harvest myself', embracing the idea of having 'control of the whole chain' as mentioned by one of her colleagues.

According to Davies et al. (2006, p. 88), [t]he 'neoliberal subject is primarily inscribed with economic discourses of survival/success, and has, as such, a commitment to the national economic project of competition and survival . . . The will to become the new subject is necessarily a personal project taken up in the interests of individual survival.' Nikolas Rose (1999) would probably denote it as an effect of an 'actuarial regime' which, opposed to the ready-made scripts of a bureaucratic one, demands people to adapt flexibly to changed conditions due to their own 'drives' of belonging. This also leads to a new identity politics in the so-called 'post-bureaucratic era', where networking is seen to be more important than fulfilling predefined role descriptions (for example, Maravellias, 2003; Ericsson and Nilsson, 2008).

The transformation of the 'naive subject' has been built on the idea that the subject has to reflect on its own becoming, and thus to challenge its naivety in different ways. But, as Davies et al. (2006, p. 91) states: 'the transforming subject we might become is not the one that can necessarily be pre-programmed, or made immune to new and dominant discourses'. Even in critical discourse analyses the 'entrepreneurial freedom' (for example, Perren and Jennings, 2005) is taken for granted.

But the neoliberal understanding of the subject, and the entrepreneurial subject specifically, is also scrutinized (for example, Ahl, 2002; Ogbor, 2000; Jones and Spicer, 2005; Perren and Jennings, 2005). Thus, it is important to critically elaborate on the issue of agency, especially regarding an embassy, and the Ambassadors acting within the hegemonic entrepreneurship discourse, where processes of subjection most significantly take place, both in constituting the subjects as 'Ambassadors', 'enter-prisers', and 'entrepreneurs', as well as conditioning their possibilities to chose 'freedom' rather than subordination (in accordance with the interests of critical discourse theory as proposed by researchers like Perren and Jennings, 2005), and simultaneously acknowledging that this kind of freedom is severely conditioned, due to its ontological assumptions.

In 'The sublime object of entrepreneurship', Campbell Jones and André Spicer (2005, p. 231), who explicitly draw on Lacan, emphasize that: 'the subject misrecognizes a coherence that represses its fragmented charac-ter'. It appears to be important to elaborate on the colonizing aspects of becoming an entrepreneurial subject, and the subjects who 'never achieves full recognition' (Jones and Spicer, 2005, p. 232), which will force them to keep on becoming.

In her book *The Psychic Life of Power*, Judith Butler (1997a, p. 30) states that: 'we must lose the perspective of a subject already formed in order to account for our own becoming'. According to her: 'becoming is no simple or continuous affair, but an uneasy practice of repetition and its risk, compelled yet incomplete, wavering on the horizon of social being.' In the case of the enterprisers, it is to (partially) recognize an agency like the Embassy and to (partially) be recognized by it (by its governmental founders) as Ambassadors. Ontologically, the subject cannot be under-stood as a given in the dialogues with governmental measures. It should rather be understood as being initiated within these dialogues. So, how can an Ambassador come about?

On Subjection

Butler's reading of Louis Althusser's[17] doctrine of interpellation, presented in his essay 'Ideology and ideological state apparatuses' (1970/1971), invites us to explore the ideological processes that constitute the making of the subject. Althusser illustrated subjection in an allegory (a 'theo-retical scene', a 'little theoretical theatre', are his own metaphors),[18] where a policeman hails a pedestrian in the street, by calling, 'Hey, you there!'[19]

While turning to the policeman, the person is subjected to the soci-etal authority (the dominating ideology, the law, family, any authority connected to the 'state apparatuses') as well as to him- or herself. What occurs is a simultaneous inauguration of the subject, and its subordina-tion to authority conducted by his or her reflexive conscience. Thus the interpellation also involves a 'turning back upon oneself' (Butler, 1997a, p. 115).

In the metaphorical 'turning' the subject is initiated by linguistic means. According to Butler, the 'subject is the linguistic occasion for the individual to achieve and reproduce intelligibility, the linguistic condition of its existence and agency' (ibid., p. 11).

The authoritative voice (of the police, the state, the Church) already has a name, or a category, an institutional sign, ready for those turning to it. Intelligibility is not a process excluded from societal power but, as Butler states, 'it promises identity' (ibid., p. 108).

Without recognizing the authority, there is no possibility of gaining social existence, and legitimacy, as an Ambassador. Disposed by her conscience, she turns, and by the act of turning, she legitimates the hailing itself.

Achieving a Voice (in Subjection)

One ideological aspect of subjection, in Althusser's view, regards skills, where learning a language means: 'not only reproduction of . . . skills, but also the reproduction of its subjection to the ruling ideology or of the "practice" of that ideology' (1970/1971, p. 133). Thus, the better one knows how to use a language, the more one is subjected to its rules. According to Butler this 'is not simply to act according to a set of rules, but to embody rules in the course of action and to reproduce those rules in embodied rituals of action' (1997a, p. 119).

Turning to *Excitable Speech* (1997b) where Butler explicitly draws on J.L. Austin's (1962) speech acts theory, she tries to bridge the theories of Althusser and Austin. But where Althusser inaugurates the subject in interpellation, Austin assumes a subject already in place, making the speech acts that may (or may not) alter meaning.

Following Austin's typology of distinguishing different kinds of speech acts – locutionary speech acts that refer to meaning, illocutionary speech acts that refer to forcing an act as one speaks, and perlocutionary speech acts that refer to 'the achieving of certain effects' (Austin, 1962, p. 120) – it is possible to discern different conditions of change.

Most interesting here are the illocutionary speech acts, also commonly referred to as performatives, that lead to physical acts while being spoken. Most often these are illustrated with examples such as naming (ships), saying 'I do', (in marriage), making a bet (for example, on a horse). Worth noting is that these examples require social presence, in one way or another, and that they are conducted according to social conventions. Saying 'I do' loudly outside its expected setting of the marriage service will not change your civil status.

Althusser's work shows how ideology permeates the constitution of the subject, and refers to naming in a way which is almost impossible to resist. Turning to Austin, Butler also recognizes the vulnerability of being named, being present or not, in an interpellation act. And according to this, she revises it, by stating that: 'The subject need not always turn around in order to be constituted as a subject, and the discourse that inaugurates the subject need not take the form of a voice at all' (Butler, 1997b, p. 31).

In *Excitable Speech* (1997b), which is often said to be a companion text of *Psychic Life* (for example, Disch, 1999), Butler explores the opportunities of political change. Thus, within a language that is not one's own, 'counter-speech' may be a way to oppose the otherwise unchallenged social power in being constituted as someone or something by speech acts.

According to Butler, the perlocutorious speech acts make change possible according to the 'gap' between utterance and effect, giving room for 'talking back' strategies, where illocutorious speech acts make the harm as they are used, and cannot that easily be countered.

ARE THE AMBASSADORS SUBJECTS (TOO)?

The feminist potential in critically 'reading' the measure, interpreting the Embassy as one of the state apparatuses that ideologically constitutes as well as regulates the Ambassadors and the commissions they are supposed to accomplish, leads me to add some comments on the prerequisites to enact change in and through subjection.

Women entrepreneurs are legitimated as Ambassadors in the very expressions of expectations put forward by the Minister of Enterprise, Energy and Communication (such as going out in the world, spreading experiences, and inspiring other women). At the same time they are required to deliver the ready-made speech acts, legitimating their position as Ambassadors.

In her essay 'The end of sexual difference?' (in *Undoing Gender*, 2004) Butler critically scrutinizes the sex difference approach that emphasizes the woman subject, although acknowledging Luce Irigaray's view that gender may well be used as a question of our time:

> As a question, it remains unsettled and unresolved, that which is not yet or not ever formulated in terms of an assertion. Its presence does not assume the form of facts and structures but persists as that which makes us wonder, which remains not fully explained and not fully explicable. (2004, p. 177)

According to Butler, Irigaray offers a critical dimension by the 'echo', constituted by women as self-ascribed subjects. In a 'critical mimesis' Irigaray:

exposes the exclusions by which certain discourses proceed; and she shows that those sites of absence can be mobilized. The voice that emerges 'echoes' the master discourse, but this echo nevertheless establishes that there is a voice, that some articulatory power has not been obliterating, and that it is mirroring the words by which its own obliteration was to have taken place. Something is persisting and surviving, and the words of the master sound different when they are spoken by one who is, in the speaking, in the recitation, undermining the obliterating effects of his claim. (Ibid., p. 201)

Accordingly, reflecting on the issues of women's enterprise means to keep the question open. Thus, rearticulations might enable the Ambassadors to challenge the power of articulation within the entrepreneurship discourse, and within the conversations on that discourse, while equipping themselves with rather conventional artifacts (such as the briefcase and the brooch). Although there are no guarantees of change, no one can be 'pre-programmed, or made immune to new and dominant discourses'; as mentioned before (Davies, 2006, p. 91), there might be hope in rearticulation.

In this last section of the chapter, I will direct the metaphorical interpretation of rearticulations. The sense-making of the subjection of women enterprisers, as well as their embodied (and disembodied, digital) Embassy, takes its main target to be the newsletter *New Tempo Special*. But I am inclined to commence it by borrowing some words from Barbara Czarniawska (2005, p. 276) when she refers to the use of Karl Weick's '"unready-to-hand mode" . . . still engaged but momentarily at loss . . . Tricky, uncomfortable, and sometimes painful, but promising' (ibid., p. 276).

'Tricky' indeed, the metaphorical use of an Embassy that is not merely a fiction, nor treated as 'real', but all the same presumes recognition, as well as action in promoting women's enterprising. Will 'giving voice' to one's experiences do? And yes, it certainly is uncomfortable to find oneself short of vocabulary when urging for changed conditions regarding women's enterprise; searching for metaphorical possibilities for that do not automatically refer to claims that women are to adapt to the prevailing entrepreneurship discourse, putting on the man's suit to be 'properly' dressed in order to get access (as a significant prerequisite for success?). And it is painful to realize that the '(de)politization of the lexicon', as once proposed by Susan Ehrlich and Ruth King (1994), is continually a process left to the social practices of language, challenging as well as reproducing the gendered aspects of an Embassy for Women's Enterprise.[20] Could the very amount of 880 ambassadors 'embody' the challenge of the stereotypical fiction of the (male) entrepreneur, by re-socializing the 'contract-like way of representing relationships' between autonomous subjects (for example, Du Gay, 2004, p. 39)? Or may the

Embassy rather constitute, and reproduce, institutionalized forms of 'verbal hygiene', as coined by Deborah Cameron (1996a, 1996b), who refers to the language adjustments women are expected to make, in order to acquire legitimacy and recognition within discourses, steadily dominated by male connotations, albeit never static, always in (slow) motion?

Finally, I think it is fruitful to reflect upon the metaphors, in order also to understand some promises of subjection; the hope for rearticulation inevitably expressed in language, but with effects reaching much further than that.

In this final part of the text I will critically elaborate upon the (de)mobilizing potential of the Embassy and the Ambassadors according to the inauguration sentences mentioned earlier. When being 'hailed' by the government, why do the enterprisers turn? As noted by Butler (1997a, p. 112), Althusser does not explain why the ones being hailed should turn, and in so doing, recognize the state apparatus as legitimate in their own claim. He rather stresses the *mis*recognition, the 'false and provisional totalization' of recognition. According to him, there seems to be as many reasons as imaginable not to turn. So, what do the nascent Ambassadors enact in subjection? I present three tentative identities, subjects for recognition and legitimacy, each of them emphasizing quite different answers as to why they turn, and thus why they accept inauguration as Ambassadors for Women's Enterprise. I start out at the tennis court.

The Embassy: An Ace-Maker?

Anyone interested in the tennis game knows the thrill of strongly smashing the ball down on the other side of the court; a winning serve which the other player fails to reach. An ace, according to both the rules of the game and to the character of the player.

Although competition on the market is seldom a dyadic relation, or would not even be regarded as prospering when constituted by aces only, the metaphor of the single entrepreneur often stands unchallenged in the entrepreneurship discourse. It draws on the neoliberal character in the instrumental use of any possibilities, be it in the view of making your own decisions, or the will of control over the chain, or the freedom attached to running a firm, as mentioned by the Ambassadors in the newsletter. The myth of the entrepreneur is almost a 'robinsonade' of our time (Nilsson, 2002), but in this study with an autonomous 'player' put in the centre (court).

The entrepreneurship discourse, ideologically influencing the turning, is more or less unchallenged. So, what are the (de-)mobilizing potentials of an 'Ace-maker'? Individual enterprisers are highlighted as role models. They come from different parts of the country, and they work with different conditions concerning their business as well as themselves. One of them copes with a handicap, another one copes with prejudices of ethnicity. But focus is put on them being enterprisers, Ambassadors, role models where other signifying aspects may be put aside. The crucial idea of doing it yourself, and at the same time maintaining the importance of role modelling, and thus gaining social recognition, makes possible the interpretation that women do adapt to requirements of the entrepreneurship discourse. The 880 autonomous 'Ace-makers' offer a match with the teachers in schools, while trying to get legitimacy from the ball boys and girls who might be expected to collect their teachers' lost arguments, handing them over for a new ace to be smashed down by the Ambassador. Thus one could indeed wonder whether the 'troublesome' pupils are the means or the destination of such an activity?

The ones saying 'Here I am!' when being hailed by the government, expect women to adapt, playing the rules of the game – as how it is set (!) by others, long before her, that is, not worrying about it, but smoothly acting according to the ruling ideals of entrepreneurship discourse the way these develop with or without 'women's enterprise' as an etiquette of their endeavour.

The Embassy: A Pace-Maker?

Rapid metaphorical steps over to the hospital. Maybe the Embassy could be interpreted to be the heart of organizational coordination for women's enterprise. A policy 'pace-maker'? A high-tech device to keep the heart beat or, better, repairing the wounds of inequality forced by an overwhelmingly functionalist entrepreneurship discourse? Do I have to state that the operation might be urgent?

It is often maintained that change must be constituted in action in order to establish itself (Czarniawska, 2005). What is regarded as action conditions, however, whether change ever occurs or not. This is to some extent overcome by the emphasis on performative speech acts, utterances that not only transfer meaning, but also constitute it in their very expression. The event of the inauguration is thus a perfect scene for governmental subjection of enterprisers, through the promising possibilities for continued arrangements in the field of women's enterprise. The measure might be facilitated by the healing (not merely hailing) device.

Of course, one could state that a pacemaker is not even thought of before the uneven heart beats call for serious attention. Thus the *New*

Tempo Special is a well-found symbol for keeping up the speed, achieved with some extra help from policy-makers and their selected experts. Some people live long, good lives with their corporeal supplements, so why wouldn't society? Overcoming prejudices of women's enterprising, clearly needs their engines (but for a period of only two years?). Operating with a (business) life-sustaining device might provoke those who would be interpellated by self-propelled subjects.

In turning, being recognized, and embodying the Embassy, the gathering of the 880 Ambassadors, from all over the country, could be seen as an imperative for 'mo(ve)ment' (Davies et al., 2006). Bronwyn Davies and her colleagues use the concept 'to signify the simultaneity of specific embodied moments and the movement toward the subject as process that can come about through the mode of telling' (ibid., p. 92). The one saying 'Here I am!' when being hailed by the government, is ready to 'give back' to society as well as to the persons she meets, telling her story within the commission of the Embassy. Her experiences are supposedly not so odd that she could not share them with others, thus mobilizing the voice of women enterprisers within the conversation on entrepreneurship discourse.

The Embassy: A Peace-Maker?

Turning back to the Embassy, the 'diplomatic relations' signify that change will be a conditioned endeavour, remembering that dialogue will occur on behalf of other parties and run according to rules of the 'receiving county'. The capacity to mediate requirements from different ideologies, when tensions appear between high school ideology and those ideals proposed by the entrepreneurship discourse, was indicated to be important by both the rhetoric consultant and one of the nascent Ambassadors. This is also underlined by the personalizing and role-modelling aspects of their task, as well as the voluntary assignments – as long as these do not 'warp the competition on the consultancy market', as noted in the newsletter.

But maintaining peace implicitly asks for moderate demands on whatever demobilizing requirements that would be put forward. The demobilizing potential of a 'peace-maker' does not promise that much regarding societal change. Radical aspects of talking-back strategies might well be counteracted already by the enterprisers themselves. Thus, the one saying 'Here I am!' when being hailed by the government, is the one who deliberately mediates the expectations from the audience, as well as from the government. And she knows how to reiterate the articulations without (explicitly) interfering with 'internal affairs', balancing the expectations of femininity and professionalism, in the gendered entrepreneurship discourse, equipping herself with both the brooch and the briefcase.

EPILOGUE

It cannot be ignored that there is a tension not only in exclusion, but also in inclusion, referring to the statement that all of these Ambassadors are supposed to act in a joint (com)mission: with the advantages of being themselves, and at the same time constituting the 100 per cent woman enterpriser role model in the classroom, as mentioned by the rhetoric consultant.

One could critically comment upon the identities proposed here by the play with signifiers of a governmental measure, as well as with the ideological 'apparatuses' that turn women enterprisers into Ambassadors. The division in 'makers' is of course an illusory way of proposing alternative identities in subjection. While constituting the 'piece-maker' myself, scrutinizing different approaches that are reiterated through speech acts in (and on) entrepreneurship discourse, the individual enterpriser, and the issues of being such a means, also for 'societal change', is somewhat challenged by a social, albeit injective device. Maybe the Embassy might support societal change by keeping the 'rhythm of enterprising' captivating enough to mobilize the alterity among as many subjects as one could possibly imagine. Promises in subjection could then mean the provisional totalization as just another way to rearticulate support services directed to 'women's enterprise' in conversations on entrepreneurship discourse.

In the newsletter there are no examples of critique, nor did I expect it in such a material. The digital website of the Embassy will need its use in practice to show whether it turns out to be a 'a minor revolution' of 'dialogue and co-construction' as concluded by the CEO who provided the service on the Web, or whether peacemakers will dominate the diplomatic relations of 880 Ambassadors and their interlocutors even if they sometimes are supposed to 'throw themselves out in the lianas' too.

NOTES

1. The article 'Topphemligt besök av Carl Bildt när ambassaden i Kabul öppnades' ('Top secret visit by Carl Bildt when the embassy in Kabul was opened'), http://www.regeringen.se/sb/d/10036/a/114794, was published on the home page of Swedish Ministry of Foreign Affairs on 3 November 2008.
2. http://www.sweden.gov.se/sb/d/4182.
3. There are no explicit declarations regarding the choice of the term 'enterprise' or why

it has replaced the former notions of women's entrepreneurship or women business-owners. One could with Paul du Gay (du Gay et al.,1996; du Gay, 2004), explore the use of 'enterprise' in its 'new' settings. 'The "economic politics of Enterprise" appears to know no boundaries either in terms of where it might be applied (schools, hospitals, universities or local governments) and in terms of who – politically – might apply it (neo-Conservatives, New Labor and Social Democrats)' (2004, p. 40). Also studies on 'new managerialism' belong to this field of critical inquiries (for example, Davies, 2003, 2005, 2006). Hence, the widened use of 'enterprise' might well have more and extended aims in diverse directions, than articulated in this (con)text.

4. '880 Ambassadors for Women's Enterprise' dated 31 March 2008. Ministry of Enterprise, Energy and Communications.

5. The sites used were government websites from Australia, Hong Kong, Korea, Thailand, United Kingdom and the United States of America was selected due to the web page information in the English language, the researchers' perception of the country as 'an opinion leader and influencer of entrepreneurship, both globally and regionally', their perception of 'the level of state intervention seeking to foster or encourage entrepreneurship' and finally according to 'the degree of influence of state mechanisms in entrepreneurial development' (Perren and Jernings, 2005, p. 175).

6. The Vienna Convention on Diplomatic Relations was ratified by the Swedish government in 1966.

7. Article 2 reads: 'The establishment of diplomatic relations between States, and of permanent diplomatic missions take place by mutual consent.'

8. In their book *Gender, Managers and Organizations*, Due Billing and Alvesson comment about one of their cases, the Danish Ministry of Foreign Affairs, that it was a ministry with high status and employees with intense interest in, even fixation with, internal ranking techniques, due to its prestigious status both among ministries and within its different departments.

9. Approximately 1500 women put forward their names for the measure, and finally NUTEK selected 880 women to constitute the Embassy. The criteria used for their selection were to ensure a variety of industries and regional distribution as well as differences in firm size.

10. Interview with an ambassador, in *Smålandsposten* (SMP). The heading was: '*Alla vill väl starta eget, eller?*' [Everybody wants to start (a firm) of their own, don't they?].

11. NUTEK presented some written information and distributed a brochure called 'Take good care of the entrepreneurship power – invite an enterpriser'. This brochure not only presents the programme, but also gives, for instance, teachers in secondary schools some advice for preparation activities (discussing films produced by NUTEK available at www.youtube.com, proposed discussion themes, and exercises – a kit for entrepreneurship communication with an Ambassador).

12. Interesting enough, *rusta* in Swedish is translated to English as 'to equip', which could associate to functional means for the task, as well as to the appropriate dress code expected by the government. But it also means 'to arm', which actually directs the associations to military services, both offence and defence.

13. What is changed is *the wording* of the questions, which will, of course, lead to different answers. Why did you want to be an Ambassador? is sometimes changed to: Why did you choose to be an Ambassador? Who has been your role model? is sometimes changed to: Who has been your most important role model? and Did you have your own role models when starting the firm? What do you want to commission as an Ambassador? is sometimes changed to: What do you want to work with as an Ambassador? and What do you want to achieve as an Ambassador? The question What good is being an enterpriser? is sometimes changed to: What is the best thing about being an enterpriser? Finally the questions What is best regarding running a firm of your own?, What is nice about being an enterpriser? and What made you take the step to be an enterpriser? were put.

14. It could have been, 'As a man sows, so shall he reap.' But it was not.

15. In comparison with the question: What role models did you have? which was put to the others presented in the newsletter, this change might be a result of the answer; thus when the answer was no, she did not have any role models, this might have resulted in a reformulation of the question in the brochure, in order to put a relevant heading here.

16. Althusser was, according to Nils Andersson (2001), a researcher who regarded scientific work as an ideological practique (2001, p. 29), and the role of scientific texts to evoke effects, rather than claiming any truth of the matter presented (2001, p. 124).

17. Louis Althusser was a philosopher and a Communist Party member in France. As Nils Andersson states in his doctoral dissertation 'The power of thought? The philosophical politics of Louis Althusser 1960–1978' published in 2001, Althusser's combination of philosophy and politics was conducted at the École Normal Supérieure where he worked. Among others, Simone Beauvoir, Jaques Derrida and Michel Foucault were his students.

18. The scene sets in motion a view of the interpellation, as if it occurs in 'real life', but according to Althusser, what 'seems to take place outside ideology (to be precise, in the street), in reality takes place in ideology. What really takes place in ideology seems therefore to take place outside it. That is why those who are in ideology believe themselves by definition outside ideology' (1970/1971, p. 174ff).

19. This doctrine of interpellation has been widely scrutinized over the years. Butler wrote that: 'Clearly we might object that the 'call' arrives severally and in implicit and unspoken ways, that the scene is never quite as dyadic as Althusser claims, but these objections have been rehearsed, and "interpellation" as a doctrine continues to survive its critique' (1997a, p. 106). It has recently been used by Campbell Jones and André Spicer in 'The sublime object of entrepreneurship' (2005) when introducing Lacan to entrepreneurship research.

20. In the mo(ve)ment of (de)mobilizing entrepreneurship, I consider theorizing to be an act of transformation in itself, a kind of 'disciplined imagination', in the words of Karl Weick (1989). But, following Judith Butler (2004, p. 204), I have to realize that theorizing, although important, is not enough for social and political change.

3. Creating the collective hero: stories of cooperative development

Erik Rosell and Henrik Hultman

INTRODUCTION

We put our faith in heroes. In the area of regional development, public authorities put their faith in entrepreneurs, who are expected to create growth in the form of profitable businesses and new job opportunities (for example, European Commission, 2003, p. 7). In order to produce this effect, confidence is placed in support services for small and medium-sized enterprises (SMEs), which are expected to have a direct effect on macro-variables such as growth, profitability and job creation. Public authorities are found to focus on quantitative growth for SMEs and policy actions tend to be based on macro-expectations (Lambrecht and Pirnay, 2005). In this way, the actors are mobilized in a strong narrative structure produced by the government, concerning the relationship between entrepreneurship and regional development (Perren and Jennings, 2005). As pointed out by Ericsson (Chapter 10 of this book) such narrative structures can be seen to shape the way in which actors think, talk and feel, and as a consequence condition their actions.

We argue that the narrative structure briefly depicted above is characterized by a strong emphasis on individual actors. The responsibility ascribed to the entrepreneurs and the support service organizations is great. Not surprisingly, the high expectations often lead to disappointment. SMEs are found to give priority to objectives other than growth (Johannisson, 1992; Johannisson and Abrahamsson, 2004). Evaluations of the effectiveness of external consultancies show mixed results, favouring the argument that consultancy has little or no effect on quantitative variables (Robson and Bennett, 2000; Lambrecht and Pirnay, 2005), leading Hjalmarsson and Johansson (2003, p. 87) to the conclusion that: 'public initiatives could not be legitimized by 'proven' positive effects'. Despite the seemingly inefficient supporting efforts, SME owners-managers using external consultants are found to be positive about the quality of the consultancy services they use (De Faoite et al., 2004; Lambrecht and Pirnay,

2005). The situation is discouraging on the one hand, and intriguing on the other. It indicates a need to rethink the expectations on support services and the effect they produce. Bill et al. (2008) rethink the alleged motives of providers and users of SME support services and suggest other motives for participating than promoting macro-variables such as growth, profitability and job creation. Another path of enquiry is to question the fairness and reasonableness of ascribing such a great responsibility to the actors. Is it fair to depict and evaluate the actors as individual heroes in the story of saving regions from economic decline? If not, what kind of deeds can we expect from entrepreneurs and the support service organizations they so often interact with? Is it possible to write another story than the one presented above, where high expectations are so soon turned into blame?

In this text such an attempt is made by: (1) examining the expectations ascribed to a support service organization (in this case a Swedish cooperative development system); and (2) interpreting the contribution of the support service organization in relation to the objectives of those they set out to support (in this case cooperating SMEs). Our purpose is to write a contrasting story to the one that is still, we argue, tainted by a heroic view of the individual actors involved on the process, putting too much explanatory force in their assumed properties. In order to fulfil the purpose we use a theoretical frame of reference drawing on actor-network theory (ANT), emphasizing 'linkages between human and non-human actors within a network, as opposed to the actions or genius of individual heroes' (Hooper and Kearins, 2007, p. 297). We also visit an organizational field that is characterized by cooperative ideals and values. The frame of reference and the organizational field chosen are argued to be fruitful in order to elaborate on a perspective that emphasizes the collective effort of alliances of actors when objectives are acted upon.

The rest of the text is organized as follows. First, we briefly present Coompanion, a Swedish support service organization targeting cooperatives. Next, a previously conducted study of how Coompanion supports cooperating SMEs is revisited and reinterpreted. The proposed frame of reference is used to analyse three stories about the development and support of cooperatives between SMEs.

THE SWEDISH COOPERATIVE DEVELOPMENT SYSTEM REVISITED

Coompanion (the Swedish cooperative development system) is a federative organization consisting of 25 local agencies. Each local agency is organized as an independent cooperative, with local and regional members (for example, other cooperatives, businesses or agencies). Each local agency normally covers a county and employs a number of advisors or consultants. The operations of Coompanion are partly funded by the governmental agency NUTEK (the Swedish Agency for Economic and Regional Growth). The state funding regulates the operations of Coompanion as it should be used for cost-free consulting services to the population and to potential cooperators, knowledge production and knowledge distribution in relation to the cooperative form. The governmental funding is conditioned on an equal amount of local funding. In addition to the matched governmental funding, a local agency can sell consultancy services and participate in local and regional projects or projects financed by the European Union (EU) by choice. The scope of this non-regulated activity varies strongly between different local agencies. The matched governmental funding has in many ways characterized the development of Coompanion. The matching mechanism balances the governmental influence on the operation of Coompanion, producing a development system that could be understood as a hybrid between a project and a permanent institution (Stryjan, 2004). It also produces a support service organization that is hard to define in a definite manner. Coompanion is a quasi non-governmental organization (NGO), and as such it offers a wide variety of consultancy services involving specialized types of training, and provision of services offering information, advice and various kinds of practical assistance in relation to the cooperative form. The activities of Coompanion are best described as a result of the specific and often unique local circumstances, for example, the funding of the specific activity, the target group, the partner collaborators in the specific situation, and the competence and interests of the Coompanion consultants involved.

In 2005, we participated in a study with the aim to evaluate the work of Coompanion in relation to one of its many target groups in society, in this case cooperatives between SMEs. This specific target group was considered to be especially interesting since Coompanion at the time had experienced a shift in focus from a strong connection to cooperatives in the social economy to increasing activity in relation to more traditional business firms organized in the cooperative form. The method of data collection was interviews, mainly by telephone, with Coompanion consultants who represented a specific local Coompanion agency. In every interview we asked the consultant to describe his or her work in relation to one specific group of SMEs. At a later stage representatives of the cooperating SMEs were contacted and their experience of the relationship to Coompanion was investigated. Representatives from the group were also asked to describe the cooperation and its development. In total, 16 interviews were conducted here. The duration of the conversation was between

45 and 100 minutes. Representatives of seven local Coompanion agencies and seven SMEs were interviewed. The study was conducted during the autumn and the spring of 2004–05 and was compiled and reported in 2006. For practical reasons, three of the initial seven cooperations described by SME representatives and consultants are picked out and reinterpreted in this text.

A theme that appeared in our conversations was that it seems to be difficult to explain to other parties what supportive work entails and how it contributes to those who are support takers. One consultant describes this as a practical problem or a dilemma:

> [Björn (Coompanion consultant):] Cooperatives can have forms of knowledge exchange that can be fruitful without Coompanion knowing it. Still, Coompanion can have participated, stimulated and contributed to a situation where the cooperatives by themselves find solutions to the problem they experience . . . and this is almost a sort of dilemma, I think, for this type of organizations. It's impossible to be perfectly clear and say that 'it's we that have done this', 'we accomplish'. This is in a way counter-productive in relation to those that Coompanion is working for. It's a question of acting without being seen in many cases. So, this is sort of a dilemma against parties who think 'but what are you actually doing, is it so important after all?'

When representatives from the cooperatives describe the work of the consultant the story is similar. Below, Ulla describes in a typical way the help that her cooperative got from Coompanion:

> [I:] But what kind of help did you receive from Coompanion and this consultant?

> [Ulla:] I don't know, I must say . . . it feels like Coompanion was around and helped us with statutes to some degree, but most of it was done by us . . . Coompanion was there in the background and I know that we were aware of this, so the help we needed we got from Coompanion . . .

Today, when we reflect upon this theme, one unpleasant suspicion suggests itself. Could it be that we, deliberately or not, approached our interviewees as individual heroes in a grand story about regional development and growth? Or could it be that this story is so permeated through society that our interviewees felt they were supposed to account for themselves in relation to the roles that they are ascribed in this kind of story? If our suspicion is right, it gives the dilemma presented by Björn a somewhat new meaning. He is expected (by parties like us, asking 'But what are you doing, is it so important after all?') to account for his contribution to those he supports in a direct and unproblematic way. This is however not easily done, since those he supports are at the same time depicted as highly capable entrepreneurs. And as we all know, a hero in need of help is less of a hero. Björn is caught in a story where he is unable to produce the kind of answers he is expected to produce. Interpreting the dilemma from another perspective, Coompanion could be seen to 'participate, stimulate and contribute' in ways that are invisible to us if we look for unproblematic, direct and measurable effects in job creation, increased sales or profit. Taken together, those two interpretations lead to the same conclusion. It seems to be problematic to mobilize support structures as principal actors in the story of creating regional growth. The expectations produced as a consequence stand out as being both unrealistic and unjust.

Based on this unjustness, our ambition is to demobilize the actors, that is, disconnect them from the 'plot' and the expectations produced by the public authorities. This demobilization is done in two steps. First, we listen to François Cooren and his propositions on how meaning is created in narratives and how narratives can be seen to organize the actors they entail. Second, we revisit and reorganize the field material produced as a result of our approach in the previously conducted study. Under the heading 'Listening to the Cooperators' a first new narrative is constructed from the perspective of the cooperators. This narrative is meaningful based on the tension between the cooperators and their objectives. We then shift perspective and, figuratively speaking, slide the camera over to the consultants. Under the heading 'Listening to the Coompanion Consultants: Opening up a Narrative Subschema' a second narrative is created. This time the story is told from the perspective of the Coompanion consultants. In this way, the actors are mobilized in two new narrative structures, one based on the perspective of the support taker, and the other based on the perspective of the support giver. Taken together, the narratives highlight the relationships between the actors, the creation of common and/or diverging objectives and the collective effort of alliances of actors when objectives are acted upon.

NARRATIONS AS STUDY OBJECTS: LISTENING TO FRANÇOIS COOREN

Actor-network theory (ANT) as a generic term embraces a variety of related but partly different theoretical contributions. Two of the more prominent contributors are Michel Callon and Bruno Latour. In their first joint article from 1981 titled 'Unscrewing the big Leviathan: how actors macro-structure reality and how sociologists help them to do so' (Callon and Latour, 1981), they explore the role of objects and artefacts in the construction of what they call collectives. In doing this, they analytically mobilize actors that are typically neglected in our accounts of social processes, that is, non-human actors. Latour has made several theoretical contributions exploring the relationship between human and non-human actors. He has also related this perspective to the concept of power, claiming that it is a misconception to believe that an actor can have power (power *in potentia*). According to Latour, power can only be exerted (power *in actua*). Following Latour, ANT can be used to describe how power (in a performative sense) is exerted as a result of the mobilization of heterogeneous actors associated in a network. Michel Callon (1986), in a slightly different vein, puts the negotiations between actors and their ability to exert influence within a network in the centre of the analysis.

In this chapter we use ANT to interpret the collective effort of alliances of actors when objectives are acted upon. Thus, our main purpose is to study the construction of collectives. In order to do this we combine ANT with semiotics, and more specifically the narrative model developed by François Cooren (2000). For an interesting example of how ANT can be used analytically differently, as a means to interpret the power struggles between actors within a network, see Lindqvist (Chapter 5 in this volume).

The semiotic work of Algirdas Greimas has been a source of inspiration for the thoughts collected under the term ANT. Greimas (1971), for example, uses the term 'actant' as a general signifier for the subjects and objects that populate a narrative. François Cooren (2000) develops a model of the organizing properties of communication where the thoughts of Greimas are central. The model reunites ANT with the lines of thought that early on helped formulate the theoretical perspective. The model is described below.

Cooren (2000) argues that a narrative is constructed around an object being circulated between subjects. There is a subject present that wants, desires or strives for an object. Narratives are built around the subject's quest for the object:

> Narrativity can be thought of as the capacity for people to throw themselves into the future, to project something in order to fill a gap or restore an order that was initially disrupted. Without this initial condition or target, no articulation can occur and no sense can be created. (Cooren, 2000, p. 60)

Cooren clarifies the general narrative structure by defining four phases (manipulation, competence, performance and sanctioning) and different categories of actors typically involved in respective phases. These are illustrated by the example below, based on the typical James Bond story. Bond is asked to recover the secret plans stolen by SPECTRE. Thanks to Q's gadgets, he gets them back and is rewarded by M:

- Manipulation phase: M gives a directive ('having to do') to Bond (to do = to recover the plans stolen by SPECTRE). Bond accepts the mission (commitment).
- Competence phase: Q gives Bond various gadgets ('being able to do') and instructions about how to use them ('knowing how to do').
- Performance phase: Bond gets the secret plans back from SPECTRE (test) and gives them back to M (gift).
- Sanction phase: M rewards Bond for his heroic performance. (Cooren, 2000, p. 71)

The manipulation phase and the sanctioning phase involve a sender and a receiver. In the manipulation phase the sender is the actor communicating the mission (having to do) or convincing the subject-receiver to accomplish the mission (wanting to do). In the sanctioning phase the sender is the actor rewarding the subject-receiver.

In the competence phase the actors helping the subject to fulfil the mission are called helpers and the actors that supposedly constitute obstacles in the subjects' way are called opponents. The competence phase typically dominates a narrative:

> As mentioned previously, the competence phases are essential to every narrative, since they usually constitute the most important parts of the story. What would a James Bond story be like if our hero had only to take the subway to recover the secret plan? (Cooren, 2000, p. 73)

The performance phase involves a subject and an object of value. In the example above James Bond is the subject and the secret plans are the objects of value. An anti-subject could be around, in the example SPECTRE which Bond fights in the final test and which also constitutes his heroic performance.

It is possible for different actors to take different and various roles in a narrative. A role can also be taken by many different actors. The roles defined above are structural positions determined by how the narrative is built up. Every phase of a narrative can potentially be analysed as a sub-schema, as follows:

- Manipulation phase: Q's mission is to provide secret agents with gadgets ('having to do', implicit in all James Bond movies, with 'to do' = 'to provide secret agents with gadgets').
- Competence phase: Q has to create, test and improve these gadgets ('being able to do', generally explicit in all James Bond movies).

- Performance phase: Q provides Bond with his gadgets.
- Sanction phase: Q is (implicitly) thanked by Bond (and more widely by Her Majesty's Secret Service). (Cooren, 2000, p. 73)

The breaking down of the competence phase in yet another narrative subschema shows that narratives tend to discriminate (or silence) certain actions and certain actors. As Cooren points out, it is this circumstance that Latour directs our attention to when he says that we tend to discriminate technical objects (technology) in our accounts of social processes. Latour (using ANT) shows us that what has above been defined as the competence phase usually involves other actors (human or non-human) that typically are given no attention in the narrative. Cooren (2000) illustrates this by analysing the writing of a book. The competence phase consists of the writer being associated with other actors (in the example pen, paper, typewriter and computer).

> Latour shows us that my new ability is actually the result of an association between any one of those three actors and me . . . .. A new collective actor has been created by our association, because, strictly speaking, the action of writing can be attributed neither to me, nor to the instrument, whatever it may be. (Cooren, 2000, p. 180)

Cooren argues that by naming this collective actor 'me' in the narrative (I write a book), one actor is given priority on behalf of all the other actors. The collective action is translated into my action.

Below we use the theoretical frame of reference to interpret the stories of the SME representatives and consultants. We start by interpreting the stories from the perspective of the cooperating SMEs. What are the objectives of the SMEs, why is a cooperative initiated, how is the development of the cooperation perceived and how can the contribution by Coompanion be understood in relation to the objectives of the cooperators?

CREATING NARRATIVES: LISTENING TO THE COOPERATORS

Lambrecht and Pirnay (2005) state that there is a need to pay attention to the micro-expectations and possibilities of entrepreneurs when the contribution of support services is evaluated. Here those expectations are analysed by telling three stories of cooperative development from the perspective of the cooperators.

The Story about the Friends Who Wanted to Start Their Own Business Together

The first example is about six friends who after their design education want to sit together and work. Here we are interested in interpreting the story from the perspective of the young entrepreneurs, that is, we place the entrepreneurs as subjects in the schema presented by Cooren (2000). In the story that we are told by Jennie, one of the friends, the common working place is important in order to make sense of the events and the formal cooperation that is eventually developed. The tension between the entrepreneurs as subjects and the premises as object constitutes the general story. The six entrepreneurs want to be able to work together in the concrete sense of sharing the same premises. It is when they begin this journey that the need to organize formally their cooperation (or friendship) arises. They want to share the responsibility of the premises and the costs that come with it. The premises (which in itself constitutes a macro-actor) can be regarded as a sender of the message that the friends need to organize themselves formally. In this case the message is more of a 'having to do'; in order to be able to share the responsibility and ally themselves with the premises under such a condition, they have to find a formal arrangement that makes this possible. In Jennie's story the majority of the events are about how the friends mobilize actors in the quest for 'the place that they want and need in order to fulfil their dream of working together'. These actions could all be interpreted as belonging to the competence phase of the narration. It is at this stage that the six friends get in contact with Coompanion.

Not surprisingly, in our study where we have deliberately focused on Coompanion and asked questions about the relationship between Coompanion and the six friends, much of Jennie's story circulates around how Coompanion was allied as a helper to the group. In total, the group met with a Coompanion consultant twice to discuss the cooperative form and how the statutes were to be formulated. Thereafter they kept in contact over the telephone and Internet, whenever there were questions concerning the formalities surrounding the cooperative form. We must bear in mind that various other actors took action together with the entrepreneurs on their mission to acquire the premises. This however does not affect the point that we want to make. Coompanion and the individual consultants are all actors who in the narrative schema that we are drawing up can be placed in the role of helpers, allying with the entrepreneurs and forming a collective actor that (at least potentially) has the competence and ability to accomplish the mission. We also want to underline that the helpers defined above tend to be neglected in the narrative. This has to do with their structural positions in the narrative schema. The subject tends to get the attention and the helpers tend to be drawn together and assembled under the subject. It is the subject of the narrative who contacts the landlord, who signs the contract and so on. These actions are however made possible by, and are in that sense performed together with, a various number of helpers. Here, we have focused on two of them. Coompanion and the formal cooperative association, together with the six entrepreneurs, form a macro-actor that takes action. The helpers are implicitly present in the following events of the story. When the six entrepreneurs are acting, other actors are put into motion. The helpers are potentially infinite in number, making this perspective hard to handle. We have only a humble ambition to focus on at least a few of them, reflecting on their contribution to the subjects' might and power.

So far, we have broken out only a fraction of the story that Jennie told us. The story thereafter continues. New tensions can be identified when the first one is resolved. For example, the six friends tell us that they have restored the premises by common funding, that they have started to make businesses together and that they want to build a common brand. This continuous development has in a sense been made possible by the alliance that was formed in the competence phase illustrated above. When the entrepreneurs take action in the following episodes, these actors are still present together with the new actors that are eventually allied to the network (for example new members of the cooperative, financial means, websites on the Internet, advertising folders, and so on).

The formal cooperative can be interpreted as a tool or means that makes the entrepreneurs more capable to reach their object of value (to be able to do). Coompanion, in a sense, brings this other actor into the alliance and contributes by instructing the group in how this new tool can or should be used (knowing how to do).

The Story about the Companies Who Had to Reduce Emissions

The story about how and why six manufacturers of plastic ship bodies form a cooperative is interesting in many ways. Compared with the story about the six design students, here we have an equal number of counterparts in the cooperation. In this case, however, there are whole companies behind the numbers instead of individuals. The group of manufacturing companies differs from the type of groups that Coompanion normally works with, by their number of employees and by the type of branch they are active in. They belong to an industry where it is unusual to start cooperatives. Norms and values about what is considered to be right or wrong, usual or different, are by institutional theory (for example, Powel and DiMaggio, 1991) brought forward as a main factor explaining why actors in a certain institutional field (branch or industry) act in the way that they do. These norms and values define what is considered to be legitimate behaviour. Legitimacy, on the other hand, affects the possibilities to acquire resources such as capital. The fact that these six companies form a cooperative is particularly interesting considering that in doing so, they go against the norms and values dominating traditional manufacturing industry.

We will now discuss what can be called the phase of manipulation in the story. Manufacturing of plastics is a business regulated by different environmental quotas. A discussion emerged among the six companies since the quotas of styrene[1] were beginning to be filled. The question was raised as to whether this type of industry was suitable in Sweden, or if the production was to be transferred abroad. Once again there is a macro-actor giving the directive (having to do, where to do = reducing the levels of styrene) to the companies. The environmental legislation is in itself a collective actor, constructed by and consisting of politicians, authorities, legislators, and so on. It is society at large pointing its finger at the six companies. The motivation behind our choice of putting the environmental legislation in the role of the sender is simple. In the story told to us by Dick (the project leader in the cooperative that was eventually formed), it was the environmental legislation that made the companies take action and organize themselves. We did not follow up that part of the story in more detail (Exactly how did they receive this signal? Who brought the message, in what way? and so on).

In discussions between the companies and representatives from the local political authorities the agreement was reached that the companies would reduce the level of styrene by investing in new production technology. The local political authorities were even backing them up by partly financing the change process. In order to accomplish the mission the companies had to mobilize a vast number of different actors as helpers. We can see a certain chronological order in this mobilization process. The investment in new production technology required capital, a resource that the companies together, and with help from the authorities, could raise. In order to do this, a juridical counterpart was required in order to facilitate the dialogue and transferring of money from the local authorities. This problem was solved by forming a cooperative association, initially with administrative support from a local law firm. At a later stage the formal documents were partly rewritten, and at this time Coompanion was contacted to support the firms. When the financial means were secured in this way, the companies could start working with the acquisition and implementation of the production technology.

All the actors presented above are in a sense required in order to resolve the tension between the subjects of the narrative (the companies) and the object of value (the production technology). At the end of the story, the environmental legislation rewards the companies by letting them continue their production in peace, without posing a threat to them.

Once again we see a story where Coompanion and the consultant are strongly associated to the cooperative as a formal structure. The formal cooperative is a tool or means for the companies to get the object of value in hand (being able to do). In the same way as in the story about the friends who wanted to start a business together, Coompanion contributes by guiding the companies in how to construct and handle this new tool (knowing how to do). We have listened to other stories where groups of entrepreneurs refuse to use the tool (they do not start a formal cooperative). This led to a somewhat different relationship between the consultant and the group.

The Story about the Entrepreneurs Who Wanted to Make Friends

In a project funded by the European Social Fund (ESF), Coompanion, being project owner, is working to support specific target groups in society, more specifically women and immigrants. In the beginning, extensive information work was carried out. All in all about 1100 persons were given information about the project. In one county the totality of the female entrepreneurs was invited to a meeting with dinner and a lecture. The interest in cooperating was investigated through a handout. Some of the female entrepreneurs showed their interest. Among these women a group soon formed which took part when more meetings were arranged within the project. In total, the Coompanion consultant had six meetings with the group, spread over a two-year period. In the narrative schema, Coompanion can be described as a sender in relation to the group of female entrepreneurs. There are however more actors who have been active when it comes to motivating and engaging the women to cooperate. Other entrepreneurs and other networks (similar projects in other locations) have obviously functioned as role models to the women. In the story that we were told, the consultant steps forward as a representative of those ideas. The consultant has the time to translate those ideas into action. We thus place the Coompanion consultant in the role of the sender in relation to the group of female entrepreneurs, bearing in mind that this is a simplification. Our argument is simply that Coompanion can be a sender (or one of many) in relation to target groups in society.

The directive that Coompanion is communicating is not a mission (having to do), but more of an attempt to create convincing arguments about the potential benefits of cooperation, thus awakening the motivation and drive among the women to work together (wanting to do). In the phase of competence the consultant is a helper to the women when it comes to administering and arranging meetings and finding more and new members of the network and its activities. When the consultant tries to mobilize more helpers in the process, something happens. The group of women want to embark on another kind of journey than the one projected by the consultant. The objective of the women is quite clear. They want to meet other people in the same situation, have a good time and support each another professionally (for example, by discussing each other's businesses and asking each other for advice). The consultant on the other hand wants to strengthen the businesses of the women in a more concrete way. Her objectives are in line with the formulations in the project plan, stating that the purpose of the project is to develop organized networks of SMEs in the form of cooperatives and, by doing this, achieve stable and lasting cooperations which in turn are supposed to lead to an increased competitive power. Another way of putting it is to say that the objects of value differ between the consultant and the group of entrepreneurs.

The point we want to make here is that the 'macro-actor' Coompanion is not allowed to play out its full register as a supporting actor in this story. The consultant perceives this as a failure. She is not allowed to mobilize all the helpers that stand 'potentially' at disposal to the group of female entrepreneurs and with the help of which the consultant could reach her objectives. The group of entrepreneurs however are pleased with the help of the consultant. She has been a helper in relation to their objectives, to connect with other entrepreneurs in the same situation, to meet and have a good time, and to exchange professional experiences. Our interpretation of this episode leads to a need to describe more precisely the potential of Coompanion as a support provider. Below we change perspective and place Coompanion and the consultant in the place of the subject in the narrative.

LISTENING TO THE COOMPANION CONSULTANTS: OPENING UP A NARRATIVE SUBSCHEMA

In our interviews with the Coompanion consultants we have had an open conversation about how they work in relation to different target groups in society, how they perceive the situation when they support a group and how they conceive their mission in society at large. In every discussion we wanted to make the description more concrete by letting the consultant relate his or her work to a specific group of cooperating SMEs. However, much of the conversation covered their work in general. Based on this general discussion it is possible to create a new narrative. A first important question is: Who can be seen to communicate objectives to Coompanion and the Coompanion consultant? Below we investigate the phase of manipulation, this time placing the consultant in the role of the subject in the schema presented by Cooren (2000).

Above we have illustrated how Coompanion can be regarded as a sender in relation to groups of (potential) cooperators in society. When we listen to consultants telling us about how they formulate initiatives and take action in relation to different target groups, a more complex story evolves. The consultant sometimes describes him- or herself as a listening receiver of signals from the target groups they later support. From this perspective, local target groups can be seen as senders in relation to Coompanion, communicating the message that there is a need for cooperation in specific situations. Coompanion reacts to those signals by mobilizing other actors, to whom Coompanion can be regarded as a sender. Another (macro-) actor directing Coompanion is the cooperative ideals and values. Those ideals and ethical principles are important to the consultant and they become clear when the consultants tell us about their understanding of their work and their relation to the target groups. The ideals partly determine what is perceived as a problem, and how the supporting work is performed in relation to various groups in society. Local groups of (potential) cooperators and the cooperative ideals and values are two examples of actors that could be described as senders in relation to the Coompanion consultant. Based on our conversations, the expectations put on Coompanion by those two actors seem reasonable in the sense that they are possible for the consultant to meet. The help that the cooperating SMEs ask for and expect in the stories presented above is not grand and challenging. They want support with the statutes and working procedures surrounding the cooperative structure and they want help in creating networks. The consultant in the different stories performs those tasks quite easily. In the story about the female entrepreneurs we see a consultant who even wants to do more. The cooperative identity is formulated within the cooperative movement of which Coompanion is a part. There is no obvious external actor evaluating Coompanion based on the cooperative values, presumably making them inspiring guidelines more than clear-cut objectives that can be met or not in an unproblematic way.

A third actor that could be placed in the role of a sender in relation to Coompanion is the public authorities financing the different operations of Coompanion. By defining the kind of activities that are allowed to be funded, and by formulating objectives for the funded operations, the will of the financier is, so to speak, 'written into' the supporting work of

Coompanion. Here, the expectations seem to be higher. In the project plan guiding the ESF project described above, and in the documents regulating the public funding of Coompanion (NUTEK, 2006), Coompanion is partly depicted as a service organization contributing to the fostering of entrepreneurship, regional development and growth. As indicated by Lambrecht and Pirnay (2005) those expectations are harder to meet, at least in an unproblematic way that is easy to evaluate quantitatively.

The operation of Coompanion is strengthened by and in a sense dependent on the sanctioning from all the actors defined above. Coompanion is rewarded by continuing financial support from the funders, and the interest in society of the cooperative identity is vital in order for Coompanion to attract new potential target groups.

The helpers available to the consultant when they act upon those objectives vary in each story. As a few examples, they can be:

- Local target groups that participate in fulfilling the more overarching objectives of Coompanion in relation to regional development and growth.
- Manuals and documents used in the process when cooperatives are established.
- Established cooperatives that Coompanion has worked with previously, later to be used as tools in the contact with new groups (as ambassadors of the cooperative model and as good examples).
- Other local and regional support structures in society, for example, the financiers of Coompanions operations.
- Legislation surrounding cooperatives and other formal associations.
- International sister organizations.

When describing what could be called the competence phase of the narrative, we would like to evoke the picture of a macro-actor being created, which with every new helper becomes more capable (at least potentially) of reaching its goals. If it were possible we would like to illustrate how the consultant on a local level mobilizes helpers from different times and different places. Decisions made on an EU level, and legislation that has been worked out in the distant past and as a result of other actors' hard work, are mobilized in a very tiny locus.

In the performance phase it is the individual consultant together with all these helpers that makes the supporting work possible. Every actor is part of a greater network (an actor-network). When someone takes action, then other actors, not only those who are present, but also actors in different times and at faraway places, are mobilized. When the individual consultant goes to work, an institution is put into motion.

CONCLUSION

One of the purposes of this chapter is to make visible the contribution of Coompanion in relation to the objectives of cooperating SMEs. So far, based on the model of Cooren (2000), our argument is that this contribution can be visualized in two different roles, that of a sender and that of a helper. As a sender, Coompanion could be understood as a catalyst activating its target groups and creating tensions (having to do, wanting to do) that can be the starting point of a new mission or quest. As a helper, Coompanion as a macro-actor allies with its target groups and constructs a new competence (being able to do, knowing how to do) that the target group did not have before and which makes it (at least potentially) more likely to reach its objectives. Below we discuss those two roles more in detail.

Coompanion as a Sender in Relation to Local Target Groups

In the story about the female entrepreneurs we see a consultant acting in relation to the wider and more 'strategic' objective of helping isolated female entrepreneurs in the region. This initiative is built on the rationale that female entrepreneurs are a discriminated-against or disadvantaged group in particular need of support in order to be more competent and capable. We can see that Coompanion, in its turn, is directed on this quest by the funding authority the ESF. The female entrepreneurs in the county are gathered around this problem and in the meeting the situation is presented to them. The consultant then tries to formulate ways for the women to handle this situation. The suggestions are that the women work together, preferably in the cooperative form. As we see in the story, this process is uncertain and tentative. Actors can choose to go along with the definition of the situation, that is, the possibilities, threats and actions suggested by the sender. Alternatively, they can refuse to take part in it. As the story about the female entrepreneurs illustrates, a third and more likely possibility is that the situation is reinterpreted or translated (Latour, 1996) in the meeting in accordance with with the will, wants and needs of new actors.

   Here, we are interested in analysing the contribution of Coompanion as a sender in relation to the objectives of the receiving SMEs. In order to do this, we return to James Bond and use the series of movies as examples of typical narrative structures, containing a number of interesting characters who all have different functions in the narrative. As shown by Cooren (2000), the character M represents a clear-cut picture of what he refers to as a sender in relation to the subject, James Bond. In the pictures, M represents the link between the global and the local level (Czarniawska and Joerges, 1996), that is, a link between the state of foreign affairs and top political contacts, and the tiny locus where the agents are actively carrying out practical agent tasks. We normally meet M in the beginning of the movie when the plot of the movie is told to the audience and to the agent. M describes the actions necessary for Bond to pursue in order to accomplish the mission (for example, take back the secret plans from SPECTRE). In this way M creates the tension of the narrative, a tension that Bond is supposed to resolve. In the words of Callon (1986) we could say that M is allying Bond and the audience in a problematization: she presents a definition of the situation and argues for a specific action-plan in order to handle it. M defines one or many obligatory passage points (Callon, 1986), necessary steps to take in order for Bond to work his way to a solution. Bond should contact certain people, visit certain important places, collect specific objects and fight specific opponents. Our argument is that Coompanion in certain situations can be understood as one actor (among many) functioning as sender in relation to target groups in society. In this function, Coompanion contributes by formulating objectives that the target groups could choose to act upon. The objectives create a tension that can be the starting point of a new mission. In this way Coompanion, in the function of sender, potentially organizes the receiving subject around a specific definition of the situation, and formulates logical actions as a response to this. It is important to note that this formulation takes place together with the various actors involved, and that the will, wants and needs of those actors are negotiated in the process.

Coompanion as Helper in Relation to Local Target Groups

In the function of a helper, Coompanion and the consultant act in a different way in relation to the target groups. Here Coompanion is not active in the definition of which path to take or how to define the situation, but active in a quest that has already been negotiated and decided upon. We have seen how Coompanion allies itself with a group of design students and enables them to rent some premises with a shared responsibility. We have seen how Coompanion allies itself with a group of ship body producers in the quest for a new and more environmentally friendly production technology. Here, Coompanion is one of the actors who make the group able to reach their objectives, and instructs the group in knowing how to do this. In both stories, the formal cooperative association is an important technological actor that is, so to speak, presented to the group by Coompanion.

Let us once again return to the typical James Bond story in order to clarify the argument we want to make. The character Q is interesting in relation to the role of a helper to James Bond. Q is not directly involved in the adventures of the hero, but he is undoubtedly on the side of James Bond in the fight against the threats posed to the world. How does Q contribute to the might and power of Bond? Q offers Bond technological innovations and instructs Bond in how to use them. These technological objects are potential tools for Bond with which he can do things that he could not do before. Being a helper in this way is closely connected to transferring abilities to someone else, giving the receiving subject a new power. The concept of power is in this case used in a performative sense (Czarniawska, 1997; Latour, 1998; Johansson, 1998).

The role of the helper is not played out be the sole consultant, nor is it played out by the individual old man Q in the Bond movie. Being a helper is performed by creating associations to other actors (human or non-human). In the case of Coompanion such other actors consist of, for example, the formal cooperative association, education material, funding or project plans (as illustrated above). These actors are, so to speak, technological innovations that the Coompanion consultant has worked with in the 'test lab' and delivers to the subject in the narrative structure. In this case, the helper (Coompanion) organizes the subject as well, as the subject is, so to speak, translated to the sum of all its helpers. The organizing dimension of this is hard to demonstrate. In the bond movie Q and his technological innovations are all helpers in relation to Bond as a subject. For every new helper that is brought into the alliance, the actions of Bond get more predictable. An agent without gadgets can fight SPECTRE in all possible ways. Every gadget that Bond is equipped with gives him a new capacity and at the same time makes his quest more predictable. If Bond uses the gadget in the fight against SPECTRE, Q and the gadget have organized Bond. In the same way, Coompanion and all the other helpers can be seen to organize the subject (the cooperators) by giving them specific competencies, making certain actions more possible and reasonable than others.

Summing It All Up

If the arguments in this text were to be formulated in one sentence it would be: let's not have unrealistic expectations about the potential contributions of individual actors in relation to macro-objectives concerning development and growth of businesses or whole regions. The story about the heroic entrepreneurs concerned with the objectives of creating growth, and the support services to SMEs having a direct and measurable effect in relation to those objectives may very well need to be rewritten or demobilized.

We have shown that putting too much confidence in the naked actor (be it a consultant or an entrepreneur) is likely to lead to disappointment.

The model of Cooren (2000) illustrates that every narrative needs a hero, a subject from whose perspective the story is told. More importantly, the model shows us how illusive this subject is. Every narrative can be broken down into a subnarrative, showing that the subject is a collective actor. By telling the same story from two different perspectives (that of the support taker and that of the support giver) we have attempted to create a collective hero in this text. Our story goes like this: sometimes entrepreneurs or organizations feel a need to organize themselves, creating macro-actors that are better equipped to conquer what might seem like small obstacles that line the path of business life. In these kinds of situations, support service organizations stand at their disposal, armed with human actors, technological innovations and instructions on how to use them. Together, and with the help of others, they take action. The practical relevance of this perspective is that if we are deceived by the phantom of the individual hero, we run the risk of placing too much confidence on the shoulders of single individuals. This, in turn, can lead to a confusing situation where those with high hopes are disappointed, and those on whose shoulders too great a responsibility is placed have a hard time justifying their operations or accounting for their actions.

The two roles conceptualized above illustrate that the contribution of the support service organization is illusive and difficult to describe in a direct and simple way. The two roles are played out together with other actors, and the contribution of a sender or a helper must be looked for in the association that is created with the subject. As Cooren (2000, p. 197) points out: 'Though each (human or nonhuman) actant performs some specific thing, the conjunction of their respective actions creates a collective performance that surpasses what they could have accomplished separately.'

NOTE

1. Styrene is an aromatic hydrocarbon used as solvent when producing plastics.

4. Seeds germinate in nature, humans gleam in cities: an exploring expedition of incorporating 'city management' knowledge

Shelley Lin and Anders W. Johansson

INTRODUCTION

In this chapter we will meet PhD candidate Shelley Lin at the time when she was still a Masters-level student. Belonging to an academic context, Shelley is also runs a business of her own, a firm with seven employees, in the city of Kaohsiung, Taiwan. The chapter is organized as follows. After this introduction, which is written by Anders, the main text follows, which is written by Shelley. The final section of the chapter is also written by Anders, where he makes some interpretive reflections about Shelley's text and how it relates to (de)mobilizing the entrepreneurship discourse. Shelley's text originates from her diary notes and was written over a time span of about one year, but has then been edited to make it more reader-friendly. Most of the editing has been done by Shelley. Minor adjustments have been made by Anders; therefore the main text represents Shelley's reflections about her life experiences in her own words.

Shelley's text appears as a story, which is made up by her reflections about what happens alongside her venture creating process. Therefore the story is an open one. A person's life story is by necessity open-ended as it reflects life, and life is always open to editing and revision. Only in retrospect can life stories be closed (Johansson, 2004a). A closed story is a finished text in the sense that the story-teller makes the plot clear. An open text is not finished as questions the text raises still wait for more definite answers. Thus an open text invites the reader to reflect upon the issues that are brought up (cf. Molander, 1996). No texts are completely open or completely closed, but the following text is comparatively open and is therefore open to different readings and closings. As any story, it is filled with meanings, contains moral judgements and emotional reactions, but at the same time it reflects an open-ended life (Brown et al., 2009).

You will meet Shelley in the third person, something that underlines that the writing of this text is part of Shelley's reflections about herself as an entrepreneur. As a reader you are invited to close the text by way of your interpretation of the text. Shelley's text starts with a story introduction and is then followed by eight chronological 'chapters' in a life-story manner. Each chapter is divided into a couple of themes which reflect Shelley's structuring of her reflections.

THE STORY

On the fourth floor of the Kaohsiung City Bureau of Human Resource Development (BHRD, Kaohsiung) building, a company known as Civic & City Development Institute (CCDI) was incubated by BHRD and the National Sun Yat-Sen University Incubation Center. The concept of incubation began from 1959, when the United States wanted to promote the development of local small and medium-sized enterprises, to stimulate an end to the economic depression, and to create employment opportunities. The government developed some financially favourable policies to subsidize academic or private institutes to provide exploitable resources for small and medium-sized enterprises to start up. Almost 2000 incubators have been set up in North America and Europe, most as academic incubation centres. They have successfully incubated numerous small and medium-sized enterprises.

The incubation plan in Kaohsiung was an innovation from the director of BHRD, who reckoned that with the coming tide of developing human resources for city management, BHRD should actively involve itself as an incubator by starting a private institute that cooperates with the government to be an efficient generator for the knowledge economy, by providing services to knowledge management industries, and to disseminate and develop city managing knowledge.

The innovative incubation plan was finally realized by a graduate student and entrepreneur, that is, Shelley.

Chapter 1: Pluralistically Creative Metropolitan

Shelley, a city dreamer, likes to work with a flexible schedule. With an easy-going personality, she enjoys communicating, as well as expressing and sharing ideas with others. She loves to wander around, appreciate beautiful things and savour the shifts and pleasures of city life.

Spending most of her time and mind on work as a typical Capricorn does, she always works with a glowing enthusiasm, genuine trustworthiness, and willingness to express and share ideas. Though she is very passionate at work, she undertakes shopping, movie watching and travelling in her leisure time as means of stimulating creativity and imagination, and as her best sources of catching the pulse of community life and observing the market tide. Other important sources of creativity from her city life include attending concerts, visiting bookstores, and admiring the ever-changing city.

Business
In her teenage, Shelley was characterized as timid, gentle, and restrained. When she studied foreign languages in university, she lived in a world of literature, and still was a timid, gentle, and regular literary schoolgirl. She started her career in international trade as a secretary for senior managers in a multinational corporation. The administrative works of a secretary offered Shelley a great chance to stand on the shoulders of giants, to learn business management and walk out from her world of literature. Influenced and encouraged by many senior managers and advisors, she left international trade and stepped into the brand promotion market in 2002. She studied all the knowledge associated with product planning she could find, and focused on work like product development, channel development, and visual advertisement planning. In recent years she focused around creativity initiation and knowledge management.

Reading
Reading has been her greatest pleasure in life; she loved reading about Western art and English and American literature in her college days and Shelley's understanding of humanity largely comes from the detailed descriptions of the characters in fiction. Before she entered higher education, Shelley also read many bestselling books about business management and product marketing, as required by her work.

With her literary sense, she watched and learned the operation of the business world in detail in her secretarial job. The strong contrast between her literature world and business reality along with her own introspection contributed to her unique opinion and perspective on business. In addition to her amiable personality and high EQ (emotional intelligence), her emphasis on communication and willingness to express herself bettered her chances to join the core group of decision-making in the company.

After decades of drifting, Shelley matured more and more; she also wanted to find her own way that was different from that of normal office workers or businessmen. She said thoughtfully:

Now thinking of it, leaving a stable job and studying in the Sun Yat-Sen University Graduate School is indeed a milestone in my life! The professional training from professors in business school and the social and political enlightenments from professors in politics and economy are getting more and more helpful to develop my own business perspectives and thoughts on social political issues more independently.

Chapter 2: A Glimpse of Business Opportunities of the City

Ponder

Shelley is always exploring, her mind seems never to stop pondering; you can tell from her face that she is always seeking answers for every question in her mind. One day, she earnestly revisited a question that had been lingering in her mind for many years: whether she should stay under the umbrella of the corporation or should carry one of her own. Being afraid of failure, she had never put her dream into practice. Was it time, yet? The pondering expression showed on her face again.

Curiosity

One early spring afternoon, while Shelley was enjoying her time in an exotically designed, aroma-satiated, and music-imbued Starbucks, her sister Sabrina called to ask her to accompany her on a visit to BHRD. That was the first time she had heard of a bureau called BHRD, which she thought should, or could, or might be something like an intelligence agency.

As the appointment was made quite hastily, she was dressed very casually when she thinks back: a black dress she had bought when she went to the Cloud Gate Dance Theatre event last winter, a pair of jeans bought in Hong Kong when she attended her sister's wedding ceremony, and a pair of designer sandals. Compared to her sister, in relatively official dress, hers was of course a bit informal. The fact was that her meeting with the director was no big deal. Her visit was solely out of curiosity, to see what the government office and its officers of different ranks looked like, just to broaden her horizons.

'God heard my prayer, you are what I prayed for', the BHRD director said to Shelley. Director Wu Eing-Ming is also a professor in the Department of Political Economy, National Sun Yat-Sen University (NSYSU).

The meeting of destiny

It is a distinguished place, with the offices laid out nicely, a coffee bar, classrooms, a dining-room, and a piano. The place is very difficult to define for a first-time visitor, however Shelley found her way into the second floor in the left wing building, to the Director's Office.

A round-faced, slightly chubby middle-aged man was there. Shelley imagined him as optimistic and open-minded, as she imagined people with figures like his usually to be. In the meeting, the Director asked her if she was interested in the knowledge management industry, after realizing that she was studying for her MBA at NSYSU. He was looking for someone who could integrate programmes about city governance and knowledge management; he wanted to incubate a 'Civic and City Development Institute' to provide a knowledge base for the development of human resources and urban planning. The passionate, direct, succinct BHRD Director and professor kindly took the initiative to propose that he would like to be her thesis advisor, and recommended Professor Stephen D. Tsai from the Department of Business Management, NSYSU, to be her co-advisor. Furthermore, he presented Shelley a ready-made thesis subject at their first meeting: '*Research of Incorporating practices from knowledge management industries into city governance*'. The thesis subject offered Shelley not only an opportunity to execute her dream of starting a business and to finish her thesis in the Department of Business Management at the same time, but also a great chance to record incorporating practices and to analyse incorporating research. It was a heavenly blessing for someone like her, troubled by thesis research and seeking advising professors.

Director Wu summoned the people in charge in the Bureau immediately, and led them to the briefing room and explained to them what '*city governance knowledge management*' is. In just half an hour, driven by the passion and excitement of the Director, and the surprise gift of advising professors and a thesis subject, Shelley agreed without much hesitating.

Intuition
Speaking on this point, Shelley scratched her head and embarrassedly said: 'Now, thinking of it, I might be a little bit sentimental and impetuous.' It sounded like a lack of consideration, to make the decision under the influence of the Director's passion and excitement. At that point she didn't have a clue about city governance knowledge, nor about how knowledge should be managed. Neither did she have any chance to weigh her own capabilities and background for the job; nor could she consider, or estimate, what Director Wu was expecting from her. Where would this decision lead her? Counting only on her intuition, she walked onto the bumpy road of incorporating businesses.

Chapter 3: Curiosity and Exploration of City Management Knowledge

Conversations

Only talking and chatting to the Director would not get Shelley to start her business. After the business idea 'seemingly' was presented, she spent eight months conversing with the political economy professor. Through conversations, Shelley increasingly began to see Director Wu's vision, to understand governmental offices, to know city governance, and what city governance knowledge Kaohsiung City Government produced.

Becoming acquainted with possible contents of city governance knowledge on the one hand, and thinking over how to find resources to start the business on the other, after eight months of ceaselessly and cautiously considering the countermeasures and executing strategies of the business, Shelley finally set up the Civic & City Development Institute. By becoming more familiar with city governance knowledge, she cares more about the city, and builds up a strong obligation to be helpful to the city's human resource development.

City governance knowledge management is a new industry. How should the new industry develop? How would the new company survive with its limited resources? These are the facts Shelley had to take into account and deal with constantly. Where is the 'way out'? was the issue Shelley had to endeavour to solve every day.

Brewing

'Every time I come up with a good idea or a thought, I keep it in mind, think it over and over, and let it brew inside my head.'

When it came to planning the future direction for the new company, in the beginning it was simply a matter of collecting the associated knowledge about city governance, and managing the process, then selling the related city governance knowledge and courses to companies or the public. However, when she wrote the operation plan, she had a feeling of emptiness, knowing it would need a certain amount of time and resources to achieve the goal. Though the resources were so limited and she was unsure deep down, Shelley still kept moving forward at her own pace.

Opportunities

On one occasion, Director Wu led a whole group of government employees to attend a Government and Education Institute Collaborating Conference at Diwan University in Madou, Taiwan. Shelley was also invited by the Director.

At the conference Shelley observed closely as part of the audience, and kept notes at the same time, also compared with the information she had;

she tried to figure out by herself how to think about the collaborating circumstances of government and education institutes. Meanwhile a lot of questions occurred to her, such as: 'What am I doing here? What are the connections between these and my business? Are these usable resources?' and pulled Shelley's thoughts away from the conference. She recovered quickly and decided to put all the doubts and curiosities away temporarily, and focused on the conference as a student does, without subjective judgement.

Some links between BHRD, the Diwan University and private actors become apparent to Shelley, such as the Garden Villa. The Garden Villa originally was the training center of BHRD Kaohsiung. However in 2006 it was transferred to the Diwan University by way of a ROT project (Rehabilitate, Operation and Transfer). The government commissions to private institutes who rent the facilities from the government, revise the facilities and then operate for a contracted period of time. When expired, they return the revised facilities back to the government. The resources around the Garden Villa are very rich, facing the native plantation-themed botanic garden, next to the Chouchai Wetland Park and Lianchitan Scenic Area; and also the railway, MRT (Mass Rapid Transport – the 'metro'), and high-speed railway are all easily accessible. With its 200-plus rooms and classrooms for accommodation and lecturing, and the abundant natural surroundings, this would be a great location to experience learning.

At this point, she had a hunch that there was a feasible business in this context. The endless curiosity and desire to explore led her into what she is now. She knew she should make use of her advantage to develop training programmes: it was the best business opportunity that integrated real estate resources with softer learning issues.

Chapter 4: The Start and Breakthrough of the Company

Initiation

When the company was just set up, Shelley did not employ any staff because of limited resources. She groped about to find the right direction on her own.

After some time she luckily found someone who was willing to invest, the 'angelic investor' who was not only a senior executive, but also an experienced mentor who was willing to provide helpful resources and patiently listened to Shelley talk about her dream. Shelley still had no idea how she could expand and promote the business.

One initiation gave Shelley the opportunity to deeply think about how to integrate the limited resources. After eight months of working with

Director Wu as a public servant, and attending eight months of lectures by Professor Wu as a political economy professor, Shelley imagined that the ambitious Kaohsiung City eagerly wanted to transform itself into an international city and to connect to the world. This showed Shelley that the city was in need of international affairs personnel.

Shelley thought that by assisting the government to develop better international affairs skills for the public servants, and planning the programmes according to their practical background, these useful and practical programmes could be related to 'city governance knowledge management'. Though developing a series of useful and practical programmes for the 'city governance knowledge management' was a nice idea for this new company, there were neither enough resources, nor qualified lecturers, not to mention the programme planning capacity. How to carry out this idea? Shelley was still baffled.

Possibility

When the company was still in a preparatory stage, Director Wu always said that the potential customers for city governance programmes were in every industry in the country. Though Director Wu had such confidence in the potential market development, Shelley was always in doubt. How does a person like Shelley who had no experience in knowledge management find suitable lecturers to plan the training programmes? Apart from the programmes planning problem, marketing was also a big issue; with such limited resources, they could not afford to stand idle while testing the market. Shelley worried about how she could go ahead at the same time as she was looking for opportunities and market.

One day an employee from Diwan University, Debbie, called Shelley and told her that the Kaohsiung City Government wanted to train some public servants in international affairs capabilities, and the BHRD hoped that universities would support native and foreign lecturers and plan the whole programme. Debbie asked her if she would collaborate with Diwan University for the project plan writing and joint bidding.

It was in the summer vacation and most of the professors were not in Taiwan. Shelley thought that there would not be enough manpower to write the project plan in the university; they should collaborate with more schools. Therefore, Shelley went back to NSYSU and discussed the possibilities with Professor Kao Ming-Rea.

Feasibility

Shelley's knowledge about management enterprises originated from taglines such as 'The duty of enterprises is to make money', and 'The duty of enterprises is to create the maximum profit for shareholders'. Books that could help enterprises to grow fast would be bestsellers, and these books would be on Shelley's reading list. However, after attending the 'Green Marketing' course lectured by Professor Kao Ming-Rea in her first semester in graduate school, Shelley reconsidered the influences of capitalism.

In Professor Kao's lecture, Shelley realized that the capitalist thinking was ruling the behaviour pattern of modern people (including herself). Are the capitalist businesses mainly built upon a series of behaviours such as taking advantage of the social vulnerable groups, stealing the resources from next generations, and destroying the future ecology of the planet? People are getting more and more profit orientated; with the capitalism notion of fast growth, we think in a straight line all the time, plan numerous strategies for business activities which waste the limited resources and damage the ecology. What if we don't change our ways of thinking to consider if they are right or wrong, and leave the profit-orientated capitalism to rule business activities without restraining it, keep consuming the earth's resources and deteriorating the ecological environment? The survival of the human race will face challenges and dangers we have never seen before!

Shelley discussed with Professor Kao that education is the means to change the ways of thinking, and that the public servants are the majority executors of urban planning. If we want Kaohsiung to be a sustainable city, by developing a training series on city governance, humanity and ecology development, the city could be set on its way to being sustainable.

That afternoon, Professor Kao not only gave Shelley another lesson on city governance, but also planned out the city governance programme and its lecturers. Because of Professor Kao's support, assistance, and encouragement, Shelley had confidence in integrating the other teams.

Integration
Next, Shelley visited the Dean of the Department of International Affairs, Wen-Zao Ursuline College of Languages, Professor Lin Jian-Hong. She took the dean's course on international affairs planning, and the courses on planning international investment, international marketing and international games (such as the World Games and Olympic Games) by Professor Lee Chin-Tarn of NSYSU, and courses on international exhibition planning by Debbie and the professors of Diwan University.

By practising and learning at the same time, Shelley gained an initial understanding of planning training programmes for 'city governance knowledge management'; the programme planning for this included developing the skills of international affairs and city governance, through introduction by specialists to enhance the capacity for international affairs such as international exhibitions, international investment, international marketing and international games. Furthermore, the programme blended in the local features of Kaohsiung to its content to make it cover not just global trends but also local ones. This programme was named 'Training Program for International Affairs'.

With best-practice lectures from domestic and foreign countries, in addition to the executive team that Shelley led, and the energetic new company and the collective resources from universities, Shelley successfully contracted with the Kaohsiung City Government for the 'Training Programme for International Affairs' project, the first case for the company.

As a result, Shelley finally had richer resources to train new employees, by collecting and managing city governance knowledge systematically, and via a group of lectures from the different countries specializing in city governance: her company eventually evolved to join the knowledge management industry.

The knowledge circle
This project gave Shelley a key to enter the knowledge management industry. With this ace of trumps, Shelley not only assembled a professional team on city governance, but also developed a series of practical lecture materials and programmes that were useful for public servants. Moreover, by executing, learning and making connections all at once, Shelley efficiently helped develop the Civic and City Development Institute into an urban planning think-tank and a training base for city governance personnel, and also expanded the training programmes for city governance knowledge and personnel of Kaohsiung into a form of public and private collaboration.

With secured resources from the government and academic institutes, Shelley could use these resources on product development and market research. The 'new venture dreamer' actively sought opportunities, including research projects for government human resources investment, promotion strategy research for the exhibition industry, government subsidies for innovative services businesses, resources integration of non-profit and profit organizations, and so on. Each of these created another possibility for Shelley's incorporating journey.

Clarify
During her term as Chief Executive Officer (CEO) in the company, Shelley gradually saw that the future of the company should be based on the notion of 'caring for the city's development'. In her daily life of enjoying the changes and joys of the city lifestyle, Shelley deliberately made detours

to the Kaohsiung Arena constructing site, to observe the construction progress. She thought it would be a perfect exhibition site in the future. Kaohsiung City was granted great support from the central government because of the World Games 2009, and these resources would be beneficial to the conference and exhibition industries. How to utilize the resources from the government, academies and industries to assist the developing industries? These were the challenges Shelley wanted to tackle. The energetic new company successively contracted with many key projects, including the City & Guilds Approved Examinations Centre, Kaohsiung City International Certificate for Project Management, and so on.

Though she knew only too well that she was not a specialist in training, and had never been involved in knowledge management before, she jumped in as the business opportunity was revealed to her. The dramatic story can be depicted by words from the Sōtō Zen priest Shunryu Suzuki: 'If your heart is empty, you are ready for everything; it is opened to it.' In a beginner's mind, the possibilities are everywhere; but a specialist only sees the limitations. She laughed and said: 'Luckily I am not a specialist, so I can jump in without much hesitation.'

Chapter 5: Crucial Questions and Clues

Think-tank

In every new project, when she drew it to a certain stage, Shelley went back to the professors seeking for advice. While executing the international conference of 'Culture Diversity and Sustainable Development: The Conversation Between Taiwan and Europe', Professor Kao Ming-Rea introduced Shelley to a French priest, Father Benoit Vermander, who has lived in Taiwan for more than 20 years and reads and writes in Chinese. Her first impression of him was marked by outward appearances like the large suitcase he carried and his damaged eye: thereafter she noticed his sensitive mind; she realised that his care and genuineness towards people was natural. He cares about Chinese people and has volunteers working with him all around the world; Shelley felt that she was meeting a 'living treasure'.

Father Vermander said sorrowfully that in the 1970s, the world saw Taiwan because of its 'miracle economy'; in the 1980s and 1990s it was the democratic progress of the nation; and now the political turmoil. What would Taiwan present to the world in the future?

The connotation

There were too many things she could do, she knew that clearly. But how to cultivate meaningful job assignments for them is what she constantly has to consider.

On one occasion, a partner from her team who has also worked for non-profit organizations for a long time, Debbie, introduced her to an English instructor certification campaign by the City & Guilds of London Institute (City & Guilds), and she saw another 'resource'.

City & Guilds is a non-profit organization with more than 100 years of history. Incorporated in 1880, it has since been dedicated to professional certificates associated to innovative development and employment, and examines personal achievement. City & Guilds is one of the largest international examination and certification-awarding organizations. The certificates awarded by City & Guilds are recognized in more than 100 countries and regions, and cover more than 600 disciplines. Now there are roughly 8500 City & Guilds examination centres around the world.

When the representatives from City & Guilds visited Taiwan, Shelley had an earnest discussion with them. They reckoned that if the city management expertise Shelley was building her company on could be recognized by international certificate, then the profession would be internationally acknowledged, creating an additional value for their education training. Furthermore, they saw the possibility that education could help the vulnerable groups to stay away from poverty. For example, there are more and more immigrants in Taiwan; if their work skills were internationally recognized, not only could they have certificates of personal achievement for their abilities, but also the immigrants could join the labour force of Taiwan. She believes that City & Guilds would be a 'trademark' to help the vulnerable groups to stay away from poverty by education and training. She travelled to the UK with her partner Debbie to meet the British, and cooperating with Microsoft Taiwan in 2008, helped introduce the City & Guilds PM-ICT (training programme for information and communication technologies) international certificate training to the World Games 2009.

Chapter 6: The Idea of Developing Southern Culture Creatives

Consideration

She is a creative thinker herself, and likes to keep company with creative people. Shelley has many friends around her who are involved in creative work. Most of them are SOHO (small office home office) workers, rich in talent and creativity, but poor in terms of marketing channels and resources. Also, they do not have the associated knowledge of business management or marketing. It has always been one of her aims to help these people start their creative businesses with government and academic resources.

There are many questions to consider. Is there any chance to help these

SOHO workers to exploit the government and academic resources, and accomplish the dream of announcing innovative ideas and products in her own NSYSU at the same time?

A budding idea had been continually cogitated, discussed, and clashed with old-fashioned thoughts and traditions. Then, integrated with surrounding potential resources, the forces of congregation and influence came into play and the 'Southern Cultural Innovation' was produced.

Space

Shelley lived near to downtown Ximending in Taipei when she was growing up. After she failed her university entrance exam, Shelley worked part-time in the Liming Art Gallery. The renowned Astoria Café was five minutes' walk from the gallery. The pressure of taking the university entrance exam again made the streets become Shelley's favourite escape; she loved wandering on the street. Shelley never made her visit into this Taiwan literature landmark on Wuchang Street; she just curiously looked inside every time she went by.

One day while she was rambling on the NSYSU campus, she came up with the idea of connecting NSYSU to the Astoria Café in Ximending. In the 1940s and 1950s, writers like Pai Hsien-Yung and Chou Meng-Tieh, who were regular customers of Astoria Café, revived the literary culture of their time. There is an Art Centre in the NSYSU by the Sizih Bay in Kaohsiung, why not make it the base for the renaissance of southern Taiwan literary culture? Why not turn it into another Astoria Café in south Taiwan, to become the locomotive for the train of renaissance, reviving the literary culture of the city.

Shelley had studied Western art history at university, and always loved Renaissance Europe. The Renaissance in fourteenth to sixteenth century had set off waves of cultural movements; also it founded the modern culture. Leonardo da Vinci, Michelangelo, Dante and William Shakespeare were all from this era, and the painting of the *Mona Lisa* was the masterpiece from the Renaissance.

The creative workers in southern Taiwan indeed needed a salon to develop the culture revival, a stage to unfold their innovations. Taiwan has gradually lost its economical advantages under the trend of globalization, and is in need of more appropriate industries to succeed. The 'creativity'-centred cultural innovation industry can bring the nation the potential growth it needs, and create new opportunities for future development and transformation. With these ideas in her mind, Shelley went to her advising professor in NSYSU, Professor Stephen D. Tsai, to discuss these ideas with him. During the conversations they came up with the idea to set up the Southern Cultural Innovation Salon.

When the Southern Cultural Innovation Salon was seeking locations for its first 'Cultural Creative Industry Entrepreneur Training Programme' event, the Art Center came to Shelley's mind. The place was ready and needed no decoration; it was a historical building that shone with its own flavour and was filled with a nostalgic atmosphere. The Japanese wooden building still has its old furniture from the Chiang Kai-Shek times, along with its art gallery, and accompanied by the visitors' discussions, agitations and interactions, this building naturally builds up into a dense literary atmosphere.

Professor Tsai was excited by this idea and contacted the Art Center immediately. Excitedly, Shelley asked if there would be any chance to record all the events happening and to publish it. The idea to write this text that you are now reading emerged from this conversation with Professor Tsai.

Chapter 7: She Always Intuitively Hires Good and Honest People

Employment
'I am too lazy to control my employees,' said Shelley. She always intuitively hires good and honest people. People with their own thoughts have a glimmer of this in their expressions, and when Shelley sees it in an interview, she knows this would be the right person.

People working for large corporations are usually stressed, but not those working for Shelley's company. She likes to work in places that look like beautiful coffee shops and restaurants rather than offices. These energetic and happy executives are inexperienced, young, creative and partners of all kinds; they are the 'dream team' of the company. They share the weariness from working on for projects together, share happiness together, share interesting articles and sometimes a nice meal together; together they make this office like a Starbucks coffee shop.

Passion[1]
Indeed, Shelley is always sincerely sharing her thoughts rather than 'making a plea' to people opposing her in order to make them support her thoughts. Amazingly, there is always mutual faith-building coming out during the process of communication this way. The work seems to be done easier and better, without unnecessary compromises.

Shelley reckons herself as a daring 'new venture dreamer', finding resources first, then creating possibilities, always looking for a stage where she could act this role. Successful or not? She always tries first without thinking much about the outcome. There is usually more than one project on hand, and she tries to make connections for different projects and see if she can find something creative from this. And she won't put all her eggs in one basket, though when she cultivates different seeds, she needs to put different efforts into each of them, but in the meantime she gets different pleasures from each of them.

Capability

Someone asked her: 'What is your core capability?' Shelley answered: 'Integration'.

The fact is that Shelley doesn't have a strong academic background. Since she doesn't have it, then she finds someone with a good academic background to work with, to integrate their resources. Meanwhile she looks for other new resources and tries to integrate them for new opportunities and new markets.

'If I had the passion for this case, and knew it would do good to others, I would just do it without worrying too much. I am always looking for mutuality in sharing communications. These mutual values can overcome many personal emotions and people can work more closely because of the mutual values. The work can be done better and easier and closer to perfect.'

And her understanding of the works of a 'project manager' is: 'To make everyone comfortable, and get them to work.'

Chapter 8: Like a Duck Paddling Under the Surface

Confusions

When the company was newly set up, Shelley's sister tried to persuade her on many occasions to stop daydreaming, be practical and realistic, find a stable job first, and seek chances for business later. Her mother, who lived in Taipei, didn't even know she was starting her own company, and her close friends and relatives had no idea what she was doing. After a while, Shelley was getting tired of explaining to them as she was struggling on her bumpy road of incorporating businesses.

Actually, she panicked for a while at the beginning stage, and didn't realize what she was doing. The fact was that Shelley was quite doubtful. She constantly estimated and envisioned any situation that might happen in the future: she couldn't find investors, there were possible failures, and so on. She worried that if she failed, she would step into financial trouble, and then she would have no choice but to go back to work in the office. Being an office worker, the stable income and regular life would soon make her content and she would stop dreaming; that would be the worst-case scenario for her.

She knows that she is often discontented at heart and she keeps challenging herself to change herself. In spite of many burdens and uncertainties that tended to make her lose control of herself and disturbed her balance of mind, Shelley still endeavoured to find a luxurious balance between her business dream and real life. Without doing so, her mind would get more and more confused.

Instinct

Shelley said that most entrepreneurs have to struggle through physical and mental tortures. Because the resources are so limited, they have to do everything on their own, and try to make connections to any available resources. Entrepreneurs are all too small, too lonely, and their lives are too tough. Aspiring to be one herself, Shelley noticed that no one is supposed to support her; therefore, she bows lower, and her heart became gentler and more considerate in working with partners from all collaborating teams.

Sometimes they just get lost in the project; when that happens, she asks herself to be a good coordinator and integrator. While interacting with others, you really need to be more considerate, gentler, and more patient. Just like an ascetic, one has to keep alert but at the same time be relaxed; most of all, behave and talk elegantly.

Shelley said: 'If I succeed in business, naturally I would remind myself to keep my mind as of a beginner's, an opened, peaceful, and ready mind to learn my way through. Because my instinct told me that many possibilities and feasibilities are there for me.'

Paddling

The brainstormings, meetings and proposals come one after another. Time after time we keep on trying, discussing, revision. Around the tabletop are beautiful smiling faces, but underneath is fierce competition. Shelley is like a paddling duck; on the surface she might look like an elegant swan, but under the surface her legs are paddling hard to keep her moving. This would be the best description for her incorporating journey.

If you asked her when she has the most creativity, she would say: 'When I am free of pressure.'

Look back

She looks back at her past journeys; she met many people who gave her opportunities to walk into their fruitful gardens. They would invite her and say to her: 'This is fertile soil; it would be flourishing under your hand.' Shelley said: 'Every time when I walked in, I saw all these varieties of plantations, I knew I had learned something, even if I failed, I would not walk away empty handed. Also I would have one more experience.'

She feels lucky that she is walking on a boulevard that is connected with her own interest and her mind. Shelley is walking toward the industry of city governance and knowledge management, and she uses her passion and vision to influence her partners from industries, academies and government to walk toward the same route. None of these achievements were known or foreseen when she started.

If the time turned back to the very first week, Shelley is sure that she would do the same. Because she thinks it would be a waste of life if one had not experienced the physical and mental struggle of the entrepreneurial journey.

She always has a smile on her face, expressing a friendly leadership nature. Frequently, she achieves her dreams before you notice any traces.

REFLECTIONS

The text above is a life story written by Shelley, while the following is written by Anders, viewing Shelley's text as reflections about herself in the context of a venturing creation. As such it provides a beginning, where her background is briefly described. In the middle we can follow the creation of the new venture and different related events. At the end of the story Shelley returns to herself and reflects upon her feelings and aspirations. As with all life stories, this life story is about the identity of the storyteller. Shelley is in the middle of her story and she does not know the end. The life plot is due to continuous re-editing as new events and experiences keep coming up (Polkinghorne, 1988). To write this story for Shelley is a way for her to tell herself who she is. As we can see, these reflections about herself are explicitly articulated.

In the introduction of this chapter it was argued that Shelley's story is an open story. The reason for thinking so is that the story does not fit with a fixed script of normative entrepreneurial behaviour. Nor does it qualify as a personal theory of what it takes to manage her firm (Pitt, 1998). Nor is her message very clear, as for example in the 'Toy Store(y)', by Allen (2007). When she reflects about the concept of 'entrepreneur' her connotations are not always very positive: 'Entrepreneurs are all too small, too lonely, and their lives are too tough.' In the sense that she wants to be an entrepreneur, she seems to look for another enactment than what the entrepreneurship discourse prescribes.

What we meet in the text is most of all a person, with her ambiguous feelings. She has a smile on her face but she also knows she is discontented and continuously challenging herself. She is satisfied, but also unsatisfied; she has control, but also much more to do than she can handle. She likes to calm down and enjoy a Starbucks café, but her legs are paddling very fast below the surface. Venture creation seems not to emphasize earning money and getting rich, but has much more to do with finding a way to realize her dreams. She wants to avoid a boring life, but apparently this leads her into daydreaming and unrealistic ideas. Not even her close friends and mother really knew she was starting a new venture. She is sharing her thoughts in dialogue with people around her rather than marketing her own business idea. Her success as an entrepreneur comes from using her abilities to relate to people, taking guidance and support from her business and academic context. We meet a living person, reflecting upon herself in the midst of her life. Therefore the story is open.

Interestingly Shelley does not close her open story with reflections about how to start and develop a new business, although this is what she has done. The entrepreneurship discourse is not mobilizing Shelley, but her story-making appears nevertheless as the self-mobilizing of an entrepreneur. To start a new venture is a tool for her to realize herself. The venture provides her with a context, networks and relationships that motivate her in her life journey. Instead of making money, this life journey seems to be about relating to a changing society in Taiwan, taking care of the environment, enjoying the atmosphere of a Starbucks café and finding space for her spontaneity and her joy in the fine arts. In other words, different big and small things that give a meaning to life. The venture is not important in itself. Thereby she is on her way constructing an identity for herself, not to be found in most textbooks of entrepreneurship. She reads the bestselling business management books, but they do not make a deep impact on her identity construction. To summarize: she demobilizes the entrepreneurship discourse and at the same time she mobilizes herself as an entrepreneur.

Following Ogbor (2000), the dominating entrepreneurship discourse is built upon the image of the male hero. Being a woman, for Shelley to reproduce this discourse would mean to masculinize herself. This is not what happens here. What happens is that Shelley has a very open and receptive response to the academic context she is part of. The subheadings of this chapter (which are given by Shelley) are a way of articulating how she strives to digest the ideas of Professor/Director Wu about city management knowledge. Thus while the academic and the city government contexts are male-dominated, Shelley's text represents a critical reflection (Berglund and Johansson, 2007a) about this context where she paves her own way. It is critical in the very sense that she constructs her own identity, not only reproduces a traditional entrepreneurship discourse, which might be (or not) in the minds of her male academic influencers and encouragers. She is positive in the sense that she responds positively to the initiatives taken by male professors, but she is critical in the way she integrates these initiatives with her own ongoing identity creation.

If generalizing from Shelley's entrepreneurial identity construction, one could argue that it might be easier for a woman not to fall in the trap of reproducing a male stereotype of entrepreneurship. If so, to understand how women create their entrepreneurial identities is important in order to understand how society at large can be changed. Referring to Chapter 2 in this book, this means that not only women entrepreneurs can benefit from other women as role models; men also can do so, as long as these role models are made a matter for critical reflection. In this way society could be renewed as new entrepreneurial identities emerge, which are less associated with traditional and stereotypic gendered patterns.

NOTE

1. As a documenter, I am really impressed by Shelley's passion for and execution of her work. Once when I discussed a case with her, she told me that as long as there is passion, as long as you know it would do good to the world, then just do it, don't worry too much.

5. Entrepreneurial successes and failures in the arts

Katja Lindqvist

Artists and art professionals[1] should be ideal protagonists of post-industrial society given the contemporary demand for innovators and creative entrepreneurs, as they are visionary, independent, innovative and highly committed to their projects. But instead of occupying centre stage, artists are largely marginalized in public discourse and space, except for when it comes to scandals. Even successful art enterprises initiated by artists or arts professionals seem to downplay the role of artistic innovativeness, independence, vision and commitment as time passes. Sometimes, as presented in three Swedish cases in this chapter, entrepreneurs founding successful art enterprises are actually contested and even taken action against. These cases recount the stories of how three entrepreneurs in the arts field are successful in resource mobilization for their enterprises, but over time face resource demobilization, including disaffiliation of themselves from their founded enterprises. Why do these conflicts occur, and are they unavoidable? These two questions will be addressed in this chapter.

THEORETICAL PERSPECTIVES ON ART ENTREPRENEURSHIP

Trying to understand entrepreneurs in the field of the arts better, there are a number of different perspectives from which to view actions which are here described as entrepreneurial. When trying to describe entrepreneurial behaviour, commitment seems vital, something which is related to the personal link between a founder of an enterprise and the enterprise itself. Also, a founder of an enterprise needs to be able to manage the enterprise through its first phase of existence and to have the skills to play a constructive role in the intricate web of factors and elements important to the survival of the enterprise. These aspects of entrepreneurial behaviour will be discussed here.

The Artist as Entrepreneur: Commitment Management

The challenges of art enterprises have only started to interest management researchers (Cray and Inglis, 2007). Mostly the tensions between the artistic rationale and the management rationale are described or discussed in this kind of research, but any perceived disorder of art enterprises is refuted (Devin and Austin, 2007; Chiapello, 1994). Rather, art enterprises follow their own aesthetic logic (Guillet de Monthoux, 2004; Zan, 2006; Lindqvist, 2007a). In the arts, personal style and judgement of aesthetic quality is essential to professional success. Style and judgement of aesthetic quality constitute the singular, personal capital of the arts professional, the vital tool for work and recognition. In the arts, quality is the end product and it is as central for producers as it is for consumers. This dimension of quality indicates the particularities of the arts in relation to politics or business: that of style-based development and centralized decision-making as regards aesthetic dimensions. As Mossetto (1993) has emphasized, aesthetic and artistic development is not functional but style-based. This means that new products in this field are characterized not by better performance or function, but by different style, and these changes relate to consumer demands. The arts field is furthermore characterized by a tradition where the artistic leader, such as producer, director or curator, has the final decision-making power as regards aesthetic as well as more general questions that in some way impact on the aesthetic output. Therefore, the artistic leader is often both artistic and administrative manager, regardless of the formal positions of other participants in the enterprise. Nevertheless, the boundaries between various professions vary over time (Becker, 1982).

Eikhof and Haunschild (2006) from a sociological perspective describe artist professionals as making lifestyle choices partly by necessity, in order to be able to work artistically. Such lifestyle choices go against many bourgeois and middle-class lifestyle choices, but are, as mentioned, not as free a choice as artists themselves might give an impression of. According to Eikhof and Haunschild, lifestyle and work activities are strongly linked, and the pursuance of *l'art pour l'art*, which is an ideal for many artist professionals, entails embracing a lifestyle that integrates personal life and work, a 'bohemian' lifestyle. Eikhof and Haunschild describe artists as 'bohemian entrepreneurs', in that they can through this lifestyle combine a *l'art pour l'art* ideal with a practice of self-management and self-marketing. Reputation is a very central element of this negotiation of ideal and practice, also described in detail in the works of Bourdieu (1979, 1993), and is the tool by which the employability of an artist professional is sustained and increased. For example, a high-prestige commission may be more important for an artist's career than a well-paid low-prestige commission. Private life is also subordinated to working life, for the same reason, and social events are as, if not more, important for an artist's working life.

Entrepreneurship Research and the Founder's Syndrome

This difference in priorities may in turn be one of the reasons for the so-called founder's syndrome described in non-profit and small business management research. This concept refers to a founder's perceived inability to manage the enterprise she or he has established and brought through its first phase of existence (from an employed new management's or the board's perspective) in a phase of stabilization or growth (Harris and Ogbonna, 1999; Ogbonna and Harris, 2001; Block and Rosenberg, 2002). For example, artists in the role of entrepreneurs or managers often do not have the aim of organizational growth. Secondly, the question of opportunity recognition becomes difficult to define for artists, who often act on knowledge and priorities that do not clearly link to a market perspective. Individual style, thirdly, is central to success in the arts, and individual style is often difficult to link to clear formulations of enterprise aims and so on. Fourthly, in the arts most of production and consumption is connected with high levels of risk, as regards quality and economic gain. Fifthly, the perspective on enterprise in the arts is often temporary, through successive projects that make up a longer-term enterprise, but with individual distinct identities, aims and organizations.

Baron et al. (1999) in a study of types of logics of organizing of founders of new technology companies in Silicon Valley in the 1990s found that there were more commitment-oriented as well as more bureaucracy-oriented company founders among the five distinct logics types identified in the sample studied (engineering focus, star focus, commitment focus, bureaucracy focus and autocracy focus), and the orientation of the founder put its character more or less clearly on the organizations even in later stages of development and growth. The commitment logic is based on love as attachment, and selection of employees was based on fit, whereas coordination and control was peer- or cultural-based, whereas a bureaucratic logic was based on work as attachment, with selection of employees based on skills, and with a formal basis of coordination and control (Table 5.1). These various types of logics of organization point to very different ways of designing an organization. Thus, the commitment type of management of an enterprise seems not to be linked to artistic training, but rather according to (certain) entrepreneurial approaches.

It seems that value judgements are employed in the perception of the 'founder syndrome'. For example Boeker and Karichalil (2002) explain

Table 5.1   Five basic employment model types on three dimensions of employment relations

Employment model	Attachment	Dimensions selection	Coordination/ Control
Engineering	Work	Skills	Peer/cultural
Star	Work	Potential	Professional
Commitment	Love	Fit	Peer/cultural
Bureaucracy	Work	Skills	Formal
Autocracy	Money	Skills	Direct

Source: Baron et al. (1999, p. 530).

the unsuitability, in their view, of certain entrepreneurs for management of their enterprises, due to limited skills or possibilities to make strategic considerations in a stage of strong growth or competition. Several small business and entrepreneurship researchers claim that founders of an enterprise may develop an escalated commitment to their enterprises in the sense of a tendency to stick to one strategy and/or a desire to hang on to the status quo, even though there is evidence that it may not be successful (Beckhard and Dyer, 1983; Schein, 1991; Brockner, 1992; Hambrick et al., 1993; and McCarthy et al., 1993, referred to in Harris and Ogbonna, 1999). But this escalated commitment by enterprise founders, which from a business management perspective is not competitive, plays an entirely different and central role for success in the art world, since commitment to an artistic vision is more about quality and aesthetic judgement than about knowledge or skills. Jansson (2008), in her analysis of aesthetic entrepreneurs, tries to describe entrepreneurship beyond traditional assumptions of such behaviour in economic research. According to her, entrepreneurship is paradoxical, and demands compliance but also deviance, in that it is both about self(-realization) and purpose outside oneself, and about becoming; and the tension inherent in that condition; making self and purpose inseparable sides of in entrepreneurial enterprising.

A limitation of entrepreneurship research is that it tends to oscillate between individual and macro perspectives in order to understand and explain entrepreneurship and its successes and failures. Newer, broader attempts at leaving the economist and the psychological approaches to entrepreneurship focus more on the ordinary dimensions of entrepreneurial action, in terms of both actors and contexts, and especially tend to focus on collectives as actors rather than individuals as actors. The collective approach is a way to approach entrepreneurship that avoids both the elimination of individual action as in economist views on entrepreneurs, and the creation of heroes when explaining entrepreneurs in psychologizing terms.

Actor-Network Theory and Translation Sociology

The hybrid collectives theory of actor-network theoreticians such as Michel Callon might help in understanding the choreography of the case studies presented in this chapter, as mobilization and demobilization of resources for particular aims (Callon and Law, 1982). Going beyond the actor level understanding of action and enterprising, actor-network theory proposes that individual actors are created by a network of actors, both human and non-human, that unify their perceived interests, or on the contrary do not unify their perceived interests, and thus act for or against the interests and aims of other actors (Callon and Law, 1997). Individual actors are made up of the active mobilized support of other actors (or rather entities) and technology as a collectivity. But this does not mean that actors in a Foucauldian sense are the product of their enclosing discourse. On the contrary, each actor or entity can act in various directions, and thus the future is variable. Originally developed within the sociology of science and knowledge, actor-network theory has over time been tested on other sectors of society as well, foregrounding the importance of non-human actors for the configuration of human actors and power to act.

Central elements of the actor-network theory are the notions of translation, displacement and representation, ultimately tools to explain power relations among social actors (Callon, 1986). Translation is the process in which negotiations of the identities and interests of various actors ceaselessly take place in social interaction. This translation process contains four analytical phases or moments: problematization, *interessement*, enrolment and mobilization. To translate is furthermore to displace, to act and speak for someone else, to be a 'spokesfigure' ('spokesman' in the original phrasing, Callon, 1986, p. 218). To be a spokesfigure is to represent others that are not present, and to silence them in the new context. This is also the challenge of translation, that the spoken-for do not keep silent, but contest the arrangement of being spoken for by the appointed spokesfigure, and do not accept the given identity and the given interests that unite them with the spokesfigure.

Another aspect of actor-network theory or science–technology–society studies is the intricate web of factors and elements engaged in the development of any social phenomenon. In their analysis of innovations and the successes and failures of technical innovations, Akrich et al. (1988/2002a and 1988/2002b) show the difficulty in deciding on who is entrepreneurial or successful in the making of history. These actors are usually constructed afterwards, given the outcome of particular processes and struggles with very complex laws of interaction. The point with the three case studies in this chapter is to describe three processes that *ex post* are defined as failures of artistic vision, but as successes of artistic visions at the time of their establishment and early years. Nevertheless, in order to understand entrepreneurship as a collective endeavour, the complexity and difficulty of identifying the criteria of success and failure in the making of enterprises is emphasized with a story form that shows the various interests at stake in the making of the enterprise.

CASE STUDIES

The cases described here are partial descriptions to the extent that only an outline of the factual events is given. The main focus of the accounts is the overall process of creation and establishment of the respective enterprises. The cases are based both on first-hand and second-hand sources, which are listed separately in connection to each case.

Edsvik konst och kultur[2]

'Edsvik konst och kultur' was the name of an arts centre that worked especially with contemporary art exhibitions, and was open to the public from 1996 to 2003. It was founded on an initiative from both politicians and local artist groups in the municipality of Sollentuna north of Stockholm, in the early 1990s, with the aim of profiling the municipality and offering its inhabitants a unique resource and attraction. As first artistic leader of the arts centre, a consultant for the municipality, who had worked with the arts in the municipal administration over a number of years was appointed. This particular consultant had a history in the arts, and had developed a concept for the new cultural centre based on high-quality, international, contemporary visual art.

The organizational form chosen for the arts centre was that of a non-profit association, with a board consisting of, among others, representatives of other local arts organizations and business life. The conservative politicians wanted culture in their municipality to be not only dependent on public support, and therefore demanded that the arts centre raise half of its running budget from sources outside the municipality. This was also well understood and agreed upon by the arts centre director. She developed an exhibition programme based on high-quality, international and national contemporary visual art. This she knew was essential in order to raise support from public bodies for artist invitations and so on.

Such a profile was also in line with the ideas of the politicians realizing the project within the political-administrative structure, as they wanted to have a high-profile arts centre in the municipality that would create attention for the municipality with a unique concept. The director knew that contemporary art does not attract large numbers of visitors, but that it was a unique and long-term investment that was to generate cultural capital that could be transformed into other benefits in due time for the municipality. However, the municipality had demanded an estimation of visitor numbers, and one of the municipality officials had made a forecast which, at the time, was deemed to be unrealistically optimistic. This forecast stated that 10 000 visitors should be the goal for the first year of operation, 20 000 the second and 30 000 visitors for the third year of operation.

The arts centre opened in 1996, and immediately won the approval of national and international critics and press. Sollentuna also very soon became a new address for lovers of contemporary high-quality art. But not all reactions were positive. Some Sollentuna citizens did not appreciate the art displayed; they were provoked by it. Eventually, politicians in the municipality were pressured to question the profile of the exhibition centre. The visitor numbers initially estimated by a municipality officer were clearly overoptimistic, yet the director was criticized for not having 'enough' visitors. Paying visitors, that is; for there were many visitors to the exhibitions, especially at the openings, but these were not paying visitors. And the municipality had demanded that the arts centre have entrance fees. So the important professionals visiting the arts centre at openings were not perceived by the municipal politicians as bringing any value for money to the municipality. As politicians they were dependent on the votes of local inhabitants, and were sensitive to local opinion. Praise in art journals and on the arts pages in magazines and daily papers nationally and internationally seemed not so important after all as time passed. Some local inhabitants felt that the arts centre showed tasteless or otherwise 'wrong' art and artists. There was never any systematic investigation among local inhabitants as to their support of the arts centre, but individuals and groups that had the opinion that other types of exhibitions would be more suitable for the arts centre made their opinion clear to local politicians.

After a few years of operation, new politicians that had come into decision-making positions in the municipality tried to persuade the director (through the municipal representative on the board) to increase educational efforts and/or to try to change the exhibitions' profile in a direction that would satisfy the opinion that was not happy with the present profile. Plainly, the wish of certain groups was that local artists should have more visibility in the exhibitions programme, and that art that was more easily understandable should be shown. The director of the arts centre was opposed to such changes, not for personal reasons, but for economic reasons. She knew that she would not be able to raise as much money from grant-giving bodies linked to the visual art field if the arts centre had a more local profile, as the overall quality of the art shown in that case would be lower, and the arts centre would no longer count as a high-quality venue in the eyes of such bodies. Secondly, educational efforts would mean a higher economic engagement from the municipality, as such activities demand more staff than just having exhibitions open to the public. The director nevertheless managed to generate external funds for some educational projects.

With time the tension between the municipality and the director clearly grew, since neither thought that the profile of the other party was successful. In this development, the change of politicians in the local government was a central ingredient, since more neoliberally oriented politicians entered the local government and more traditional, conservative politicians became fewer. As agreement on a profile for the arts centre was not reached, the municipality eventually decided to withdraw its support to the arts centre, with the motivation that it did not agree to adapt to changed priorities in the municipal government. This decision was the peak of a development where discontent from politicians towards the director of the arts centre was suddenly flanked by a discovery of a deficit in the budget of the arts centre, due to previous miscalculations. Economic deficit is a common reason for politicians to express their distrust in a director, and it is worthwhile to ask if the discovered deficit would have created the same reactions if the attitude towards the arts centre management had been positive from the side of central local politicians.

This situation resulted in the director and the staff of the arts centre being dismissed, and the arts centre temporarily closed in 2003. After a while, another director was found for a period of time, who continued activities with exhibitions that had already been planned. With the shift of director and the reopening, the municipality was suddenly so anxious to increase the number of visitors that the entrance fee was abandoned. Eventually, the activities of the arts centre were discontinued, and in 2005 the association was formally dissolved. The municipality later opened the premises of the previous arts centre with a new management and staff. The new arts centre receives about a third of the operating budget as the original arts centre, as municipal support, and is oriented towards local professional and amateur visual art. The contemporary municipal government states that it is happy with the current profile of the arts centre, as it has a clearly local orientation.

Tensta konsthall[3]

'Tensta konsthall', an art gallery (*Kunsthalle*) in Tensta centrum, a suburb of Stockholm built in the early 1970s, opened its doors in 1998 and is still active. It was established on the initiative of artist Gregor Wroblewski, who himself lived in the district, and wanted to establish an arts venue in his local neighbourhood. He had previously been involved in an art school for children (Järva konstskola) in the local neighbourhood that had been very popular but which had had to terminate its operations. When Stockholm was the Cultural Capital of Europe in 1998, Wroblewski managed to get financial support to hold an exhibition in an unused space under the entrance of the metro station in Tensta centrum, which is located one floor up from ground level. The space, in which the gallery is still located, faces an unused square that was previously a parking lot, and which was mostly frequented by drug dealers.

In the following years, Tensta konsthall managed to generate more short-term funding from the City of Stockholm through the District Council and directly from the Cultural Board of the city government. The exhibition programme received very positive comments from national and international critics and arts connoisseurs, and a new art public found its way to Tensta. The inhabitants and politicians were also happy with this achievement. Even though many of the visitors to the gallery came from outside Tensta, its success managed to generate a sense of pride among local inhabitants. The self-esteem of Tensta was increased due to the local and international work of the gallery and its small staff.

In order to secure long-term existence and funding for the gallery, its founder wanted to establish a foundation. The gallery had initially been run by its founder Gregor Wroblewski, a curator and a person responsible for education, and its exhibition programme had been designed by an artistic board formed by Wroblewski as manager, the gallery curator, Celia Prado, and Sune Nordgren, a director for a number of arts organizations in Sweden and at the time the director of the Baltic Centre for Contemporary Art, near Newcastle in England. The City of Stockholm had some money left over from their engagement in the Stockholm European Capital of Culture year in 1998, and decided to donate a few million Swedish crowns to Tensta konsthall, if it was established as a foundation. A foundation was established, with statutes and a board. The board was made up of a number of well-known people from both the arts field and business. The artistic board was still to be the active body for the long-term exhibitions programme, and Wroblewski the manager of the gallery.

The success in terms of appraisal from critics and audience continued for Tensta konsthall, but a sound financial footing was not actually secured by the donation to the foundation of the gallery. This Wroblewski discovered as he used the capital of the foundation as partial funding of the expenses of the gallery in the coming years. This led to a discussion with the board of the gallery, and with the City of Stockholm as the enabler of the foundation through its donation. Wroblewski did not see it as a problem to use the capital of the foundation for the expenses of the gallery, as it was used to produce good exhibitions. He probably relied on obtaining additional funding in the future through the good name that the gallery was building. But the board of the foundation felt it their responsibility to suggest alternatives to spending the capital of the foundation. They suggested that cheaper exhibitions be produced, or that the gallery could show exhibitions produced by others, such as larger museums.

These suggestions the manager of the gallery, however, interpreted as interference in artistic decision-making from the board, and he did not want to change his exhibition profile to include shows produced elsewhere. The Friends of Tensta konsthall association, which was a separate association established to support the activities of the gallery, engaged strongly in work for further funding. Eventually, a civil servant at the Arts Board of the City Administration was asked by the politicians of the City Hall to conduct an evaluation of the alternatives for a sound financial footing of the gallery. The report was perceived as a betrayal of the idea of the gallery, according to the gallery founder and manager, and by many other supporters of the gallery. They meant that by showing exhibitions produced elsewhere, the unique identity and quality of Tensta konsthall would be erased. The conflict escalated throughout 2003. In June, the board decided to withdraw the right to approve expenses of the manager of the gallery, as he refused to comply with their demands on more restrictive economic programming. The positions were locked, and the founder and manager was dismissed just before Christmas that year. There was an outrage on the arts pages of the daily papers published in Stockholm. The media attention was enormous during the most heated phases of the conflict between the board and the director of the gallery (Hedstrand, 2003; Persson, 2003; Herbert, 2004; Kihlström, 2004; Hernadi and Poellinger, 2005).

According to the founder and manager, the role of the board of the gallery was to support the artistic leader's visions and ideas, his project, but they came to support the foundation as a formal organization, its statutes, and its activities from the formal documents of the formation of the foundation. In a comparison with the founder, the board seems to have prioritized organization and structure above persons or individuals and personal visions, as good administrators and bureaucrats. But the majority of the members of the board were not bureaucrats. Most of them were business or public organization managers, and some of them had very long experience in the cultural and arts field.

Six months after the dismissal of the founder of Tensta konsthall, in the spring of 2004, a new management took over at Tensta konsthall. It consisted of three young creative professionals who had experience from a number of projects within the field of arts in Stockholm. They were given a free hand, at least according to their own statement, by the board regarding the future profile of the gallery. Under their management, the gallery hosted more process-oriented projects, and they also worked intensively with educational activities for local children and youngsters. They resigned in early 2008, however, after finding out that the board had assigned one of its members to do a consultancy service for the foundation, without informing the management. During 2008, a new manager was appointed with a background in marketing, and Tensta konsthall continues to operate, but its presence in the daily papers is not at all comparable to the first phase when Gregor Wroblewski was manager and artistic leader of the gallery.

Dalhalla[4]

'Dalhalla' was initiated by the former opera singer and radio producer Margareta Dellefors. The story of Dalhalla started with Dellefors looking for a possible Swedish open-air opera scene in the early 1990s. She 'rediscovered' an old limestone quarry in the Siljan area in Dalarna in central Sweden. Through personal contacts and stubbornness, she developed a network of supporters, who little by little developed what was to become Dalhalla. Comparatively small investments were made in the industrial heritage landscape, but with professional management, the enterprise was perceived to be an opportunity for more activities and thus more turnover.

Dalhalla was officially inaugurated in the summer of 1994, and met with immediate success from public and professionals internationally and nationally. The events in the summer engaged a large number of volunteers, so many that the engagement could even be perceived as a bit too demanding by the rather few local inhabitants. As the success of the enterprise made by the organization grew, in 1996 a sub-company with its own chief executive officer (CEO) was established, managing all operative matters at Dalhalla. The first CEO was replaced by another less than two years after his appointment. In an attempt to secure financial stability, the new management decided to prolong the season. But prolongation of the season did not prove to be as easy a strategy as imagined, since it entailed a broadening of the repertoire to include popular music, something which in itself threatened the exclusivity and the classical music audience's interest. The Dalhalla enterprise found itself burdened by self-inflicted costs in the form of CEO and star artist wages, large technical solutions and staff, and unpredictable Swedish summer weather.

Dalhalla was a project that Margareta Dellefors had embarked upon after her retirement. In 2001, in the midst of what was going to be the beginning of the economic problems of Dalhalla, she celebrated her 75th birthday. During this period, Dalhalla was celebrated as a successful arts enterprise that aimed at very high artistic quality, but the economic strategy started to change with the new management. Dellefors had worked on very restricted expenses, and succeeded partly through her large professional and private network, and through no unnecessary expenses. With time, however, the deficits started to grow due to increasing expenses, including management salaries and engagement fees for singers and other performing artists. Dellefors had agreed to resign as artistic leader in early 2001, but was to remain a resource for the enterprise as a consultant acting within the artistic board, which planned the programme for each year. But shortly thereafter she found out that the CEO of the enterprise was now artistic leader, and that the artistic board, that she herself had introduced, was now reduced to a parenthesis in the general management of Dalhalla. It was now the CEO who made all the central artistic decisions.

The economic year of 2001 turned out to be disastrous, as economic and accounting mistakes created a deficit that threatened the whole enterprise with liquidation. The finance director appointed a year earlier was dismissed, and the disastrous result of this year was blamed on him. The result of these events was that Dellefors was reinstalled as artistic leader in the spring of 2002. But not for long. In the meantime, Dalhalla – and Margareta Dellefors as its founder was the first to be informed about it – received a donation of 10 million Swedish crowns, from private donors. This was an extremely appreciated and needed economic support that obviously was personally linked to the person of Margareta Dellefors.

During 2002, the relationship between the CEO of Dalhalla and Margareta Dellefors became more difficult. In the autumn Dellefors decided to discuss the things she saw as mismanagement within the organization at a board meeting. Later the same year, she was dismissed from her position as consultant to the enterprise.

Dalhalla has managed to continue its activities, even though the financial results have not been very good. What has been an important issue are the economic margins of the enterprise. The Association of the Friends of Dalhalla (Föreningen Dalhallas vänner) decided in 2006 to increase the long-term assets that create economic stability by inviting public and private actors to buy shares in a new limited company that was to be the organizational foundation of the activities at Dalhalla. By this new issue of shares, a number of municipalities in the immediate surroundings of the site, as well as the region, and private investors became shareholders in Dalhalla. The Association of the Friends of Dalhalla nevertheless remain major owners, due to their ownership of the site itself, being the most valu-able asset in the new enterprise (Nilsson, 2006; *Dalademokraten*, 2006). The Association of the Friends of Dalhalla have also been quite successful in attracting funding from various public bodies locally and in the field of the arts, both towards investment in the facilities, and in the develop-ment of a repertoire. In a survey of the impact of visitors to Dalhalla on the local and regional economy, a study undertaken in 2008 showed the importance of the site and its events for visits to the Siljan region (Jones, 2008; Gilbertsson, 2008). An interesting detail in this study is that almost nine out of ten visitors to Dalhalla in 2008 attended non-opera events; but it is known, and marketed, almost exclusively as an opera arena.

CONCLUSIONS FROM THE CASES

All the cases show some common elements: an idea of a high-quality arts venue, located in a spot with non-existent physical as well as social current value but with considerable potential, that could put a deprived or anonymous area or region 'on the map'; a physical location for a cul-tural enterprise that would generate resources and its specific social value from the unique combination of physical location and cultural quality, with very low infrastructure investment, and with an initiator who knew the local limitations and had a position or the persistence to mobilize resources for a new art enterprise. As the enterprises became successful, questions of long-term funding became more pressing, and this is where the enterprises needed more formal support from their political, social and economic contexts, but in which the original ideas were questioned as a strategy for the enterprise to gain solidity. All the cases show initia-tors that are clearly quality- and content-focused in their enterprising, not so much quantity- or structure-oriented. They thus have experience in enterprising, but in enterprising usually on a project basis, as this is the normal form of enterprises in the aesthetic field. Common for all three cases is also the fact that the artistic leaders had to leave their positions at a stage where the respective organizations had reached a certain level of stability. This level of stability also posed increased pressure to ensure longer-term funding and economic stability. The conflict between artistic leaders and boards and principals can be said to be due to differing ideas of how to prioritize among aims, and the need for reorientation of activities.

The entrepreneurs, initiators, assumed that all contributors shared their priorities, whereas managers and board members assumed the entrepreneurs, initiators, to be complying with, in their view, normal management procedures and conditions.

The cases also stand as examples of enterprises creating spatial, social and cultural value in locations which had none of these previously, at least in the specific field they became known for. The enthusiasts or entrepreneurs that have created the enterprises presented here, Tensta konsthall and Dalhalla, have created space for art that also creates a space that is socially utilized in the physical landscape, a landscape that previously has not had any social identity. With the social identity (and capital) created, economic capital is also eventually created, something which paradoxically in these cases threatened to endanger the whole enterprise. The social value of these enterprises was instantly recognized by the audiences to which the enterprises were oriented. But this valuation of the enterprise was not shared by the political and governing actors engaged in the enterprises. Edsvik konst och kultur created a visiting spot out of the mansion at the Edsvik Bay, that was in the ownership of the municipality of Sollentuna but was classified as cultural heritage and therefore could not host just any activities. The arts centre could fill unrenovated buildings on this site that were not suitable for rent as offices or similar, with activities that generated social as well as cultural value and space. The future director of Tensta konsthall spotted an unused space in the centre of the Tensta district that was an absolute non-existent social space, and changed interaction in this previously avoided public area. The value of the social space created by Tensta konsthall can be measured in the way that the new owners of the facilities, the international company Boultbee, gradually demand increasing rent for the premises, which, before 1998, had been non-existent.

If an actor-network approach is applied to the three cases presented, we are able to understand the development of the art enterprises in a way that does not heroize any party, but that still manages to acknowledge the achievements of efforts of various actors as actor-networks. This will also allow a description of the enterprises as processes rather than as structures. Callon identified four analytical phases in the translation process: problematization, *interessement*, enrolment and mobilization. The first phase, problematization, is characterized by a particular actor trying to 'become indispensable to other actors in the drama by defining the nature and the problems of the latter and then suggesting that these would be resolved if the actors negotiated the "obligatory passage point"' (Callon, 1986, p. 196). The second phase, *interessement*, refers to the ways in which the actor in question tries to lock other actors into roles that have been proposed for them in the proposed script. The third phase, enrolment, describes the strategies which the actor in question tries to define and interrelate the roles given to others in the script, and the fourth and final phase, mobilization, refers to the methods used by the actor to ensure that spokesfigures for collectivities concerned are really able to represent those collectivities and thus have their commitment, so that the collectivities do not betray the spokesfigure and refuse its assumed commitment to represent them.

In all three cases, it is clear that various artistically trained and experienced individuals start a process of translation, in which the proposed drama or script or solution is an art enterprise where they are the artistic leaders and directors. The success of these enterprises depends on the continuous success of keeping the interests of the various necessary contributing actors along their own lines of interest. It is this continuous negotiation that after an initial success turns into controversy when the roles and interests ascribed to the various contributors are challenged. In the end, all enterprises turn out to be arenas for shifting power relations where the enterprises shift identity from one defined by their initiators to one defined by other actors in these dramas.

The initiators first manage both to raise interest and to create mobilization, but then are contested and by force given quite unforeseen and unwanted roles by other actors creating different alliances and other definitions of interests and identities. What unfolds in these cases is a series of negotiations about the identity of the enterprises established, negotiations that for the founders mean a loss of power regarding the identity definition to other actors having been enrolled and mobilized for the realization of the enterprise. The enterprises, due to the scripts clearly defined in the fields of management and politics, are with time redefined in other terms than originally intended and envisioned by their founders. The founders or initial directors are eventually 'outdefined' from the enterprise project by other actors connected to the work with the enterprises. They are even rejected in situations of heightened conflict, pitting the various proposed or preferred identities of the enterprises against each other. These situations with emphasized contradictory suggestions for the profile of the enterprises, their identities, turn into a nightmare for everyone – the initiator, the board and management, and supporting politicians. The founder or initiator sees their proposed identity as hijacked by others mobilized to the enterprise, and struggle to ensure a continued identity for the enterprise as stipulated by them. The other contributors to the enterprise, having been enrolled during the course of establishing and managing the enterprise, may perceive the initiator's or founder's suggested identity for the enterprise as not as well integrated with their own idea of the desirable identity of the enterprise, and therefore work to enrol and mobilize other actors for a different identity and profile of the enterprise, more in line with management or political scripts for well-run and publicly accessible enterprises.

Significant also is the power of the boards of these enterprises to act even against the will of the director, due to laws stipulating the various decision-making powers of various position holders in organizations, such as foundations or public organizations. These laws in these cases clearly played into the hand of the boards of the three enterprises, when it came to situations where different preferences for the identity of the enterprise in question became evident, with a power struggle as a result. The trust that the initiators of the enterprises had in the respective boards of the enterprises to act according to their own preferences was, when it came to be tested, not something that the boards, or certain members of them, were willing to accept as more important than the freedom to choose alternative identities for the enterprise, according to their own preferences, once the enterprise was up and running.

In the case of Dalhalla and Tensta, the initiators with their long experience in their respective professional communities, and with various other contacts established in the geographical location (especially political contacts), managed to create interest, and to enrol and mobilize a number of actors working for the realization of an art enterprise and a venue that would function for the enjoyment of art. This was also the case in Sollentuna with Edsvik, even though the initiator there was not so easily singled out as in the other two cases. What all initiators and directors of these art enterprises eventually had increasing problems with was the continued support for their visions, their scripts, and the identity they gave to the enterprise, to themselves, and to others in the organization of this enterprise. In all cases, the initiators encountered increasing unwillingness to accept their definition of the enterprises and their purposes and profiles. The identities of the enterprises were challenged by the other allies, and the ensuing power struggles in all cases ended with the initiators being the ones left outside the transformed alliances of the enterprises. This was because so many significant other actors had more in common than with the initiators, whose only link with the other initial actors had been through the envisioned enterprise. But with the enterprises already established, the initiators could be left out of the alliances. What remained were the renegotiated enterprises, that for the winning parties in the power struggle continued to have an important role to play in their respective collectivities.

In the case of Tensta konsthall, the collectivity identified as the Friends of Tensta konsthall voiced their commitment to the director, as did the collectivity of art journalists, even to the extent in the case of Lars O. Ericsson of being dispelled from his work as art critic at *Dagens Nyheter* (a major daily newspaper in Sweden). But the board and funders, in the form of the politicians of the City of Stockholm Cultural Board, acted without their collectivities raising any voices. Also in the case of Edsvik, some local inhabitants who did not accept the orientation of the director voiced their challenging views on the gallery, whereas the majority of voters in the municipality, as well as the collectivities that the other board members represented, did not voice any opinion, whether supportive or challenging relative to their representatives on the board. In the case of Tensta konst-hall the board, having accepted the role of keepers of the statutes of the new organization, did not accept the director's suggested script of using the capital of the foundation for running expenses. They did not accept the identification of the most important task of the organization as being to produce high-quality art exhibitions according to the judgement of the director. They saw the long-term survival and funding of the organization as superior to that of artistic quality. Thus they acted as the board with the mandate given them in their role as the board, by the general legislation of foundations, to act in the interest of the organization, as interpreted by them, not by the director.

Different scales for measuring success create tension between an artistic leader with a qualitative vision, and management with a more administra-tive and quantitative approach to the enterprise. For the politicians and board members criticizing the directors of the three enterprises, the success in qualitative terms was measured through credit given by the professional art field nationally and internationally, and by their audience. For most of these politicians and bureaucrats and businessmen, the long-term secur-ing of a sound financial footing and direct utility for local inhabitants was more important than the highest artistic quality. In all cases, the two parties were not willing to negotiate their positions, and both had good reasons for their arguments. The question is whether this is unavoidable. This is not the place to discuss other positive cases, but research on such positive examples would certainly be important for future art enterprise directors and managers, and for the publics that appreciate different kinds of art enterprises, including those with very high artistic ambitions. Skills and resources of the founder are evidently central to the success of the enterprises described.

The personal vision and feeling for quality is of course also central to the success of these enterprises described in their initial phases. These two ele-ments are essential to success in the arts field. Nevertheless, it seems they are not deemed as central elements of the management of a going concern, of an established enterprise, by professional managers, especially outside of the arts field. Experience from production of artistic work seems to be vital for an ability to balance management with artistic *Fingerspitzgefühl*. Therefore it is not surprising that the founder-entrepreneur becomes possessive of his or her project and vision. All three directors of the arts enterprises presented here say after their dismissal that they trusted other people engaged in the enterprise to support work towards realization of the qualitative, artistic vision. They all felt completely let down in this respect by the people they had taken on board the project as it grew larger. This naive faith in the sharing of artistic vision is what generated their own energy for the enterprises, and also what actually managed to mobilize resources for them. All three directors and artistic leaders realized that they needed good managers and board members to run the enterprise, but they all felt gravely betrayed by the actions of boards to separate them from the day-to-day management of 'their' enterprises. They had all assumed that the other actors shared their engagement in the artistic vision, and saw the enterprise as the realization of that vision, rather than as an enterprise with a vision that could be negotiated. This is probably a significant difference in arts enterprises compared to business enterprises.

CONCLUDING REMARKS

A question that remains after a Callon-based interpretation of the three cases presented is whom the board of Tensta konsthall actually represented, or spoke for. Did and does the board represent anyone but themselves? The same doubt can be raised regarding the boards of Dalhalla and Edsvik konst och kultur. The board is in theory the representative of the owners of an enterprise, or in relation to political organizations, the voters. But Tensta konsthall was organized as a foundation. In other words the board was the supreme decision-making organ, being accountable only to the tax authorities and to funders. So, on behalf of whom were they acting, when finding continued cooperation with the initial director impossible? Not on behalf of the director who had appointed them to their positions as members of the board – so much is clear. The Friends of Tensta konsthall acted vigorously during the conflict and long after the dismissal of its first director. But they had no influence on the decisions of the board, and their appeals to politicians resulted in no more than clarifications that politicians could not in any way command the board of the gallery. In the case of Edsvik konst och kultur the interests of the board are also unclear. On the board of Edsvik there were representatives of a private music school hosted in facilities adjacent to the gallery. Their connection was foremost with the municipality of Sollentuna. There was also a member representing a local history association, having facilities likewise at the premises of the Edsbergs mansion at Edsviken. They could best be described as competing with the gallery for municipal resources.

The recurring problem for art enterprises is the infinitesimal margins for undertaking activities, especially over a longer period. This is a striking element in all three cases. High-quality art in particular, which often is not as accessible as more traditional art, may be perceived as unnecessarily expensive given the difficulties in assessing its quality for many individuals including politicians. A quantitatively large response or financial basis seems more important for politicians and board members in general, who see the enterprise from the perspective of a going concern. This is an issue still largely unstudied in business and public sector management.

Is there a solution to the dilemma? Probably not, as artistic leadership is closely tied to aesthetic and artistic decisions that need to be taken in close contact with the actual production of art. There is still a need for boards and managers to help consolidate successful art enterprises, and to release artistic directors from unnecessary administrative burdens. Thereby the risk of institutionalization processes immediately enters the enterprise, and more so with public support, where politicians judge an enterprise from their political perspective which does not always recognize the social and cultural values of art enterprises to their full extent. A conclusion both from literature on the influence and role of founders in start-up organizations that become established, and from the cases investigated, is that it seems a true dilemma. It is a problem, from a management point of view, that founders have such a strong commitment to their enterprises. From the point of view of the founder and artistically engaged stakeholders, however, too much formality in management easily kills the value of an art enterprise. The enthusiasm of art enterprise initiators seems, according to boards and management, to be problematic as long as it is not available for more rational, more instrumental aims of politics and formal structures. The entrepreneurship, compassion and personal engagement so sought after in institutional contexts, government and public administration today is not accepted as it is (too) passionate and personal.

In a number of chapters in this volume there are stories featuring structural agents as well as entrepreneurs. The former are defined as possessing various kinds of structural resources, whereas the latter are characterized by visions that seek realization. In the stories of Coompanion (Chapter 3) and the Embassy for Women's Enterprise (Chapter 2) as well as that of Shelley Lin (Chapter 4), the structural agents need other 'entrepreneurial' actors in order to fulfil a predefined function. However, the stories told in these chapters, as well as the stories of this chapter, highlight the different narratives in which their respective figures manage to make sense.

What is remarkable is the difference in the structural agents' narratives for mobilization of support on one hand, and the entrepreneurial narratives for mobilization of support on the other. This becomes especially clear in the cases of failed mobilization of support and even demobilization of support, as in the three cases of this chapter. Where organizations and structures tell stories of aims and resources and development of the region, the entrepreneur tells a story of desires, feelings, action and thoughts. These different narratives phrase the tension between enterprise as a lived individual project in Jansson's (2008) sense, and as aggregate regional strategy projected on a structural (administrative) level. The entrepreneurs of Edsvik konst och kultur, Dalhalla and Tensta konsthall were not willing to accept the mission suggested by representatives of the existing model of structure and organization, but wanted instead to offer structure and organization to a mission, that of helping in the construction of a dream come true. This division of roles and power, quite obviously, was challenged when structure and organization was settled upon for the new enterprises. In this sense, the cases of this chapter serve to show that the rules of the game can effectively prevent entrepreneurial potential being exercised and released, as discussed in Chapter 11 of this book. If the plot of the narratives of the structural agents in Chapters 2 and 3 is about how the entrepreneur can be animated, the plot of the narratives of this chapter is how to kill the entrepreneur without anyone objecting to it – rather an awkward mission in this era of heroization of the creative entrepreneur.

NOTES

1. Professionals more or less directly related to artistic production, such as producers, creators and similar.
2. The case is based on detailed study of both first-hand and second-hand sources, combined with extensive interviews with the former director and other involved parties. The case is presented in detail in Lindqvist (2007a) and also discussed in Lindqvist (2007b).
3. This case is based on first-hand and second-hand sources including official documents, interviews with civil servants, members of staff of the gallery, newspaper articles, a university thesis (Englund, 2004), and other publications (Andér, 2003; Epstein, 2004; Ericsson, 2005), but also on personal contact with several of the actors involved in the management of the gallery during the period 2000–2003.
4. The case is based on first-hand and second-hand published sources, including a book written by Margareta Dellefors (2008) herself, various research reports, and newspaper articles and some municipal public documents.

PART II

. . . Mobilizing the Entrepreneurship Discourse, . . .

6. Entrepreneurship, space and place

Björn Bjerke

INTRODUCTION

As an academic subject, entrepreneurship has come a long way in its 300 years of existence. Many theories have come and gone, many models and interpretations have been proposed, of which some have been accepted, some rejected. Today entrepreneurship is a hot topic, indeed, but it seems to be at an academic crossroads, having many different directions to choose from in the future. One pair of concepts spreading across the social sciences today is space and place. It should, in the light of the title of this book, be of interest to discuss to what extent these two concepts, if applied more consistently, could be an armament in mobilizing the entrepreneurship discourse, fighting for various academic positions in the future.

This chapter contains such a discussion. The purpose is not, however, to replace the ruling entrepreneurship discourse, to the extent that it exists, with a space–place determinism, but to broaden the possibilities of the subject, adding more of the conceptual pair of space and place (some of it exists already, even if fragmentarily).

'Space' and 'place' (as well as 'time') are trivial in a sense, of course. Almost anything we do as human beings occupies space and takes place (and takes time). However, the idea here is to look at space and place as active factors in the sense that a situation would not be the same without considering them. I want to bring space and place into the open and turn them into analytical categories in order to explain or understand entrepreneurship better. In the entrepreneurship field (as well as in the field of business in general) I look at 'space', like Hudson (2001), as mainly an economic evaluation of location based on its capacity for generating profit; and 'place' as a mainly societal evaluation of location based on its capacity to provide meaning.

Let us start by summarizing how the conceptual pair of 'space' and 'place' has been looked at in literature and thinking over the years; this in order to provide a perspective on my aims in this chapter. I will then continue by presenting how it would be possible to discuss various aspects of entrepreneurship using these concepts, and finish by giving my opinion of how the entrepreneurial discourse could be strengthened by incorporating these concepts.

SPACE AND PLACE

The concepts of 'space' (*Raum* in German; *espace* in French) and 'place' (*Ort* in German; *lieu* in French) are basic components of the lived world and we take them for granted. We notice the absence of space when we are pressured, and the absence of place when we are lost (Tuan, 1977). And just because we take them for granted, we normally deem them not worthy of separate treatment. Also taken for granted is the fact that we are 'put in a situation' in space and place to begin with, that space and place existed a priori of our existence on earth. Just because we say that we cannot choose in this matter, we believe we do not have to think about such basic facticity to start with (Casey, 1997). However, when we think about the two concepts, they may assume unexpected meanings and raise questions we have not thought to ask (Tuan, 1977). In fact, space as well as place can be very complicated concepts, which is all the more confusing because, at first glance, they appear so obvious and commonsense. After all, it is impossible to think of the world without the two (Cresswell, 2004, p. 124). To look at the world as space and/or place is to use dimensions to characterize the world into a special fashion and, like using any criterion, a special way to talk about and to understand the world. According to Cresswell (2004, p. 27): 'by taking space and place seriously, we can provide another tool to demystify and understand the forces that effect and manipulate our everyday life'.

Looking at the world as a world of places, for instance, we see different things:

> Looking at the world as a set of places in some way separate from each other is both an act of defining what exists (ontology) and a particular way of seeing and knowing the world (epistemology and metaphysics). Theory is a way of looking at the world and making sense of the confusion of the senses. Different theories of place lead different writers to look at different aspects of the world. In other words, place is not simply something to be observed, researched and written about but simply part of the way we see, research and write. (Cresswell, 2004, p. 15)

Space is normally seen as the more abstract one of the two concepts. When we speak of space, we tend to think of outer space or possibly spaces of geometry (Cresswell, 2004, p. 8). Space is something deterritorialized (de Certeau, 1984). It can be discussed without considering that it might contain any social life, inhabited by actual identifiable people. It is an opening and a result of possibilities, for instance, from a business point of view. Spaciousness is closely associated with the sense of being free. Freedom implies space, enough room in which to act (Tuan, 1977).

Space is generally seen as being transformed into place as it acquires definition and meaning. Brenner (1997, p. 137) expresses it such: 'Space appears no longer as a neutral container within which temporal development unfolds, but, rather, as a constitutive, historically produced dimension of social practices.' Considering antonyms to place, we refer to words such as 'remove', 'take away', 'dislodge', 'detach' and 'take off' (Rämö, 2004). When space feels familiar to us, it has become place (Tuan, 1977). In other words, place is then a meaningful location, to which people are attached (Altman and Low, 1992).

Places are significant to human life. We might even say, like Cresswell (2004, p. 33), that: 'there was no "place" before there was humanity but once we came into existence then place did too'. Places are being made, maintained and contested. All over the world, people are engaged in place-making activities (ibid.). Nothing we do is unplaced (Casey, 1997, p. ix).

However, places are not isolated. Cronon (1992) argues that we must pay attention to their connections. Places are something we occupy. The relationships between people and places are at least as complex as relationships between people, but of another kind. As mentioned, places give meaning to people. This is where people learn to know each other and themselves. Places become points which stand out in every individual's biography, and a set of feelings for different places develops through social interaction (Ekman and Hultman, 2007). Altman and Low (1992, p. 7) phrase it such that: 'the social relations that a place signifies may be equally or more important to the attachment process than the place qua place'.

Even though the term *Homo geographicus* has been coined (Sack, 1997), place is more than geography. It is something, the meaning and usefulness of which is continuously created in social relations and networks, that is, in meetings and flows between people and objects. This is something which has gained increasing response within social as well as within human sciences (Ekman and Hultman, 2007). To put it differently, place is culturally defined (Casey, 1993, p. 33).

The political geographer John Agnew (1987) has outlined three fundamental aspects of place as a 'meaningful location': (1) location; (2) locale; and (3) sense of place.

'Location' has to do with fixed objective coordinates on the Earth's surface (or in the Earth's case a specific location vis-à-vis other planets and the sun). By 'locale', Agnew means the material setting for social relations – the actual shape of place within which people conduct their lives as individuals. By 'sense of place', Agnew refers to the subjective and emotional attachments people have to place. Place can vary in size from being very large (for example, the Earth, universe or nation), mid-sized (for example, cities, communities and neighbourhoods), smaller (for example, homes or rooms) or very small (for example, objects of various kinds) (Altman and Low, 1992). It may even be something completely imaginary such as Utopia. A place can be called a 'room for activities' (Massey, 1995) or an 'arena' (Berglund and Johansson, 2008). 'Home' is an 'exemplary kind of place' (Cresswell, 2004, p. 115).

One concept that frequently appears alongside place in geography texts is 'landscape'. In most definitions of landscape, however, the viewer is outside of it. Places, on the other hand, are very much things to be inside of (Cresswell, 2004, p. 10). Another concept of interest here is 'region', which became very much a part of our vocabulary during the twentieth century (Curry, 2002, p. 511).

Some Views on 'Space' and 'Place' over the Years

For Aristotle place was 'prior to all things'. To be for Aristotle was to be in place (Casey, 1993, p. 14). Aristotle's view on place was dominant for more than 1500 years.

Descartes identified space with matter. To him, place was also a subordinate feature of matter and space (Casey, 1997, pp. 152–6).

In Motte and Cajori (1934, pp. 6–7) we can read that Newton claimed that 'absolute space, in its own nature, without relations to anything external, remains always similar and immovable', and that 'place is a part of space which a body takes up, and is according to space, either absolute or relative'. According to Newton, places do not exist on their own; they exist in name only. Newton's ideas of absolute space became dominant for several hundred years. His contemporary 'competitor', Leibniz, trying to promote the idea of a relative space, never had a chance (Casey, 1997).

The increasing obsession with infinite space from the thirteenth century onward, due to the dominant position of the Catholic Church in the Western world at that time and supported by Newton's theories, had the predictable effect of putting place into the shadows (Casey, 1997). The subordination of place to space culminated in the seventeenth century (Casey, 1993). Renaissance thinkers remained capable of equating space with place and vice versa. However, space eventually took over. From the end of the eighteenth century, place was virtually excluded from the scientific discourse (Rämö, 2004, p. 854). It did not come back, and then in full force, until the mid-twentieth century.

Kant tried to demonstrate that space, as well as time, are conditions under which sense perceptions operate (Jammer, 1982). To him, space was no longer situated in the physical world but in the subjectivity of the human mind (Casey, 1997). Space was not something 'out there', but existed as a sort of mental structuring (Curry, 2002).

According to Curry (2002), two opposing intellectual movements, one deconstructive and one constructive, which gave rise to the recasting of thinking of space and, above all, place were coming up during the latter part of the twentieth century. The first of these, the deconstructive, is perhaps most clearly seen in the work of Heidegger. According to him, everything in the world could and should be an object of empirical inquiry. Place is the same as authentic experience, according to Heidegger (Cresswell, 2004, p. 22). Another body of work that took a deconstructive tack toward the concept of space was the later work of Wittgenstein. Words, including 'space' and 'place', only have meanings within the contexts of the individuals and groups that use them, in particular situations and particular places (Curry, 2000). Before 1960, place was seen ideographically and space was seen nomothetically. However, from the 1970s, constructive notions of place, which were as universal and theoretically ambitious as approaches to space had been, became more and more common. Some attempts in this direction already existed before, for instance Jacobs (1961), who discusses the notion that in social planning one needs both to look at the everyday activities of people who live and work in urban neighbourhoods, and to attend to them as places constructed through these everyday activities; and Hall (1959), who pointed to the ways in which people interact with one another when in close proximity. More central to constructive attempts to move place to the centre of scientific inquiry, however, were geographers like Tuan (1974, 1977), Relph (1976) and Buttimer and Seamon (1980). One element in this movement was a desire to rethink the role of people (and bodies) in the construction of places. Examples of such contributors are the post-structuralist Foucault, the phenomenologist Merleau-Ponty, the historian de Certeau and the Marxist-architect Lefebvre.

Foucault's historical inquiries reveal an alertness to space, or, more precisely, to the way in which spatial relations – the distribution and arrangement of people, activities and buildings – are always deeply implicated in the historical processes under study (Philo, 2000). He claimed in one interview (Foucault, 1980, p. 149), that 'the history of powers' would at one and the same time amount to a history 'written of space'.

Merleau-Ponty claims that places we inhabit are known by the bodies we live. We cannot be implaced without being embodied. Conversely, to be embodied is to be capable of implacement (Casey, 1997). He teaches us that the human body is never without a place and that place is never without body; he also shows that the lived body is itself a place. Its very movement constitutes place, brings it into being (ibid.).

De Certeau may seem to have a kind of opposite understanding of space and place to what is the most common one. To him, place is an empty grid over which practice occurs, while space is what is created by practice (Cresswell, 2004). While we have to use the rules and structures of language to make sense, the same applies to place. As we live in places that become pre-structured, those places are not operational without practice in them. He stresses that tactics operate through a sense of timing (movements) whereas strategies operate through place (fixation) (Hjorth, 2004).

Lefebvre presents a theory that an 'urban revolution' is supplanting an 'industrial revolution' and that this urban revolution is somehow a 'spatial revolution' as well (Merrifield, 2000). He talks about construction of space through a spatial triad: representations of space (also called firstspace – empirically measurable and mappable phenomena), representational space (secondspace – the domain of representations and image, a felt and cared-for centre of meaning) and spatial practices (thirdspace – the lived world, which is practiced and lived rather than being material/conceived or mental/perceived) (ibid.; Cresswell, 2004).

There is a close interconnection between the technologies available for communication and representation and the ways in which space and place are conceptualized. The modern region was in important ways a product of new technologies like the printing press, modern transport and the breakthrough of statistics in social life (Curry, 2002, pp. 508–9).

A genuine rediscovery of place, alongside space, in most of the social sciences today is obvious (Casey, 1997), as in the course of history (for instance, Foucault), in the natural world (for instance, Berry), in the political realm (for instance, Lefebvre), in gender relations and sexual difference (for instance, Irigaray), in the production of poetic imagination (for instance, Bachelard), in geographic experience and reality (for instance, Tuan), in the sociology of the city (for instance, Arendt), in nomadism (for instance, Deleuze and Guattari), in architecture (for instance, Derrida) and in religion (for instance, Nancy). We can see it in economics (for instance, Krugman) and there are examples where space and place are used in business studies in general (for instance, Rämö) as in entrepreneurship in particular (for instance, Hjorth).

The Use of 'Space' and 'Place' in this Chapter

How does 'time' come into this chapter? Places are never finished, but are constantly being performed (Thrift, 1996). Whereabout is always whenabout (Casey, 1993). The old Greeks separated *chora* (space) from *topos* (place, or rather, region), but also *chronos* (dated time) from *kairos* (valued time). Rämö (2000, 2004) makes a four-field classification out of this, of obvious relevance to entrepreneurship. Being aware of the difficulties of separating time from space and place, however, I still do not discuss separate concepts and perceptions of time explicitly in this chapter (it would lead too far). One excuse for this 'neglect' is possibly that in modern and postmodern times we are so inured to the primacy of time that we rarely question the dogma that time is the first of all things. This modern obsession with time may have blinded us to the presence of place in our lives (Casey, 1993).

As mentioned already, in the continuation of this chapter I would like to use the concepts of 'space' and 'place' the same way that Hudson (2001) does. To him, 'space' is an economic evaluation of a situation based on its capacity for profit, while 'place' is a societal situation based on meaning. Spaces are therefore valued predominantly through the lens of production and consumption based on supply and demand, use of factors of production and operations on markets. Places, on the other hand, are situations of meaningful societal life where people live and learn; they are situations of socialization and cultural acquisition. Places are made up of a complex system of societal relations. They create a distinct culture, have meaning and build up identities (ibid.). Thus, while space is the situation of enterprise, place is the situation of societal life. Occasionally, situations thrive both as spaces for profitable business and as places with a rich societal fabric. Under these circumstances, the situation appears to combine the best of economic and societal life (Florida, 2002). In such situations, there is a synergistic relationship between space and place (Johnstone and Lionais, 2004).

Using the concepts of space and place when analysing entrepreneurship can have several advantages according to Hjorth (2004), including: (1) it brings into focus an often-neglected but basic element of everyday life; (2) power becomes naturally included in our studies, which is something rarely happening as part of entrepreneurship research.

Paradoxically, place has become even more important in our modern society with increased mobility (Ekman and Hultman, 2007, p. 21). Today we can witness a multitude of what might be referred to as 'non-places', like airports and other temporary dwellings, which Augé (1995) sees as different from genuine (what he refers to as 'anthropological') places. Our view on place has importance for such important issues today as migration, cases of refugees and asylum.

OUR ENTREPRENEURIAL SOCIETY IN TERMS OF SPACE AND PLACE

In terms of where entrepreneurship is going on (or could go on) in society, I see three types of situations, which can be discussed in terms of space, place or both (Figure 6.1): (1) business situations (where entrepreneurship is going on in markets), (2) common situations (where entrepreneurship is going on in institutions), (3) social situations (where entrepreneurship is going on in public places).

This broad orientation goes along with the call made by Steyaert and Katz (2004): (1) to say that entrepreneurship takes place in multiple sites and spaces; (2) to claim that these spaces are political places in the wide sense of the term; and (3) to state that entrepreneurship can be seen as a matter of everyday activities rather than just as actions of elitist groups of entrepreneurs.

It is important to realize that Figure 6.1 is not intended to be more than a classification of various types of situations in society, where entrepreneurship is going on. To what extent these three types cover all possibilities and pre-empt all entrepreneurial efforts in a society, I dare not say. I also do not want to refer generally to these types as sectors. From an entrepreneurial point of view, the distinctions between various sectors in the society of today are rather blurred. Furthermore, thinking of entrepreneurship as

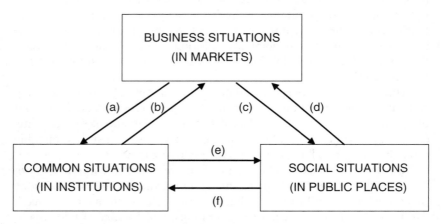

Figure 6.1   Types of entrepreneurial situations in our society

something going on in between (*entre* – as part of the originally French term *entreprendre* = 'inter' in English), moving between the above types of situations can be seen as entrepreneurial movements. Examples of connections between the three situations in Figure 6.1 can be:

(a) One consulting company is helping one city with its 'place marketing'.
(b) One local community is privatizing waste collection.
(c) One company is serious in applying corporate social responsibility, not just in words.
(d) One voluntary organization is supporting women to start their own businesses.
(e) Three employees in a local government institution are starting a soccer club among teenagers.
(f) Two social entrepreneurs are running a seminar on what they are doing, where the participants are members of the dominant local political group.

However, moving between the situation is not straightforward. Working in the common 'sector', running business and operating in the social 'sector' are based on partly different logic. It is important in this context to realize that: 'increasing the connections between entrepreneurship and society, we . . . get the chance to see the new multiverse of entrepreneurship with its variety of social, cultural, ecological, civic and artistic' possibilities (Steyaert and Katz, 2004, p. 193). However, for the sake of clarity, I intend to discuss the three above types of situations of the society one by one in the following order: (1) business situations; (2) common situations; and (3) social situations. I will then continue to discuss two further phenomena of our society related to entrepreneurship in terms of space and place, that is: networking and social capital; and urban and regional development.

Business Situations

Most theories of entrepreneurship we have are market-based and space-based. Historically, theories of entrepreneurship have been built on the economic discourse (Steyaert and Katz, 2004). And most of them are positioned neither in time nor place. Just a few examples:

● Entrepreneurs are achievement-motivated, have a risk-taking propensity, have an internal locus of control, have a need for autonomy, are determined, creative and self-confident and take the initiative (Bridge et al., 2003).

- Many entrepreneurs seem to think counterfactually, live more in the present and in the future than in the past, and become more involved when making decisions and evaluating things, underestimating costs as well as the time required for succeeding (Baron, 1998).
- Positive consequences for entrepreneurs of starting a business include creating one's own future, having a high degree of independence, being responsible only to oneself and following in the family's footsteps (Coulter, 2001).

Two things come naturally with such theories: (1) discussing 'growth' as something primary (which is possible only in space, not in place); (2) looking at 'opportunity recognition' as a distinctive and fundamental entrepreneurial behaviour (Gaglio, 1997; Kirzner, 1979; Stevenson and Jarillo, 1990; Venkataraman, 1997).

I have in one publication (Bjerke and Hultman, 2002) presented entrepreneurship research today in four areas: the role which is played by entrepreneurship in society; the characteristics of entrepreneurs and their thinking; entrepreneurial environments, including intrapreneurship; and entrepreneurial courses of events.

I have in another publication (Bjerke, 2007) outlined four existing schools of entrepreneurship today. They are mainly space-based and are aiming at explaining facts: (1) macro and micro schools; (2) entrepreneurial description schools; (3) supply and demand schools; (4) psychological and behavioural schools.

In the same publication, I suggested four alternative research orientations, place-based on an understanding discourse:

- Entrepreneurs as sense-makers (for instance, Weick, 1995; or Sanner, 1997).
- Entrepreneurs as language-makers (for instance, Normann, 2001; or Arbnor, 2004).
- Entrepreneurs as culture-makers (for instance, Redding, 1993; or Bjerke, 1999).
- Entrepreneurs as history-makers (for instance, Spinosa et al., 1997).

When market-based entrepreneurship theories are discussed in terms of place, this is commonly done by using narratives (for instance, Johansson, 2004b), by bringing networking and social capital into the picture (see later) or by discussing cases like indigenous entrepreneurship (Anderson et al., 2006). When space and place are combined in discussing market-based entrepreneurship, this is commonly done by introducing networks and/or social capital. We will come back to this later.

Common Situations

What I refer to as common situations are situated in what has traditionally been called the public sector and the term 'public entrepreneurship' is still used in the English-speaking world in this context (Osborne and Gaebler, 1992; Osborne and Plastrik, 1997; Cohen et al., 1999) (I will come back to my own version of 'public' entrepreneurs later, when discussing social situations). However, the traditional distinction between public and private in terms of ownership seems less adequate when discussing entrepreneurship today (Hjorth and Bjerke, 2006, p. 99). Traditionally public duties like schooling, sanitation and official transportation are in many countries often taken care of by private enterprises, and various traditionally private businesses are often run by governments, nationally or locally. Common situations can be looked at in terms of space as well as in terms of place. The public sector (which contains such situations) has occupied a space to act economically by requiring people in a society pay taxes, tariffs and charges to an amount which in a country like Sweden is more than half its gross national product (GNP). However, at the same time, activities in common situations (entrepreneurial or not) take place in institutions like schools, hospitals, courts and common political and quasi-political offices at national, regional and local levels. Movements like labour unions and consumers' cooperatives have today become rather institutionalized and may very well be seen as belonging to common situations (or to business situations in the latter case), even though they once started in social situations.

Common situations at the central political level of a nation can be understood in terms of space and seen as a more collective form of entrepreneurship that focuses on broader actions and outcomes as a response to changes characterizing the global age (de Bruin, 2003).

It is clear that there is a need for a new terminology to be developed to convey better the nature of the state and to conceptualize the reconfiguration of the role of the state in this new era. The 'welfare state' concept is now outmoded. Jessop (1994, p. 251) argues that: 'a Schumpeterian workfare state is more suited in form and function to an emerging post-Fordism state'. Similarly, Audretsch and Thurik (1999) observe that industrialized countries have changed from the 'managerial economy' of the previous industrial era to a knowledge-based 'entrepreneurial economy'. De Bruin (2003) suggests the term 'the strategic state': 'The strategic state could be the principal actor in laying the foundations for building a strong, socially inclusive economy within the globally connected world' (p. 156). Some small city-states are doing just that. According to Pereira (2004), the Singaporean government has chosen to evolve from a developmental to an entrepreneurial state.

There are ten features which characterize the new form of entrepreneurial government in general, according to Osborne and Gaebler (1992). These are promotion of competition, empowerment of citizens, measuring performance through outcomes, being driven by goals, redefinition of clients as customers, prevention of problems rather than offering services later, putting energies into earning money rather than simply spending, participating management, preference of market over bureaucratic mechanisms and focus on catalyzing all sectors into solving a community's problems.

When going to the local level of government, the discussion becomes different from the above. Place then takes a front position:

> Economic processes are often regarded as provoking a more basic level of explanation, while cultural and political change is interpreted as a dependent variable which is caused or heavily conditioned by the economy. While there is no doubt that what is conventionally understood as 'the economic' has important effects on all aspects of urban life, the view of the economy as foundational is flawed for a number of reasons. First, it is based on a false division between economic, cultural and political realms. None of these areas is independent of the others. Second, the very idea of a foundational explanation is suspect. Even if it is possible to explain some aspects of (say) political change with reference to economic processes, this does not exhaust the explanatory task, since the economic processes themselves require explaining. Third, economic changes always have a wide range of preconditions, some of which may well be cultural and political.Thus an entrepreneurial urban economy will only emerge if certain preconditions are in place. The precise specification of these preconditions is likely to vary from case to case, since it is possible that slightly different combinations of conditions could be compatible with the emergence of entrepreneurial cities. (Painter, 1998, p. 266)

I will discuss more of this in a later section, called 'Urban and regional development'.

Social Situations

Locating some entrepreneurship in social situations as well as in the other two types of situations is related to the idea, mentioned earlier, that entrepreneurship can be seen in the whole society, not only in its economy. Another term covering social situations sometimes used is therefore to talk about a 'third sector' (outside the market and common situations). In almost all industrialized countries, we are witnessing a remarkable growth in this sector (Defourney, 2001, p. 1). Westerdahl (2001) suggests three hypotheses why this is so:

1. The vacuum hypothesis: the shrinking common sector and the decline in the business sector over vast areas of the society have provided scope for other actors.

2. The influence hypothesis: we are witnessing a questioning of the way in which the common sector handles tax monies coupled with a desire for an increased influence over the forms for handling them.
3. The local-identity hypothesis: parallel with globalization, we notice a quest for local and regional identities.

A concept sometimes heard here is 'the social economy'. Assuming that actors in the social economy have the common good or the good of their members, not private interests, as their principal driving force, the definition of social economy selected by the European Union (EU) confines itself to four types of organizational forms: cooperatives, mutuals, associations and foundations. The historical roots of social economy are in eighteenth-century France, which was marked by violent class conflicts, leading up to the French Revolution. Economic thought in France became focused on 'finding a compromise, on restraining the market and crass individualism by launching the pedagogical and political programme which came to be known as *l'économie sociale*' (Trädgårdh, 2000, p. 6). Other names used for the social economy are non-profit sector, not-for-profit sector, solidarity economy, alternative economy or third system (Westlund, 2001).

There are several problems with using the concept 'social economy' for 'social situations' in the context of this chapter:

1. It is a very space-based concept with the restrictions that follow from this.
2. I can see cooperative, mutuals, associations as well as foundations operating in both the other two types of situations outside my social ones, and I can see entrepreneurs in social situations that have derived their impetus from voluntary work and operating under a wide variety of organizational forms not restricted to the four covered by the EU definition. Those ventures covered by the EU definition could be called 'social enterprises' (Defourney, 2001), where only some of them could be understood by my view of 'social situations'.
3. The modern concepts and the theories behind the social economy (there commonly referred to as the non-profit sector) come from the USA. The understanding of the social sector in that country is, however, very different from the European one (Defourney, 2001).

Talking about public entrepreneurs in social situations allows a novel discussion of entrepreneurship as a societal force (Hjorth and Bjerke, 2006, p. 99). And as mentioned already, it is not the same as entrepreneurship in situations, in what is traditionally referred to as the public sector, which I refer to as 'common situations'. I use 'public' in a broader, historically contingent sense. 'Public' entrepreneurship may look the same as 'social' entrepreneurship, but there are differences. The social can be seen as an invention (as mentioned, originating in revolutionary France) meant to make visible the specific problems related to inequality and poverty in a society founded on civil and political inequality (Dean, 1999). Whereas 'social' entrepreneurship produces the 'social' as something needing to be fixed, however, 'public' entrepreneurship creates 'sociality' as something missing in local communities or something which is seen as marginal, concerning only a few. 'Social' entrepreneurship is today used primarily when discussing how to 'fix' problems with a withering 'welfare state' (Dreyfus and Rabinow, 1982), including 'reinventing government' (Osborne and Gaebler, 1992). Public entrepreneurs do not try to do the institutions' job better or replace the market. Public entrepreneurs are not producers or institutional offices approaching consumers or clients where the laws of supply and demand are ruling, but citizens involving other citizens, aiming at making some marginal phenomena more central (public) in the society. Another term for public entrepreneurship could be 'citizen entrepreneurship'.

Citizenship is a composite concept that includes individuals and groups, and discussions of citizenship always have to deal with rights and values and societal practice in which forms of citizenship are practised (Petersen et al., 1999). Citizenship in today's society is less of an institution and more of an achievement. Citizenship is therefore a matter of identity.

I use 'public' in the original Greek sense of something accessible to all and something which all should feel responsible for. Public entrepreneurs operate in public places. Public places could be defined as physical, virtual, discursive and/or mental arenas which are, in principle, open to everyone. At the same time, these public entrepreneurs are often missing on the institutional policy-makers' agenda (Hjorth and Bjerke, 2006, p. 120).

Going back a bit in modern academic history, it 'started' as social entrepreneurship. This phenomenon, discovered only in the mid-1990s, has already got several names, for instance, 'civic entrepreneurship' (Henton et al., 1997) or 'mundane entrepreneurship' (Rehn and Taalas, 2004), to mention a few. It originates in the US, where it was immediately incorporated as another form of management. Some examples:

- Bornstein (1998, p. 36) characterizes social entrepreneurs as: 'pathbreakers with a powerful new idea, who combine visionary and real-world problem-solving capacity, who have a strong ethical fiber, and who are "totally possessed" by their vision for change'.
- Schulyer (1998, p. 1) argues that social entrepreneurs are: 'individuals who have a vision for social change and who have the financial

resources to support their ideas and who exhibit all the skills of successful business people as well as a powerful desire for social change'.

- Boschee (1998, p. 1) presents social entrepreneurs as: 'non-profit executives who pay increased attention to market forces without losing sight of their underlying mission'.
- Thompson et al. (2000, p. 238) describe social entrepreneurs as: 'people who realize where there is an opportunity to satisfy some unmet need that the welfare system will not or cannot meet, and who gather together the necessary resources (generally people, often volunteers, money and premises) and use these to "make a difference"'.

To summarize the American view on social entrepreneurship, we can say:

- The models focus on individual entrepreneurs.
- The models are very rationalistic. If you have the right characteristics as a person and apply the correct set of activities, you will make it as an entrepreneur, social or not.
- The entrepreneurs are presented as super-persons. Only some people can be entrepreneurs.
- In the same way, entrepreneurship is presented as extraordinary activities, not as everyday activities.
- Entrepreneurship should use as much as possible of established business knowledge, the more the better. A social entrepreneur is seen as another kind of entrepreneur, but he or she should act as much as possible as a business person.
- Definitions of social entrepreneurs are given either as their mental profile or in terms of what they achieve, not so much as how they actually operate, that is, the definitions are more in space than in place terms in my vocabulary.

These are not the public entrepreneurs I talk about, that is, citizen entrepreneurs who try to do good for other citizens.

NETWORKING AND SOCIAL CAPITAL

Some say that Piore and Sabel brought business networks into entrepreneurship theory through their 1984 book heralding the industrial districts in Northern Italy as an alternative economic model (Piore and Sabel,

1984). They defined industrial districts as geographically concentrated communities of mostly small businesses, each specializing in particular production or service components of an end product (I will come back to industrial regions in the next section). More profoundly, it is a common understanding that we have a network society today:

> Networks have existed in all economic systems. What is different now is that the networks, improved and multiplied by technology, have entered our lives so deeply that 'the network' has become the central metaphor around which our thinking and our economy is organized. If we cannot understand the logic characterizing the networks, we cannot exploit the economic change which has now started. (Kelly, 1998, p. 10)

> The diversity of networks in business and the economy is mind-boggling. There are policy networks, ownership networks, collaboration networks, organizational networks, network marketing – you name it. It would be impossible to integrate these diverse interactions into a single all-encompassing web. Yet no matter what organizational level we look at, the same robust and universal laws that govern nature's own webs seem to greet us. The challenge is for economic and network research alike to put these laws into practice. (Barabási, 2002, p. 217)

> Networks are the new socio-morphology of our societies and the diffusion of the logic of networks is, to a large extent, influencing the function and results of production processes, experiences, power and culture. (Castells, 1998, p. 519; my translation)

'Networks' and 'networking' are important entrepreneurial tools that contribute to the establishment, development and growth of small firms (Shaw and Conway, 2000, p. 368). Some say that without networking, there is no entrepreneurship (Johannisson, 2000).

Typical discussions of networks in terms of space would be:

- A more developed network is more beneficial to a start-up than a less developed network (Larson and Starr, 1993).
- The advantages of network membership accrue to large and small businesses alike, but given the limited resources of small businesses relative to large ones, network membership is more important to small business survival (Szarka, 1990; Pyke and Sengenberger, 1992).
- Networks allow the owner-manager of a new business venture access to resources that are not possessed internally (Ostgaard and Birley, 1994).

However, there is a difference between discussing networking as a way to improve business (a discussion in terms of 'space') and networking as a necessary social organic existence (a discussion in terms of 'place'). Discussions of network in terms of the first often leads to technical discussions like good or bad networks, more or less functional networks and so on. Networks have an economic as well as a social content. They consist of weak, calculative ties (mainly a space concept) as well as of strong, emotional ties (mainly a place concept). In the latter case, we sometimes talk about embeddedness (Granovetter, 1985). Southern (2000) offers some relevant points on the embedding process which every small firm goes through:

- The embedded nature of their business is not simply a property of an economic transaction but of the concrete social relations which are built up between participating actors.
- A social relationship must exist between the business owner-manager and business contacts before an economic transaction can take place.
- A moment of lack of trust, opportunism of the worst kind or disorder is always possible in all business transactions.
- It is difficult to discuss a single business activity in isolation without considering its predecessors and its followers (related to the same firm).

A concept of high relevance here is 'social capital' which, unlike 'human capital', is a place concept. Broadly, analysts of social capital are concerned with the significance of relationships as a resource for social action (Nahapiet and Ghoshal, 1998). This reflects the emerging concern about the role of social relationships in understanding business activities. An actor's embeddedness in social structures endows him or her with social capital through networking (Portes and Sensenbrenner, 1993; Oinas, 1999). In the literature, social capital is broadly defined as an asset that inheres in social relations and networks (Burt, 1997; Leana and van Buren, 1999).

The characteristics of urban concentrations and regions (the subject of the next section) that to progress successfully probably include a more diversified social capital in which new growth and closure of actor-networks is continually going on. This implies social capital that is fairly heterogeneous but at the same time has a sufficiency of links between the various actors' and groups' own networks not to collapse into numerous competing funds of social capital at the urban or regional level (Grabher and Stark, 1997).

URBAN AND REGIONAL DEVELOPMENT

Talking about urban concentrations and regions from an entrepreneurial point of view could have been done when talking about the common situation mentioned earlier, but entrepreneurship at urban and regional level has its own merits to justify its own discussion. It is common to hear the terms 'entrepreneurial city' or 'entrepreneurial urban space' today. It is hard to find a generally accepted definition of an entrepreneurial city (or an entrepreneurial urban space), but the notion of cities (and urban space) being run in an entrepreneurial manner is widely subscribed to (Beyes, 2006, p. 260). Painter (1998, pp. 260–61) provides a list of some ideas of the meanings of the words 'entrepreneurial city':

- The city as a setting for entrepreneurial activity.
- Increased entrepreneurialism among urban residents.
- A shift from public sector to private sector activity.
- A shift in values and meanings associated with urban living in favour of business.
- A shift in urban politics and governance away from the management of public services and the provision of local welfare services towards the promotion of economic competitiveness, place marketing to attract inward investment and support for the development of indigenous private sector firms (this is Painter's own focus).

Painter (p. 262) also provides a definition of an entrepreneurial urban regime: 'A coalition of interests including the public sector and private firms which is organized through partnerships and whose goal is the enhancement of the competitiveness of the urban region.' Painter asserts that entrepreneurial institutional governance does not arise automatically, but is socially, politically and culturally produced. This points at the importance of 'place' alongside 'space' here:

> The new urban entrepreneurialism typically rests on a public–private partnership focusing on investment and economic development with the speculative construction of place rather than amelioration of conditions within a particular territory as its immediate (though by no means exclusive) political and economic goals. (Harvey, 1989, p. 9)

This also indicates that occasionally urban politics can be seen as moving away from institutionalism and into governance:

> Urban politics is no longer, if it ever was, a process of hierarchical government in which decisions by local politicians are translated straightforwardly by

public bodies into social and economic change. Rather it involves a complex process of negotiation, coalition formation, indirect influence, multi-institution working and public–private partnership. This diffuse and multi-faceted form of rule has come to be termed 'governance'. (Painter, 1998, p. 261)

According to Jessop (1997), governance is associated with a particular form of rule. Unlike the hierarchical rule provided by the local state and the anarchy of the market, he argues that governance involves 'heterarchy', which might be defined as 'rule through diversity'.

In entrepreneurial cities, political agency is not unitary or singular, but heterogeneous and complex. Furthermore, entrepreneurial cities should not require risk-taking, but a focus on opportunities (Dupuis et al., 2003, p. 134). Learning to be an entrepreneurial city involves, among other things (Painter, 1998, pp. 268–9):

- The acquisition of specific skills, such as those associated with place promotion, auditing, commercial accounting, negotiation with private sector institutions, and the preparation of funding applications.
- The development of new self-understandings which may involve, for example, a subordination of the role of 'welfare provider' to that of 'business supporter', or the role of 'bureaucrat' to that of 'strategic manager'.
- Acquiescence (rather than active resistance) in the face of centrally imposed requirements to shift to more entrepreneurial practices of governance.
- The acceptance of change and of 'challenges' as inevitable, or even desirable, in contrast with a previous expectation of stability.

Inspired by Lefebvre (1991) again, we can talk about three kinds of city place. The first kind is the physical aspects of the city, like public places, amusement parks, shopping malls, and gated communities as well as shanty towns or other islands of poverty. This kind is perceived. The second kind is rather conceived. It is the product of the creative artist, the artful architect, the utopian urbanist and the philosophical geographer, among others. This is a type of imaginary city, constituted by an abundance of images and representations (Hubbard and Hall, 1998). The third kind is the 'directly lived' place, an enacted city. This third kind is the most interesting one in entrepreneurship studies, as I see it. To use Beyes's (2006) words: 'A theatre of entrepreneurship has a lot more to offer than commerce and economic drive' (p. 270).

A common trend in local government in developed countries has been greater activism in promoting local approaches to local conditions (Dupuis et al., 2003). Urban places may be regarded as potential 'lived places' – as potential sites for reorganizing the established and crafting the new. 'Communities have within themselves the ability to foster entrepreneurship by defining it at the level of every person and every interaction' (Steyaert and Katz, 2004, p. 191), or to phrase it differently: 'crossing research on entrepreneurship and entrepreneurial cities with thoughts on and observations of socially produced places' (Beyes, 2006, p. 255). However, researchers seldom consider the lived culture of entrepreneurial cities or the changing textures and rhythms of everyday life in their work (Hoggart, 1991, p. 184).

One situation where the difference between space and place is obvious is when we talk about depleted communities, that is, places which are inhabited by people with strong feelings for the local situation, at the same time as they are places which are less developed in economic terms. If such communities are to develop (economically), it must most likely take place by alternative forms of entrepreneurship that are adapted to their particular circumstances (Johnstone and Lionais, 2004). For such places to succeed in terms of gaining an economic space through the application of business techniques and practices at the same time as they strengthen the sense of place among their inhabitants is sometimes called 'community entrepreneurship' (ibid.).

Moving up in space, there is today a considerable interest in clusters, regions, regional development and so on. There are several reasons for this.

During the 1970s, the conditions for economic development in industrialized countries changed dramatically. Previously it had been taken for granted that mass production gave winning advantages. Now this growth model ran into trouble (see, for instance, Nyström, 2002). The industrialized countries could no longer compete with low-cost countries when manufacturing standard products. Companies in the Western world instead had to compete through innovation, flexibility and productivity, which did not turn out to be easy for large companies. Small and medium-sized firms proved to be better at handling this situation in decentralized systems in geographically limited areas.

In a globalized production and finance economy, countries' central governments have lost control of the flow of investments and labour. At the same time a more knowledge-intensive economy has developed. Regions supporting processes of learning and innovation have been identified as a key source of competitive advantage (MacKinnon et al., 2002).

Localization has become a competitive factor. Thinking about competition and competitive strategy has previously been dominated by what goes on inside companies. Yet the prominence of clusters suggests that much of competitive advantage lies outside companies, residing in the locations at which their business units are based (Porter, 1998). Companies may actually benefit from having more local companies in the same business field as themselves, in spite of the tendency to believe that this will create more local competition, drive up input costs and make it more difficult to retain employees.

Geographic concentration occurs because proximity serves to amplify productivity and innovation (Porter, 1998). Transaction costs are reduced, the creation and flow of information is improved and local institutions turn out to be more responsive to the specialized needs of companies, when there are more of them and peer pressure and competitive pressure are more keenly felt.

> Paradoxically, then, the enduring competitive advantages in a global economy are often heavily local, arising from concentrations of highly specialized skills and knowledge, institutions, rivals, and sophisticated customers in a particular nation or region. Proximity in geographic, cultural, and institutional terms allows special access, special relationships, better information, powerful incentives, and other opportunities for advantages in productivity and productivity growth that are difficult to tap from a distance. (Porter, 1998, p. 11)

Knowledge is a non-rivalries production factor which, when used more, will not lead to decreasing returns but can be used by a large number of actors at the same time. Several studies point out the fact that knowledge-intensive production tends to organize itself in clusters (Braunerhjelm et al., 1998).

Many theories and models have been presented to explain and to assist in improving regional entrepreneurship. Some of them are Marshall's 'industrial districts' with spillover and agglomeration effects (1898); Polanyi's 'tacit knowledge' (1966); Porter's 'diamond-clusters', based on the synergy of four groups of production factors (1990); Feldman's 'regional technological infrastructure' (1994); and Normann's list of characteristics of successful regions (2001). They are all, more or less, space-based.

In my opinion, there should be more of place discussions in studies of successful entrepreneurial regions. Along this line, I would like to raise five questions as a kind of criticism against established regional theories (Bjerke, 2007, pp. 220–22):

1. What is an Industrial Region?

There are many who claim that what is happening when specific senior actors get together is that industrial regions are constructed rationally using plans, decisions and coordinated action. An alternative (and in my opinion more fruitful) view is a social constructionistic one (compare Alberti, 2003) or a phenomenological one. An industrial region gradually comes into existence through repeated discussions and materializes as names and labels come to be given to those events and activities that take place and by endorsing supportive organizations with the name of the region (Berg, 2001).

One is 'invoking' (Berg, 2001) and one 'makes sense of' (Weick, 1995) the region in such a way. An industrial region then becomes a sense of belonging (Alberti, 2003), a way of thinking, a discourse and an epistemic community (Håkanson, 2003) more than anything else.

2. How Important is Entrepreneurship in the Society-Wide Meaning of it to an Industrial Region?

As I see it, all kinds of entrepreneurship are crucial for the success of the industrial region. Nothing happens if nobody acts. Entrepreneurship is, after all, about coming up with things that the environment can use.

However, one should look at entrepreneurship in all varieties that exist in the modern society. It appears (or should appear) in all parts of society, that is, in the common, business and social situations.

3. Is it Possible to Successfully Build an Industrial Region Top-Down?

Industrial districts have almost exclusively been studied and treated as objective phenomena, on the assumption that it is possible to identify the crucial parameters that are necessary to succeed and then work (hard) to apply them (Acs, 2002).

Human abilities such as will-power, passion and empathy have hardly been considered at all. Social capital is assumed to be produced by formal institutions, which generate trust and absorb uncertainty (Hjorth and Johannisson, 2002).

A more realistic alternative is to discover the unique, organic conditions existing in an industrial region and then to support and participate in dialogues in creative and constructive networks, where key actors move forward together. The enabling role of authorities then becomes more important than the task of providing service (Karlsson et al., 2001).

Industrial regions (and clusters) are extremely difficult (or impossible) to create from the outside or top-down. Existing regions have a history and have taken time to develop, from within and bottom-up.

4. Is it Possible to Successfully Pick the Geese that will Lay the Golden Eggs to be Part of the Industrial Region?

Too many power-holders in incubators, industrial villages and local community institutions believe they can decide beforehand which types of industries ('They shall belong to the future') and business firms ('They shall have a growth potential') should be included in their region, and also that they can pick out those that will be most successful.

This contradicts everything we think we know about how innovation works. Innovative processes cannot be planned in a rational way, they behave randomly, almost arbitrarily and they are practically unpredictable.

The task is rather to do one's best in an industrial region to create even more turbulence, even more variety, to 'let a thousand flowers bloom'. Participating actors then have the best conditions in which gradually to build something more meaningful and more sustainable.

5. How to Humanize Visions, Networks, Ideals and Systems in an Industrial Region?

People interpret their belonging (or lack of belonging) to an industrial region in different ways, which may seem coherent and meaningful only to themselves (people are 'embedded' in their social context). There are, however, several problems associated with the dominant, super-rational view on how to develop successful industrial regions (Hjorth and Johannisson, 2002):

- There is a need for a gradualist approach, social constructionism or phenomenology.
- One should listen to local 'storytellers'.
- One needs a local 'world-view', think and act 'glocally'.
- One should study local history.
- One should invoke and make sense of a collective identity.

EXPLAINING AND UNDERSTANDING, SPACE AND PLACE

We can find some interesting similarities between talking in terms of space and place and talking in terms of explaining and understanding. I have talked about explaining and understanding earlier in this chapter. According to von Wright (1971) and Apel (1984), the German philosopher of history Johann Gustav Droysen (1808–84) was the first, within science, to introduce the difference between 'to explain' and 'to understand' (in German, *Erklären* and *Verstehen* respectively), to ground historical sciences methodologically and to distinguish them from natural sciences. He did this in *Grundrisse der Historik*, which was published in 1858: 'According to the object and nature of human thought there are three possible scientific methods: the speculative (formulated in philosophy and theology), the mathematical or physical, and the historical. Their respective essences are to know, to explain, and to understand' (Droysen, 1858/1987, p. 13).

Droysen's term *Verstehen* can be traced back to the modern founders of hermeneutics, Friedrich Schleiermacher (1768–1834) and Auguste Boeckh (1785–1867), and was made more generally known through Max Weber (1864–1920). A historically significant form of the debate between understanding and explanation began with Wilhelm Dilthey (1833–1911). He utilized the dichotomy between understanding and explanation as the terminological foundation for distinguishing between natural sciences and *Geisteswissenschaften* (the humanities) as a whole. Initially understanding gained a psychological character, which explanations lacked. This psychological element was emphasized by several of the nineteenth-century anti-positivist methodologists, perhaps above all by Georg Simmel (1858–1918), who thought that understanding as a method characteristic of the humanities is a form of 'empathy' (von Wright, 1971). But empathy is not a modern way of separating understanding from explanation. Understanding can today be associated with 'intentionality' (a phenomenological term), for instance, in a way which explanation cannot.

Generally we can say that natural sciences require concepts which permit the formation of testable laws and theories. Other issues, for instance those deriving from ordinary language, are of less interest. But in the social sciences another set of considerations exists as well: the concepts used to describe, explain and/or understand human activity must be drawn at least in part from the social life being studied, not only from the scientists' theories (Fay, 1996). Scientific concepts then bear a fundamentally different relationship to social phenomena from that which they bear to natural phenomena. In social sciences, concepts partially constitute the reality being studied; in relation to natural phenomena, concepts merely serve to describe and explain (ibid.).

'It is possible to explain human behaviour. We do not try to understand an area of low pressure because it has no meaning. On the other hand we try to understand human beings because they are of the same kind as we are' (Liedman, 2002, p. 280; my translation). No one today claims that only natural sciences should aim for explanations and that only social sciences should aim for understanding. In practice, attempts at both are made in both areas. Researchers are also conscious of the differences between the two approaches, although in everyday usage it is harder to distinguish between what is meant by 'explain' and 'understand'. While it seems relatively clear that 'explain' means, by and large, to figure out the external circumstances around what has happened or what is happening, there is, however, a wide variety of opinions as to what we could mean by 'understand':

- 'To understand' means to find out more details.
- 'To understand' means to get access to subjective opinions.
- 'To understand' means to get a picture of the larger context in which a phenomenon is placed.
- 'To understand' means to get a picture of relevant circumstances which have taken place earlier in a specific situation.

To me, none of these equates to understanding; they are each just more detailed, more circumstantial or deeper aspects of explanation. As I see it, the crucial difference between explaining and understanding is that explanation sees language as depicting reality and understanding sees language as constituting reality.

Thus, explaining-oriented researchers look for factual (objective and/ or subjective) data and use a depicting language; want to find cause–effect relationships; and build models. While understanding-oriented researchers deny that factual and depicting data exist (at least in the human world); want to look for actors' views on meaning, importance and significance and use a constituting and forming (even performing) language; and come up with interpretations.

In this, models are deliberately simplified pictures of factual reality and interpretations are deliberately problematized pictures of socially constructed reality. It is natural for explaining-oriented researchers to build models and for understanding-oriented researchers to come up with interpretations.

So, why have I brought this up here and discussed 'explaining' and 'understanding' at some length? There are four reasons for this:

1. It is important to understand that there are different incompatible research paradigms around.
2. It is equally important to understand that there is no neutral point from which you can choose objectively between paradigms.
3. So, when 'choosing' (if that is the word), you must by necessity be situated in one of the options, thereby looking at your own paradigm differently from what proponents from other options (paradigms) do.

4. There might be a huge difference between everyday language and research language, for instance, between 'explaining' and 'understanding'. I have often heard the question: 'Can we combine explaining with understanding in one and the same research effort?' My answer is: 'Yes you can, but, then you do not mean the same thing with the words as I do. Furthermore, trying to be eclectic rarely leads to wisdom.'

Above all, the main reason why I have introduced this discussion in this chapter is that I think we can discuss 'space' and 'place' in similar terms as 'explaining' and 'understanding'. The two may bring different kinds of (incompatible) thinking to the researcher when using them. If so, it is not a matter of choosing between them, because they may (in a strictly scientific sense) look at the world differently and there is no neutral point from where you can choose objectively between the two. Of course, we can use 'space' and 'place' in the same research effort. However, if so, we are not discussing 'space' on premises of its own, and discussing 'place' on premises of its own. This, in my opinion, is not very constructive and may even lead to confusion.

WHAT GOOD CAN 'SPACE' AND 'PLACE' DO TO THE ENTREPRENEURSHIP DISCOURSE?

As a summary, in the spirit of this book, I can see several possibilities by incorporating the conceptual pair of 'space' and 'place' into the entrepreneurship discourse more extensively and more consistently than has been the case so far. Above all, I can see three possibilities:

1. Having the opportunity to use a lot of theories, models and interpretation from 'neighbouring' subjects when researching entrepreneurship, subjects which have been discussing their research areas through this pair of concepts for quite some time, for instance history, political studies, human geography, architecture, urban studies and regional economics.
2. Truly being able to live up to the vision that entrepreneurship belongs to the whole society, not only to its economy.
3. By using such broad approach, unshackling the entrepreneurship paradigm from such 'hangover biases' such as that entrepreneurship primarily has to do with economic growth, that the subject is a predominantly male gender issue, is associated with a hero focus, and does not have to consider culture and mundane activities in everyday life (aspects which are discussed in several other chapters of this book).

7. Innovation, creativity and imitation

Anders W. Johansson

INTRODUCTION

In this chapter it will be argued that entrepreneurship discourse is highly influenced by the idea that innovation and creativity is separated from imitation in a hierarchical pattern. According to this discourse a few innovators are the most valuable for the society – and imitators in a descending order appear in greater and greater masses as less and less valuable for the change of society the further down in the hierarchy of imitators they appear. This discourse serves to prevent the mobilizing of entrepreneurship in the sense that it does not encourage ordinary individuals to contribute to societal change, unless they behave creatively. The deconstruction of this aspect of the dominating entrepreneurship discourse is therefore a mission in itself as it raises an awareness of what may prevent ordinary men and women from becoming entrepreneurial.

It will be argued that creativity and innovation is a life necessity. There is a basic human tendency to imitate others at the same time as coming up with personal variations of such imitation. To increase innovation and mobilize entrepreneurship in the society might therefore not be a matter of finding men and women with creative talents or of training people in creativity only. It is rather a matter of allowing and encouraging the fundamental capacity every man and woman has to combine creativity and imitation without stressing the first (Ricoeur, 1984).

Imagine a ski jumping hill like the big one in Garmisch-Partenkirchen. You stand at the top of the hill with long skis on your feet. There is a distance of about 100 metres down the hill to reach the take-off ramp and then you are expected to land on your skis after an air voyage of 125 metres. The speed at the take-off ramp is about 100 km/hour. What are your feelings if you imagine yourself standing at the top of this hill right now? A spontaneous response is probably that most ordinary men or women would not even think of risking their lives in this way.

Imagine a young person. Imagine further that this youngster has a couple of handicaps like epilepsy and stammering. He is bowlegged and a chain-smoker. Our man was born in Koskuskulle, a village with less than 1000 inhabitants in the north of Sweden. There is still a ski jumping hill in that village. At the time he was born, 1966, there were quite a few ski jumpers living here. So as a boy he could watch older boys jumping down this hill. This hill was not at all as big as the big one in Garmisch-Partenskirschen. And he did not need to make his first jump from the top of the hill. So our man started to jump down this hill. He tried to imitate the older boys as well as he could. And he managed to come down on his feet. He also found out that he liked this sport and started to exercise, which means he started to imitate other ski jumpers. In gaining experience he did not only imitate others, however. When he had done a successful jump, he tried to jump the same way the next time, aiming at gaining in perfection. Simply stated, he imitated his own success in order to improve his jumping continuously.

The name of this man is Jan Boklöv. At the age of 19 he was a promising ski jumper by Swedish standards, which was not that good in competition with Norway and other eminent countries. At this time, during the summer of 1985, however, something happened that eventually came to affect and change the whole sport of ski jumping as a new jumping technique was born. Before, the Daescher technique was dominant, which means that the skis were kept parallel to each other throughout the jump.

Jan was practising on the plastic ski jump in Falun. On one of the jumps he did not manage to keep his legs tight, so they spread and shaped a V-form. Remember that he was bow-legged. It looked so funny to the spectators who were watching that they started to laugh. But when he landed, the jump measured 90 metres, which was 20 metres more than he used to jump. This event incited Boklöv to new trials and after some time he had developed a new style, a style which is usually considered to be the main reason why he won the World Cup in ski jumping in 1989. Today every ski jumper in competition uses the V-style. It is usually considered that this technique increases the jumping distance by approximately 10 per cent (http://en.wikipedia.org/wiki/V-style). Further, this style means that the ski flight is closer to the ground, which makes the jumping safer for the jumpers. There are now fewer accidents in ski jumping.

The invention of the V-style was an accident, something that happened by chance. This has been acknowledged by Boklöv himself in interviews. He himself does not recognise it as a 'real' invention. However it must be added that the V-style probably would not have been invented at that time had it not been that Boklöv tried to jump in the same way again as the 'accident' caused him to do. He intentionally imitated his 'error' and so the

V-style was born. Not only did the spectators laugh at him the first time he jumped this way, but in the beginning this style was not acknowledged by the judges and was given low style points. This did not stop Jan Boklöv from winning the World Cup.

The moral of this story is that a more or less average ski jumper can change the whole sport by chance. This is however not the important part of the story. The important thing is that this man was not hindered, despite his handicaps, from starting ski jumping. And during his career he was an enthusiastic imitator of other jumpers as well as of imitating himself. He was living out his imitative behaviour and this caused him to be creative, not just once, but continuously, as he continuously strived to improve his performance. This is more or less the experience of every athlete. The same is also true for every man and woman in any occupation as long as they have a passion for what they do.

Entrepreneurship discourse has incorporated ideas that go against the idea of the potential of every man and woman as an innovator. This chapter starts by recapitulating some of Joseph Schumpeter's ideas about entrepreneurship. It is argued that Schumpeter's early ideas, which convey a rather narrow conception of the entrepreneur, have permeated the discourse on entrepreneurship. Some of his later ideas about innovation, which go in a quite different direction, still stand on the sidelines supplanted by the image of the spectacular entrepreneur. Using Schumpeter's later ideas about entrepreneurship as a starting point, it is argued that in order to understand innovation as a common and collective phenomenon, another understanding of imitative behaviour than Schumpeter's is needed. Here the work of Gabriel Tarde and Paul Ricoeur is drawn upon as they offer quite a different view of the link between imitation and innovation when compared to Schumpeter. Both Tarde and Ricoeur hold that innovation emanates from imitation. First, Tarde's argument is recognized as well as the attention given to imitation in contemporary organization theory. Then, Paul Ricoeur is drawn upon as he offers a theoretical lens to understand innovation as an intentional act based upon imitation.

DIFFERENT VIEWS OF ENTREPRENEURSHIP: SCHUMPETER I AND II

Today 'entrepreneurship' is a catchword not only on the lips of economists but is used by all kinds of scholars and practitioners in a diversity of contexts. But what is it? If only one author is to be chosen as having greatly influenced the meaning of entrepreneurship it is not very controversial to

suggest Joseph Schumpeter (1883–1950). Without doubt he was successful in attributing to entrepreneurship a fundamental function within the
economy and in social life, namely the function to bring the market out
of equilibrium and move the whole economy and thereby change society.
Entrepreneurship was generally assumed to be the key to economic
growth.

Not that Schumpeter was very clear about what entrepreneurship
actually is or was. He actually changed much of his thinking during his
life, therefore it is more relevant to associate him with two quite different
theories of entrepreneurship (Gratzer, 1996, 2009). The early Schumpeter
articulated the individual entrepreneur as the hub of and the engine behind
the change in the economy (Schumpeter I). In his later works (Schumpeter
II) he was much more concerned with innovation as a phenomenon than
with the entrepreneur as an individual. While still recognizing a time in the
early capitalist industry where there was a type of entrepreneur that was
best described as a 'fixer', he thought of modern milieus as less resistant
towards new methods and new goods (Schumpeter, 1947). This means that
while entrepreneurship by Schumpeter I was much associated with the
individual entrepreneur, in his later writings entrepreneurship turned out
to be more of a team effort. Innovation was something which he associated
with teamwork of specialists or whole organizations. From a historical
point of view he meant that the economy was in the process or bureaucra-
tizing itself and thus the entrepreneur (as an individual) loses his function.
Thus Schumpeter experienced as well as predicated a quite different social
structure.

Today's discourse on entrepreneurship is still much like the ideas of
Schumpeter I, where there is one crucial element of all economic activity
and that is the entrepreneur. This is not really true to Schumpeter though,
as the ideal entrepreneur has come to be equated with the manager of fast-
growing or 'gazelle' firms. The role of the entrepreneur in Schumpeter's
thinking was rather to develop innovations, thereby initiating new activities (Landström, 1999). However, in his early writings he was careful not
to equate the entrepreneur with the firm:

> The carrying out of new combinations we call 'enterprise'; the individuals
> whose function is to carry them out we call 'entrepreneurs'. These concepts
> are at once broader and narrower than the usual. Broader, because in the first
> place we call entrepreneurs not only those 'independent' businessmen in an
> exchange economy who are usually so designated . . . As it is the carrying out
> of new combinations that constitutes the entrepreneur, it is not necessary that
> he should be permanently connected with an individual firm; many 'financiers',
> 'promoters' and so forth are not, and still they may be entrepreneurs in our
> sense. (Schumpeter, 1934/2000, pp. 74–5)

Nevertheless, since Schumpeter entrepreneurship theory has been preoccupied with associating the entrepreneur with the firm and not with the innovation process. While researchers belonging to the influential Research Center in Entrepreneurial History at Harvard in the 1950s related entrepreneurship to team activities, a common unit of analysis has been new business ventures (Larsson Segerlind, 2009, p. 32). Thereby the Center took a stand to be independent of Schumpeter. The strongest tradition in entrepreneurship research today is probably what Gratzer (2009) refers to as the 'business school approach'. Within this approach entrepreneurship is operationalized by measuring attitudes to start-ups, the number of new ventures and growth in existing ventures. As Gratzer argues, the underlying assumption is that starting new ventures is supposed to change the economy. More and more, this preoccupation of entrepreneurship scholars with the firm is now questioned. O'Connor (2009) points out how entrepreneurship research, while using Schumpeter's ideas about entrepreneurship and the entrepreneur, has deviated from the idea of entrepreneurs as those who carry out new combinations thereby changing the economy. Sarasvathy (2004) recognizes this tendency and she urges scholars to ask new or other questions in order to understand better what entrepreneurship is all about, especially what entrepreneurs do when they are 'entrepreneuring' (Steyaert, 2007).

Thus mainstream entrepreneurship theorists have lost Schumpeter's interest in distinguishing between entrepreneurship and running a business. Except for one thing: the idea of the entrepreneur as an extraordinary individual, the Schumpeter I idea, has been firmly adopted; while the Schumpeter II idea of innovation as a team effort has formed a research stream of its own, innovation system research (Ylinenpää, 2008). Within entrepreneurship research the idea of the extraordinary man still prevails (Ogbor, 2000).

While mainstream entrepreneurship theory still is preoccupied with the firm, entrepreneurship studies no longer solely deal with economic growth (Steyaert and Katz, 2004), they also deal with social, cultural, civic and ecological issues. In some ways this development harmonizes with Schumpeter II. Entrepreneurship is constituted by a number of different roles and these roles most often are not materialized into one single individual but rather a team of individuals who together carry out the roles of 'the entrepreneur' and act as market disrupters. We then see entrepreneurship as a collective of individuals carrying out new combinations. Further entrepreneurship is not exclusively situated within private firms but takes place in the whole of society. Schumpeter II seems to have been ahead of his time when he shifted perspective from the individual to innovation as a phenomenon.

Technological progress is increasingly becoming the business of teams of trained specialists who turn out what is required and make it work in predictable ways. The romance on the earlier commercial adventure is rapidly wearing away, because so many more things can strictly be calculated that had of old to be visualized in a flash of genius . . . Thus economic progress tends to become depersonalized and automatized. Bureau and committee work tends to replace individual action. (Schumpeter, 1942/1950, p. 132)

Schumpeter radically abandoned his earlier ideas. Entrepreneurship in early capitalism he saw as embodied by a single extraordinary individual. Later innovation, within the hegemony of the world of the big firms, was increasingly institutionalized and routine. These ideas have also greatly influenced research and policy, although as already stated mostly within a separate stream of research. The 'triple helix' idea is one expression which assumes that when universities work together with private firms and public organizations, innovations could be planned and carried out. It should be noticed, however, that this more innovation-oriented stream of research and policy also tends to be excluding. It is typically based upon technology innovation and large firms. Service development, public organizations, small firms and women-dominated businesses tend to be excluded.

To sum up, Schumpeter II shifts focus from the individual entrepreneur to the phenomenon of innovation in order to understand the function of modern entrepreneurship better. While this shift emphasizes entrepreneurship as a collective phenomenon not necessarily related to venture creation, it is still a perspective where large groups of the society are excluded as innovators and entrepreneurs. It should be added that it is not really fair to divide Schumpeter into I and II as his writings are much richer and varied than such a simple division suggests, yet it is done here in order to make the argument in this chapter clearer. In the following sections of this chapter it will be argued that Schumpeter, in his understanding of innovation, separated innovation and imitation while still not helping us to see innovation as it happens. Following this separation, innovation has been associated primarily with creativity as an inherited human characteristic and/or as a capability to be trained; while imitation has been degraded to second-order behaviour when associated to innovation. Thus mainstream entrepreneurial discourse has nurtured a view of innovation as a super-normal instead of a normal human behaviour. Thereby entrepreneurial discourse has demobilized entrepreneurship as action – discouraging ordinary men and women from recognizing their entrepreneurial behaviour. By viewing imitation as a fundamental human behaviour and imitation as inseparable from creativity, a different conception of innovation is made possible, one that mobilizes entrepreneurship in thinking as well as in action.

IMITATION

One main difference between Schumpeter I and II was that in order to grasp the essence of entrepreneurship he shifted focus from the entrepreneur to innovation. To understand innovation became the same thing as to understand entrepreneurship. Even in his early works he found it very important to distinguish between enterprise and business, what innovation is and is not. Running a business as a manager is not entrepreneurship. It is the person who undertakes an innovation, and only him or her who is an entrepreneur. In fact Schumpeter argues that entrepreneurs appear in clusters (1934/2000, p. 228). Only one or a few of the beginners, however, will succeed. Others can then follow these pioneer entrepreneurs/ innovators, because success has now been shown to be possible. So, more people will follow as it has now become easier to succeed, and finally the innovation becomes familiar. Schumpeter (1939) here made a distinction between the entrepreneurs and the followers or imitators, which is fundamental to the main argument of this chapter: 'And those who follow the pioneers are still entrepreneurs, though to a degree that continuously decreases to zero' (p. 414).

The imitators were more like ordinary people, while real entrepreneurs had a leadership capability not many people have. The later in the chain of innovation managers appeared, the less gifted leaders they needed to be. Schumpeter continually insisted that incremental change and discontinuous change were completely different phenomena (Becker et al., 2006, p. 356). Even if Schumpeter was not clear on the borderline between these two, his claim was still there (Gratzer, 2009). Referring back to Boklöv, if we follow Schumpeter's distinction, Boklöv was temporarily an entrepreneur. He was so from the summer 1985 until other ski jumpers had started to jump in the new way. My view is that Boklöv was an entrepreneur in ski jumping throughout his ski jumping career. The Schumpeter-like invention was an 'accident' that happened. However, it would not have happened had he not been an entrepreneur according to the logic I argue for.

While others have followed in Schumpeter's footsteps and, like Winter (2006), adjusted his theory to a more evolutionary process, the argument here is that in entrepreneurship discourse imitation is seen as a completely different behaviour than innovation. Imitation is paid much less attention to in entrepreneurship texts. A review of papers published between 1996 and 2006 in the *International Journal of Entrepreneurial Behaviour and Research* showed that creativity is much more frequently associated with innovation than imitation. Imitation is described primarily as a strategy which can be used by the second-best entrepreneurs. In Schumpeter's world these are not entrepreneurs; the imitators are those that bring equilibrium back to the market. The imitators are important to spread the innovation but not important for the innovation to happen in the first place. Many more people are able to imitate, but imitation is not related to 'true' creativity, it is rather the opposite. And the further down in the chain of innovation we look, the less talented individuals need to be. We have on one side the rare creative people and on the other side the imitators 'en masse'.

The separation of innovators from imitators is something that the entrepreneurship discourse has incorporated from Schumpeter. There have been few attempts to link innovation with creativity and imitation in the entrepreneurship literature. One early exception is Lowe (1995). Lowe argues that previous studies have researched innovation using perspectives and methodologies which have been unable to reveal what people actually do when they are innovating. Lowe uses 'creative imitation' to describe innovation as a social process. This term was used by Drucker (1986), when he proposed 'creative imitation' as a very useful strategy for entrepreneurship. But when Drucker uses the concept it is in harmony with Schumpeter's distinction between the entrepreneur and the imitators. Creative imitation is a strategy that a manager could choose to use in order to be successful. It does not take a (Schumpeter I) entrepreneur to do that. Drucker does not help us much by discussing creativity and imitation and how these two are linked. He reduces imitation to a matter of choosing one strategy or the other. Similarly Schollhammer (1982) relates imitation to one type of strategy and van de Ven (1986) relates it to management. Also Yu (1999, 2001) goes in the footsteps of Drucker, explaining the success of Asian businesses as an outcome of imitative strategies.

The way Lowe (1995) uses the concept 'creative imitation' is different. He argues that the basic social processes involved in innovation itself have been overlooked by researchers (p. 54). Most of Folkoperan's (the studied context in his case) innovative ideas were shown to be imitations of good practices elsewhere, which were 'copied' and transferred to a new context. However Lowe does not further explore imitative behaviour theoretically.

To find an explicit discussion about imitation we need to go outside of contemporary entrepreneurship research. In the field of organization theory there is a recent rediscovery of the works of the sociologist Gabriel Tarde. While being contemporary with Durkheim, his works for a long time have been in the shadow and recent literature on Tarde in English remains very limited (Barry and Thrift, 2007). For Tarde, imitation was one of the social laws (Tarde, 1903). He was a forerunner to Schumpeter by emphasizing the importance of ideas and invention in economic life (Barry and Thrift, 2007). Sundbo (1998, p. 48) finds Tarde to be the first great theorist of innovation and entrepreneurship. For him, in order to understand innovation the crucial thing was imitation.

Characteristic of Tarde are the analogies he drew between natural sciences such as astronomy, physics and biology and social sciences. Thus he stressed the fundamental characteristics of each science. For sociology this was the social individual. Fundamental to understanding the social individual is imitation. The human individual is most of all an imitating creature: 'imitation plays a role in societies analogous to that of heredity in organic life' (Tarde, 1903, p. 11). If human beings comply with one law, it is the law of imitation. This argument may appear as essentialism, but no more so than the idea that creativity in itself is essential for innovation.

For Tarde, imitation was the source of innovation. This means that innovation need not be an intentional act – it is rather a spontaneous effect of imitation: 'for the individual often innovates unconsciously, and, as a matter of fact, the most imitative man is an innovator on some side or another' (Tarde, 1903, p. xiv). Imitation is crucial for innovation and not the other way round. While Tarde distinguishes between imitation and innovation he maintains the interdependent relation between the two. Imitation can never be exact, as imitation always contains a surplus which allows an event or an action to deviate into invention (Lepinay, 2007).

While a discussion of Tarde's ideas of imitation and innovation is more or less missing in the field of entrepreneurship, it is present in the field of organization theory. One example is Sahlin-Andersson and Sevón (2003). Their message about innovation is covered in the introductory paragraph of their chapter:

> we live in a world in which nothing is absolutely new, in which there are no truly original ideas or actions. In such a world, every act is related to one's own ideas, experiences and actions and to those of others. At the same time, however, no idea or action is a perfect copy from other organisations or individuals, for ideas are adopted and translated into something that fits one's context. In this way, actions, although imitated, may become different. (p. 249)

Imitation means to act like someone else, Sahlin-Andersson and Sevón write. Therefore innovation is more or less the opposite of imitation. The two authors confirm that innovation used to be seen as something better and more heroic than imitation. Imitation was an act of the peripheral and the weak. Further, they confirm the picture that today what is new is not that radically new. Innovative ideas are often a combination of new and old ideas, see Lowe (1995) and van de Ven (1986). But for many researchers imitation still is treated as the cause of diffusion, as the way innovations are spread – and imitation as a consequence is reduced to mechanical repetition.

Drawing from Tarde, Sahlin-Andersson and Sevón underline that pure imitation of the repetitive kind does not exist. Instead they see imitation as an ongoing translation made by individuals, whose identities are in the process of being transformed. When individuals translate, they combine what they have seen others do with their own ideas of how to do it in their own context. Therefore, in practice, imitation is neither solely a copy of something nor a completely new way of doing things, but something in between.

Sahlin-Andersson and Sevón make it an important issue that imitation is connected to identity constructions. People imitate prestigious groups, this is an underlying force in Western civilization in the search for 'heroes'. But not only do ordinary people strive to imitate the heroes: so also do the heroes imitate the less prestigious, and we all imitate ourselves. Further, the 'heroes' need not be men and women of flesh and blood: they can also be 'best practices'.

To sum up, Sahlin-Andersson and Sevón challenge the common distinction between imitation as copying on the one hand, and innovation on the other. They hold that processes of imitation may be highly innovative. Processes of imitation on the one hand lead to organizations that behave very similarly, but they also lead to variation and change on the other. Sahlin-Andersson and Sevón bring us much closer to what individuals and organizations do when they are imitating, providing another understanding of innovation, something that we can expect to occur frequently and among ordinary men and women. Still, as they have organization and organizing as the prime framework we primarily meet the individual as an organizational member. So, how can we further their discussion, having the innovating individual(s) and innovations as the prime focus?

INNOVATION

Schumpeter illustrated innovations, such as the Bessemer engine (a Schumpeter I kind of innovation) or Deerfoot sausage (Schumpeter II), more than making visible how these innovations came about. The story about Jan Boklöv above emphasizes how Boklöv was an entrepreneur as well as how he once acted in a way that resembles Schumpeter's view of innovation. Schumpeter defined innovation as the carrying out of new combinations (1934/2000, p. 66). He mentioned five cases:

1. The introduction of a new good.
2. The introduction of a new method of production.
3. The opening of a new market.

4. The conquest of a new source of supply of raw materials or half-manufactured goods.
5. The carrying out of the new organization of any industry.

This list illustrates how Schumpeter was recognizing economic development and innovation as something which was related to material goods and the manufacturing industry. We could say that the V-style meant the introduction of a new jump (1), the introduction of a new way of jumping (2) and the opening of a new market for longer ski jumps (3). Still the comparison limps, because here we are not concerned with the manufacturing of products but with performance of a specific sport. But just as the Bessemer engine was a good example of the innovation of a new product and the Deerfoot sausage was an innovative branding shaping a new market, so the V-style was a Schumpeter-like innovation in ski jumping, an innovation that completely changed the way ski jumps are carried out.

The V-style as well as the Bessemer engine and the Deerfoot sausage can be visualized by pictures or direct observation. However, the story about the invention of the V-style also visualizes how this innovation came about. We can come close to understanding what actually happened. By this we can illustrate what Tarde stated, namely that innovations stem from imitating individuals who sometimes deviate from their imitating behaviour. We could not expect an innovation such as the V-style from any amateur jumper, but rather from a dedicated sportsperson who was used to intense practising. Boklöv recognized the deviation as a potential innovation and started to imitate the deviation instead, and we can say that he started to imitate his own behaviour.

I agree with Lowe that previous studies of innovation have used perspectives and methodologies where it remains unarticulated what people do when they are innovating. In the Boklöv case, we can easily comprehend how the innovation occurred. Innovation as originating from a deviation of an imitating behaviour is a more radical idea than 'creative imitation' of others, because deviation happens seemingly just by chance, while strategy is intentional.

A counter-argument is that not all innovations are like the invention of the V-style. The taming of nuclear power and its diverse applications appear as involving knowledge complexity of a completely different kind compared to ski jump technology. However, in our times we have stronger reasons than did the late Schumpeter to recognize the imitators also as entrepreneurs. While Tim Berners-Lee can be recognized as the creator of the World Wide Web, it is also apparent that what has been made of the Web could not be associated with one man only. The Web has opened a space for increased, never-ending innovation, a space enabling more and more people to enact entrepreneurship. Further, we now live in a society where social change is to a much larger degree carried out by collective processes rather than by exceptional individuals. The work content of most professional workers of today is such that it can best be developed and adjusted by those who perform their tasks (Eliasson, 2006). While on early industrialist assembly lines the work content could be designed and measured by engineers and leaders, this is hardly the case any more. So also does the daily life of a ski jumper or any passionate athlete contain continuous innovations, even if very few events will change a sport the way that Boklöv's jump on the Falun hill did.

At this point it needs to be admitted that my reading of Tarde is not in accordance with his view of society. Tarde has been criticized by Clark (1969) for holding an elitist view. For Tarde it was an upper-class function to decide how society was to develop. He was also criticized by Durkheim for attributing change to individuals, while Durkheim stressed that individuals are always subject to collective structure. There was a battle between the two, and Tarde was the one who lost.

In my interpretation of Tarde, I take his idea of innovation as emanating from imitative behaviour that by chance deviates into an innovation. And what is more, my argument is that the potential to innovate does not exclude individuals because of class, gender, race or inherited talent. But there is one restriction in the Boklöv case. You need to be dedicated to imitation to be an innovator. However, all individuals cannot be innovators by being dedicated to something.

Schumpeter was careful to distinguish the 'real' entrepreneurs who brought new combinations to the market, and was less concerned with the imitators, although he changed his mind over time. For Tarde it was the first bold imitators (those who were among the first to copy Boklöv's new style) that he saw as crucial for innovation. Following Tarde we can recognize this boldness in Boklöv too. The conclusion is that even if every individual is an imitating individual and potentially an innovator, sometimes this potential will end up with innovations and sometimes it will not. Innovation as something that occurs by chance or accident is thus also something which is restricted by the 'braveness' of the imitating individual or the (dis)encouragement of the 'audience'.

This conclusion brings us to the intentional aspect of innovations, and in the last part of this chapter, I will elaborate on Paul Ricoeur and his threefold mimesis, because he provides a framework to explain more fully how something which starts as a deviation from imitative behaviour becomes an innovation that is intentional. The deviation as such is not intentional, but threefold mimesis helps us conceptualize how deviation is turned into intentional behaviour.

INTENTIONAL INNOVATION

Following Tarde, the birth of an innovation is caused by unrestrained imitation. It happens as an unintended act but is caused by imitative behaviour. It will not become an innovation, though, without intention. In this last part of the chapter I will discuss the intentional aspect without losing the interdependence between imitation and creativity. In doing so, I will use Ricoeur's concept of 'threefold mimesis'.

The French philosopher Paul Ricoeur (1913–2005) cannot compete with Tarde and Schumpeter as a seminal scholar of innovation and entrepreneurship theory, although his ideas about imitation are very similar to Tarde's. His field of interest was literary theory. Ricoeur's (1984) seminal work bears the title: '*Time and Narrative*'. In this work he brings innovation, creativity and imitation together in the context of narrative and (literary) texts.

For Ricoeur a text is not only a text because it is related to the lived life. Ricoeur (1981) suggests that meaningful action should be regarded as text and vice versa, and that text and action are mutually mediated. When someone describes a personal action, a 'text' is produced in the form of a narrative. This narrative is told, but is also lived. Thus action and representation are mediated in this way. This means that text (what is narrated or represented) is an imitation of action, but also that action is the imitation of what is narrated. Therefore when an entrepreneur tells a story about his or her life, this story is an imitation of lived life but also a story that will be lived out in the future. This means that when Boklöv tells stories about his ski jumping, this mirrors what has actually happened. And also, his stories affect his ski jumping.

The idea of a text as an imitation of action, Ricoeur gets from Aristotle. According to Aristotle, (tragic) poetry is the imitation of action. This central idea is accepted by Ricoeur not only for poetry but for all kinds of texts. The term Aristotle uses for imitation is 'mimesis'. But mimesis means more than just a 'hard copy' of an act, since it involves the organization of events by 'emplotment'. This means in turn that creativity must be involved as well; creativity and imitation are thus mutually mediated. In his interpretation of Aristotle, Ricoeur separates three 'moments' (or levels; Laitinen, 2002) of mimesis. To begin with, time is prefigured, which means that as humans we have a preunderstanding of human action (mimesis1). We therefore imitate and represent action through a narrative mode. Through emplotment we actively and creatively construct meaningful stories from events and incidents (mimesis2). When we read or listen to a story, our experience is modelled through the plot (mimesis3). Through mimesis1, mimesis2 and mimeis3 Ricoeur introduces Augustine's *aporia* of time, the threefold present (past, present and future) into his analysis of Aristotle's mimesis. Ricoeur's threefold mimesis means following 'the destiny of a prefigured time that becomes a refigured time through the mediation of a configured time' (Ricoeur, 1984, p. 54).

Ricoeur is in fact stating the very same things as Tarde, also elaborated upon above with reference to Sahlin-Andersson and Sévon (2003). But he does this by linking the lived life to storied life, making the intentional aspect of innovation clear without losing the interdependence between imitation and innovation. Ricoeur's explication of mimesis1, mimesis2 and mimesis3 is quite extensive and it is built upon a circular argument. This means that the three parts of mimesis go round in circles. I will not follow the details of Ricoeur's rich elaboration of the threefold mimesis here, but rather make a rather free interpretation of some of his thoughts applied to the Boklöv case.

Time is prefigured – mimesis2 – which means that as human beings we have a preunderstanding of the world of action, which is narrative. We understand anything we do in narrative terms. As soon as we explain something we do, we tell this in the form of a story with a plot and underlying motives (Raz, 1999, from Laitinen, 2002).

So also with Boklöv. It would be impossible for him to isolate action, the imitating of other ski jumpers, from narratives about ski jumping. He not only watched older boys jumping down the hill in Koskuskulle, he also heard them and others telling their stories about what they did, stories that in turn imitated their actions. So before he started to jump himself he had a pre-understanding of ski jumping in narrative form, that is, stories from others and imaginations of his own future actions.

When Boklöv started ski jumping his preunderstanding involved using the Daescher technique, because this was the cultural norm (that is, implicit in mimesis1), the proper way of jumping. By this norm the referees judged whether or not a certain jump was good or not. Implicit in mimesis1 is, further, the human ability to reflect upon actions. Of course Boklöv had this capacity – ready to use – to reflect upon how he had been jumping. In this reflection his preunderstanding caused him to rely on cultural norms regarding ski jumping. We need to remember that the output of this first phase of mimesis is not more than a partial or implicit understanding of external events (Zelazo and Lourenco, 2002).

Ricoeur uses the concept of mimesis1 to isolate the capacity of humans to make sense of what they are doing, before they actually do so. The concept highlights that human beings indulge into action predisposed and deemed to make sense of actions through narratives (whether they are spoken, written down or not). By mimesis2 Ricoeur moves to the active and creative sense-making – the configured time. In constructing mimesis2 Ricoeur borrows the concept of emplotment from Aristotle. In three ways, emplotment is a way of mediating. First, the function of the plot is to construct a meaningful story from events and incidents. A plot transforms events and incidents into a story. This makes the plot a mediator between events and a narrated story. Second, emplotment means bringing the components that are prepared for ordering (mimesis1) into a syntagmatic order (the making of the structure of the 'text'). Third, plot is mediation because of its temporal characteristics.

We can imagine Boklöv making sense of his ski jumping from the beginning. Every jump more or less asks for a new story as no jump is exactly like any previous jump has been. Any story created induces a creative act. Every small deviation from what was expected demands an explanation and this explanation requires creativity. It is from a pedagogical point of view easier to see this when we think of the event at Falun, because this deviation was so great, so extremely visible, that the necessity of creative sense-making is more obvious, but the same thing relates to every jump. We can imagine Boklöv constructing a meaningful story from the incident on the plastic hill at Falun. What was happening by chance was given a meaning. This meaning was expressed by way of a story (text). The past, the present and the future were linked together. He knew and could make it a clear intention that he had by accident (the past) invented a new style (present), which he intended to use in his jumping (future).

The configurational act of emplotment (mimesis2) requires productive imagination. The presentation of circumstances, characters and episodes in a story is guided by intuition. The imagination has a synthetic function, connecting intellectual understanding and intuition. Stories tend to be told in a way that is rule-governed, however (for example, a tragic story follows a pattern typical of tragedies). There is thus interplay between innovation and tradition. Consequently creativity is a necessary part of making and telling a story (as well as living a life). This means that mimesis2 is not unrestricted creativity, but there is always room for creativity. At the same time creativity is a rule-governed activity just as stories tend to follow a particular tradition.

It required imagination from Boklöv to create a story where he could make sense of a jump that by chance was 'incorrect' according to tradition. Intellectually and intuitively he could understand and feel that there must be something he could do with his experience. Using creativity he could turn his experience into an intentional innovation which helped him overcome the resistance from tradition. Interestingly, when Boklöv tells about the 'incident' he views it not as a 'real' invention, as it was by chance. Apparently he tells the story following a plot line in line with the entrepreneurship discourse.

Finally, mimesis3 marks the intersection of the world of the text and the world of the hearer or reader (Ricoeur, 1984, p. 71) – the refigured time. It is when we read or listen to a story that the plot can model our experience. It is the joint work of the text and the reader or hearer that allows emplotment to become an act of judgement and productive imagination (creativity). The reader/hearer is also involved in completing the story as the written text consists of holes and lacunae that he or she can fill through their own engagement. Zelazo and Lourenco (2002) refer to the third phase as trans-figuration – actions can be understood differently in light of the story.

Following the constructing of a meaning with the experience Boklöv had and the story he thus constructed, he could continue to let this story model his further experience. The story was not finished at once, nor was the new technique. There was interplay between the story Boklöv could tell himself at first and his further experience in imitating his 'incorrect' jump while he kept modifying the new technique into something that eventually made him the World Cup champion in 1989.

So, how does threefold mimesis help us to explain innovation as rooted in imitation, further than just a deviation from imitative behaviour that happens by chance? Firstly, Ricoeur confirms imitation as the most basic behaviour of human beings. Secondly, he makes explicit the interdepend-ence between imitation and creativity. As human beings keep imitating by necessity this leads to creativity. Bringing in the narrative aspect is the key to this. As individuals not only imitate or try to copy certain behaviour, they need to explain what they do for themselves and others and do so by telling stories. And as exact imitation of an act is impossible, so it is impos-sible to tell a story about something that does not involve creativity. It is the necessity by which an imitating individual must also be a creative indi-vidual that is especially elaborated in Ricoeur's analysis. The individual is not only by nature imitating, but as a consequence also creative.

Thirdly, Ricoeur connects what we do with what we narrate. When we start to narrate the world by an altered discourse of entrepreneurship, we also start to change the world, as we live out our stories. So the individual is an active individual, not only imitating fashions and slightly adjusting to them. In Riceour's text we can, in fact, clearly see the agency and the potential of each individual to do something completely new and unex-pected. The innovation, initially caused by 'accident', becomes at the end highly intentional.

IMPLICATION

The discussion in this chapter can be summarized as follows. Entrepreneurship has to do with processes that change society. Changes are driven by innovation. What is at stake is whether the innovators are to be found within a small minority of the population or if most people are innovative by nature. It has been argued that the entrepreneurship discourse has favoured the former view, while in this chapter the latter view is taken. In order to make this argument, innovation has been explained as emanating from imitation. When imitation is regarded as the prime prerequisite for innovation the consequence is that innovative behaviour need not be rare.

The important issue is not to find those few people with creative talent or capacity, for all humans have this capacity. What is important is that innovations are allowed. Culture and structure tend to prevent creative behaviour. An innovative society is a society which allows creative actions to become innovations. A society that encourages people to become passionate imitators and allow 'accidents' to happen will experience much creativity and – as a consequence – many innovations.

Unfortunately the dominating entrepreneurship discourse tends to demobilize entrepreneurship in action. In order to mobilize entrepreneurship we need more stories – stories building upon other discourses. We need stories about imitation and creativity. When innovation is understood as an everyday phenomenon and when imitation and creativity are released, this understanding can contribute to the mobilizing of a kind of entrepreneurship which is inclusive, a kind that is in tune with the time we are living in and not past times. Most innovations are not that radical, but when a society is characterized by many 'small' innovations some of them will be more radical automatically. We live in a society with more and more places for innovations, but we need to free ourselves from the ideas that innovations are rare and a result of creativity only.

8. Entrepreneurship requires resistance to be mobilized

Karin Berglund and Johan Gaddefors

INTRODUCTION

It's Friday afternoon at 5 p.m. on a spring day in 1983. Michel Foucault is strolling down a lane in Berkeley on his way to a lecture on Kant, Socrates and Seneca. One undergraduate Philip Horvitz, who is studying to become an actor and a dancer, attends the class. According to James Miller, the writer of the biography *The Passion of Michel Foucault*, Horvitz was obviously also interested in mastering 'the currents of avant-garde thought' and thrilled and curious enough after Foucault's guest lecture to decide to visit him during his 'open office hour' (1993/2000, p. 351ff). The dialogue between Horvitz and Foucault comes to be about power, resistance and changing structures; not surprisingly, perhaps, as Foucault is the philosopher who has made an enormous impact during the last century by practically turning upside down our thoughts on how we can perceive power. Power, Foucault claims, is 'everywhere', producing not only knowledge but also the Self. Contrary to the idea of power as a function that makes a person do something he or she would not do otherwise, this view of power puts it the other way around. As Sunesson (1987/2003, p. i) elaborates in the preface to Foucault's path-breaking *Discipline and Punish*, 'the twist is that our body is imprisoned by our soul, and not the other way around – as we most often understand it – that our body makes up the prison of our soul. Consequently, it is our thoughts that determine what we can do with our bodies.'

Compare this with our normal thoughts on entrepreneurship. We usually think of entrepreneurship first of all as an effort, which one way or another changes structures. For instance, Schumpeter (1934/1968) pointed out that by radical innovations a necessary destruction of existing economic structures is entailed, whereby new economic structures can develop. He viewed the entrepreneur as a creative destructor (only in his later writings did he give the entrepreneurial process as a whole more emphasis, not only looking at the entrepreneur; Lindgren and Packendorff,

2004, pp. 86ff), as what disturbs the economic equilibrium (or the circular flow according to Keynes), leading to development of society. Schumpeter is focused on changing economic structures, while Spinosa et al. (1997) highlight the aspect of changing our thought structures. They talk about history-making as a way to describe how entrepreneurs change the way we see particular things.

In this chapter we start from the idea that entrepreneurship provokes structures to change as well. However, as we see it, talking of entrepreneurship and structure, one aspect of it is left too much in the background, that is, resistance to change. This is the focus of this chapter.

The case we will discuss in this chapter is a project which aims to put a red small cottage on the surface of the moon. The project is formalized by the non-profit association Friends of the 'Moon House' and the company 'Luna Resort', but can above all be seen as an extensive informal network consisting of numerous activities. Inspiration and the birth of the moon house can be traced years back in time to the artist Mikael Genberg's thought of creating a trilogy of housings. The idea of the house on the moon, and some of the actions taken, have encountered resistance and support. We argue that resistance is important in moving the project forward as it is met by counteraction. The project, as we have understood it, simply requires resistance to move on. By discussing the moon house, the link between entrepreneurship and resistance becomes obvious as this case shows how ideas and actions meet resistance, and that the process requires resistance to continue, as well as that entrepreneurial action is an act of resistance. Accordingly, we find the dialogue between Foucault and Horvitz intriguing as it opens up for us to think about what role resistance plays in entrepreneurial processes in general, and in the moon house project in particular.

Entering the room of Foucault, Horvitz finds the master wan, tired and surrounded by students eager to ask him detailed questions. Horvitz patiently waits for his turn while Foucault waves aside the students' questions with laughter. Finally his turn comes: 'Does the artist have an identity, or is he a powerless "type" who in the last fifty years has become more powerless than ever, due to the manipulation of technical media like television? Can the artist transcend "The Structure"? Or is he doomed to commodization, puppetization?' (Miller, 1993/2000).

Foucault pauses and does not give Horvitz an answer. Instead he invites him to come back the next day as he wants to think about this question. When they meet again, Foucault argues as follows: 'Freedom can be found, but always in a context. Power puts into play a dynamic of constant struggle. There is no escaping it. But there is freedom in knowing the game is yours to play. Don't look to authorities: the truth is in your self. Don't be scared. Trust yourself. Don't be afraid of living. And don't be afraid of dying. Have courage. Do what you feel you must: desire, create, transcend – you can win the game' (ibid.).

Horvitz waits a while and dares then to press the philosopher further: 'What about the economic constraints on the artist?' (ibid.).

Foucault then responds: 'Well you can't have a perfect world. Revolution doesn't work. Still, it's an ideal. Playing with the structure – transforming and transfiguring its limits – is different from playing inside the structure. Artists have more freedom than ever. . . . See how much freedom you have, use it, to get still more' (ibid.).

As we read this dialogue, power and resistance are inevitably entangled in processes of changing structures. Where there is power, there is always resistance. Power is productive, hence resistance is also productive. There are always openings for change of direction, for playing with the rules differently, for shaping the future in new creative ways. Translating this to entrepreneurship, power and resistance are always part of entrepreneurial processes. Bearing in mind Schumpeter's (1934/1968) concept of 'creative destruction' we use his thought as an illustration of how 'the new' is created and 'the old' is destroyed in processes of creative destruction. Arguably 'the old' could both be seen as something that we agree upon to destroy or something that we do not agree upon destroying. In the latter case, resistance is clearly part of entrepreneurship.

In this chapter we are interested in the more unorthodox meanings that are ascribed to entrepreneurship in diverse contexts (Dimov, 2007; Steyaert and Katz, 2004). We see the moon house as a context that constantly develops in different directions, creating space for playing with the structures, often by actors who are within the structures. Hence, the notion of 'playing with or within' the structures makes up a nice metaphor for describing the sometimes thin line between reproduction and change. Clearly we equate playing with the rules of the game with intervening in the world by way of entrepreneurial action.

The case of the moon house could indeed be interpreted as the ultimate and grandiose entrepreneurship story. However, we do not intend to reconstruct the grand story of entrepreneurship coloured by the ideological orientation of a 'rational European/North American male model [who] exhibits the propensity to take risks, to conquer the environment and to survive in a Darwinian world' (Ogbor, 2000, p. 618). Instead our ambition is somehow to tear this story apart by looking at what role resistance plays in doing entrepreneurship, or 'entrepreneuring' as Steyaert (2007) has named it. As Berglund et al. (2007) have demonstrated, this is also a story with many aspects which make it possible to turn everything upside down and end up with a most unorthodox entrepreneurship story. By adding the notion of resistance and power we argue that new questions could be raised considering what it means to 'do' entrepreneurship in everyday life. We believe that it will create conditions for new understandings of entrepreneurial, not only in theory, but also in practice. Our ambition is thus to mobilize the entrepreneurship discourse to some extent.

Next we continue with a theoretical discussion on resistance and how it links to entrepreneurship, power and changing structures. Then we present the case of the moon house. After that we discuss the role of resistance in shaping the moon house project. Eventually we end up by discussing resistance as an important piece of the puzzle in entrepreneurial processes. In short, resistance shapes the future by provoking identities.

ENTREPRENEURSHIP AND RESISTANCE IN THE GAME OF POWER

In this section we will develop our theoretical framework combining entrepreneurship and resistance. In society entrepreneurship is generally discussed as a pro-phenomenon, a positive power that we want to have more of. It has become a concept synonymous to desired change and development (Berglund and Johansson, 2007a). With few exceptions, in entrepreneurship studies the notion of resistance and destruction seems not to have intrigued researchers. For example, the popular understanding of entrepreneurship as the discovery (Shane and Venkataraman, 2000) or the creation (Gartner et al., 2003) of opportunities is primarily focused on how opportunities grow, and do not discuss resistance in this same process. What is 'destructed' as a result of entrepreneurial action is seldom discussed. On the contrary narratives of entrepreneurship often end when the new organization has successfully replaced the old one or has found its place in a previously new and empty space.

One alternative view is presented by Berglund et al. (2007) when they discuss how Genberg's artistic installations, such as the house on the moon, have been organized. For instance they argue that the ideas of his artistry did not appear to Genberg as *the* great discovery – which by the way seems to be an assumption that mainstream entrepreneurship research seldom questions (Gartner et al., 2003, pp. 103ff) – but instead as a movement back and forth in the borderland between imitation and creativity, the old and the new, and between Genberg and other people. We should therefore talk about entrepreneurship in terms of creative imitation rather than looking for naive forms of creativity that never exist when we are dealing with processes of creation in social settings. Likewise, we argue, it would be wise not only to look at how opportunities are created in an air of total consensus, but also to learn about how resistance shapes entrepreneurial processes.

Consequently, we argue resistance to be a sound companion to entrepreneurship. In our perspective the concepts are intertwined, tangled together and thus impossible to disconnect. This is particularly pertinent when entrepreneurship takes on challenges that will affect structures. We thus argue for a more thoroughgoing investigation of combining entrepreneurship and resistance. We now turn to two examples of how resistance is implicitly discussed in entrepreneurship theory.

Rehn and Taalas (2004) use the concept of entrepreneurship in a most unconventional way in their work. They argue that the 'blat system' in the former Soviet Union could be described as the most entrepreneurial society – ever! *Blat* is described as 'the practice of friends and acquaintances being tied together in an intricate weave of favors and counter-favors in order to facilitate access to commodities or services in short supply' (ibid., p. 239). It is the effectiveness of the *blat* system that allows the authors to claim that the former Soviet Union could be regarded as the most entrepreneurial society ever. Arguably, resistance towards the official system has played a crucial role in forming the entrepreneurial *blat* system. To us, the Rehn and Taalas approach illustrates how entrepreneurship works in opposition to an existing structure. There is no effort made from either side for a dialogue that might change the established structure. Instead the two structures exist side by side.

Another approach to our topic is the conceptualization of 'embeddedness', a metaphor used for discussing how entrepreneurship meets and handles resistance, preferably related to a particular place (Johannisson et al., 2002; Jack and Anderson, 2002; Steyaert, 2007). This perspective emphasizes the dialogue between entrepreneurship (the new) and the established (the old). The dialogue works on different levels: for example, there is the immediate, angry resistance that can easily be evoked, but also a more subtle form of resistance like a gentle conversation that can go on for long periods of time. This approach emphasizes the interplay between the entrepreneur and the environment, the new and the old. As such, embeddedness illustrates how the people involved try to handle resistance in order to reach consensus.

If we turn to organization theory and resistance we discover that it is a rich concept holding many connotations. By putting your knee firmly against a door you resist the wind's opening it. In other words, there is always an opposing power of some kind involved in resistance. Someone must take a position and something must be at stake in order to awaken resistance. In an organizational setting resistance often has its root in a dislike of an idea, resulting in opposition towards someone or something.

This shows why resistance is often related to obstinacy towards authorities, a refusal to obey. It explains how resistance is a concept reserved for the weaker or the threatened part in a relation, and thereby that resistance is relational, but also how it is related to power.

What is often problematized in the organization literature is employees' resistance to management efforts (Jermier et al., 1994; Fleming and Spicer, 2003; Mumby, 2005). In this vein Alvesson (2002) problematizes 'the production of the appropriate individual', indicating the doubtful relation between management and employee. Another example focuses on the struggle between power and resistance within an organization (Mumby, 2005; Fleming and Spicer, 2007). Mumby's (2005) main concern is with workplace resistance: 'The focus is typically on the everyday struggles of workers to carve out spheres of autonomy through various informal (often guerrilla-like) practices', (Mumby, 2005, p. 25). He identifies a binary opposition in research between organizational control and employee resistance. Fleming and Spicer (2003) show how employees resist identifying with management and the organization through dis-identification. Here cynical employees practice the corporate rituals, but simultaneously remain autonomous. The most frequent strategy in this endeavour is culture change programmes of some kind; that is, how management can handle such (presumably) unproductive situations (Badham et al., 2003). These are only a few examples of how resistance is problematized in organization theory. Accordingly, resistance and power are related, and our example shows how resistance and power are in opposition towards each other, creating a deadlock position. Relating to the introductory discussion, the game to play seems, at least in these cases, to be within the structures without changing them.

Another approach rather than to accept the resistance–power dichotomy is to discuss it as a dialectical relationship where control and resistance are co-produced (Mumby, 2005; Zoller and Fairhurst, 2007). Here, focus is not on how power can handle resistance but rather on how resistance can be constructive and change structures. Resistance might not necessarily come as a reply to domination. It is possible to think of resistance without putting focus on the struggle for power. Zoller and Fairhurst (2007), for example, examine the role of leadership in mobilizing collective resistance. In their approach, neither resistance nor leadership of resistance are a priori existing. Instead, they emphasize the mutual mobilization of resistance and leadership of resistance. Here resistance and entrepreneurship are growing in a process-changing structure. This dynamic perspective on how novelty comes about combines entrepreneurship and resistance.

Also investigated in the literature are more subtle forms of resistance. In critical management studies it is framed as a critical response to destructive institutions or (managerial) colonizers; destructive for an individual, a group, an organization or society at large (Alvesson and Willmott, 1996; Nord, 2003; Styhre, 2008a). In these cases resistance is making something, as well as someone, move. Again, relating to the introductory discussion, the game to play seems in the latter cases to be with the structures by changing them somehow.

To sum up, we have discussed three approaches to entrepreneurship and resistance. First, entrepreneurship and resistance can be discussed as in opposition to something else, a binary approach. For example, in Schumpeter's version of entrepreneurship the other has to be destroyed, and in the resistance literature the battle stands between organizational control mechanisms and employee resistance. Second, a dialectical approach is present in theory. In the entrepreneurship and the resistance literature co-production is emphasized in different ways. Finally, the third approach is the critical, elaborated as a response to destructive institutions in society.

To develop further our understanding of entrepreneurship and resistance related to the moon house the dialectical approach will be our point of departure. Consequently, we think that resistance is important for entrepreneurship in multidimensional ways that go beyond the notion of resistance as something that should be handled or something that is a response to destructive powers in society. Our argument is that the whole spectrum of resistance is present in entrepreneurship, in dialogue, as well as in shaping and moulding the future. Our ambition is therefore to investigate resistance as a constructive, entrepreneurial activity.

A HOUSE ON THE MOON AS AN ACT OF RESISTANCE

The story about creating a moon house is a multifaceted story of entrepreneurship. The 'House on the Moon' is not the first 'house', built by the artist Mikael Genberg but the final piece in a trilogy of housing alternatives. The two first houses have already been installed and have already become well-known hotels, not only by locals but by many visitors from around the world. 'Hotel Woodpecker' is situated in an old oak tree in the central park of Västerås and the underwater hotel Otter Inn, found in Lake Mälaren, is visible from the waterside in the same town.

On the one hand we could address the traditional plot by putting forward the entrepreneur Mikael Genberg as possessing some special traits (or to be a bit provocative, an unknown entrepreneurial gene). In such a story Genberg would be the one who persuades people to buy his 'product', that is, the idea of the moon house. The resistance in that situation would come from the venture capital market when competing for financing the house on the moon in order to be able to make a profit on commercial rights and thereby creating an empire.

However the story could also be read quite differently, where nothing would have happened in the project without all of the co-entrepreneurs that have been involved from the beginning in 2002. Without them Genberg would still sit in his tree house dreaming of a house on the moon. Because without all the collective action taken, the project would have been impossible to accomplish.

Resistance in this story is more about how questions are raised that force the actors involved to construct new answers. One of the questions raised was what Genberg would do with all the money that the moon house could result in after the installation. The answer that came up was to create the 'House on the Moon Foundation for Mankind' in order to contribute to making the world a better place. The overall aim for the foundation is to provoke people's ideas about what is good in the world today, as well as what it means to create a better world, by engaging in and encouraging thoughts and actions that cross borders between art, business, science and technology.

In the story that follows we do not aim to arrange the story according to either of the alternative readings. All we wanted to do in this introduction was to make clear that there are several possible readings of the story, and we hope to encourage some more in the text that follows.

Mikael Genberg as the Artistic Phantom

So where does it all begin, then? Of course, with Genberg's artistry. It would be ridiculous to tell the story of the moon house without including the story of Genberg. In the book *Moonstruck – Genberg and the Thousand Musketeers*, written by Anders Lif (2008), a number of anecdotes are told from the life of Mikael Genberg. One is from the time before the election in September 1991 when Genberg, on a dark night together with friends who acted as lookouts, painted the Phantom (a masked comic-strip character fighting evil) on political campaign posters all around the city. When people woke up the next day the candidates were all masked in the disguise of the Phantom, which caused a lot of discussion.

So is Genberg the Phantom? Well, perhaps in one way. Not least, we can see some similarities between Genberg's eagerness to provoke the artistic establishment – or as he often says himself, 'the artistic room' – in making art become closer to each and everyone, by creating space for both thought and action; and in the Phantom's continuous battle in fighting evil and creating space for the weak and oppressed. Could it be so that Genberg sees people in general as, if not weak and oppressed, then occupied by and locked into everyday routines? This side of the story goes very much in line with the persona of the artist, the rebel who wants to break with the old myths, opening up possibilities for new thoughts and scope for action, and who is trying to wake everyone up – themselves included – from our routine, sleep-walking life and to consider new ways of how to move on. With such a view it is not difficult to see how resistance is invoked.

Hence, the story about the third piece in a trilogy of housing alternatives is also a story about the artist Mikael Genberg. One could say that the two are inseparable, even though the project involves so many more actions than one single person is capable of pursuing. Despite all the actors involved, a traditional plot could easily be reconstructed consisting of the rebel artist on a mission. The Phantom in a new version. However, changing the world by putting a house on the moon involves so much more than one single rebel artist and is therefore also, simultaneously, a break with the plot involving the lone artist painting on canvas. As we stated earlier, both stories could be told. So far the project has progressed by a continuing pulse that moves between action and resistance, linking Mikael Genberg with other actors.

Genberg's artistry however did not start by provoking the artistic room. He started by painting portraits, which he also made a living from for several years. After a while, though, the interest of challenging the artistic establishment took over and, besides painting the Phantom on political campaign posters all over the city during election time, he enclosed his old comic papers (probably some of the Phantom) in plastic, making a writing-table and a chair. He also made rag rugs by weaving stripes of torn up paintings. The idea was to make art functional – useful. The carpets would be worn by time and the furniture could serve as a source of inspiration during work. Ironically, the plastic furniture is today exhibited at a museum, and the carpets are hung up decorating walls as paintings do.

Another example comes from an exhibition in November 1995. Västerås citizens rushing for lunch were surprised by what appeared to be a crime scene on one of the streets. 'Is this art? I was sure it was the place of a recent murder', one shocked bus driver passing by uttered. A place on the pavement was marked with roses, torches and a tower of sugar lumps, where the whole scene was supposed to be a sign of a murder. Obviously questioning, as well as irritating and provoking, came to be a trademark of Genberg's artistry, which also moved his artistry towards entrepreneurship in many ways (see Berglund et al., 2007).

Woodpecker and Otter Inn: Exceptional Hotels or Artistic Installations?

In 1998 the small cottage, Hotel Woodpecker was inaugurated 13 metres up in the largest oak tree in Vasaparken in Genberg's home town of Västerås, located about 100 kilometres from Stockholm. Hotel Woodpecker has come to set a mark on the park, but it has also become a trademark for Västerås. A couple of years after Woodpecker it was time to create the second house in the trilogy, namely the underwater hotel Otter Inn, inaugurated at Lake Mälaren in Västerås. The creation of the two small red houses has changed the silhouette of the town of Västerås. When the local newspaper *VLT* presented the new city silhouette the three traditional houses – the city cathedral, the skyscraper and ASEA Brown Boveri (ABB)'s head office town Ottar – were accompanied by a small red cottage surrounded by a big red heart. A warm dot in the midst of the local giants. The spectacular hotels thus seem to have become distinguishing marks for Västerås.

In 2004 Mikael Genberg was awarded the local marketing prize, a prize he didn't know whether he should perceive as an honour or as a slap in the face considering the fact that he was actually an artist and that the commercial arena should be kept apart from the artistic arena. He decided to stick to the first-mentioned alternative, which goes in line with Genberg's interest in provoking the artistic establishment and moving art into the larger societal room that we call society. What could then be better than getting attention for the houses as a marketing phenomenon? The houses are not only visible during Sunday strolls in the park, or by the side of Lake Mälaren, but pictures of them have also been used in a variety of ways to create attention. For instance they have been used in advertisements to attract people to visit Västerås, as well as by a number of companies who somehow connect their business idea to the small red houses; and also the pictures of the small red houses have been used (without permission) in advertisements by an estate agent. If people do not look for art, art has to look for people, seems to be a proverb that drives this artistic Phantom.

Genberg's installations, which challenge our conceptions of housing, appear as both creative and new thinking, but simultaneously fall back on his previous artistic expressions where houses in different shapes have been recurrent elements. Among Genberg's earlier works of art, that in one way or another comment upon basic human needs, Café Koala can be mentioned, a 'cafe' where up to eight people can enjoy freshly brewed coffee on 5 metre high chairs. The question to figure out is: does it taste the same? Another example is the Toilet Closette where the visitor, thanks to a spy glass can watch everyone outside, but from the outside no one can look in. Guaranteed to be unpleasant, according to Genberg himself.

Moreover there is also a small house made of gingerbread on the scale of a small garden shed, completed with the help of many friends.

Putting up a House on the Moon

When the work to realize the third and last installation – the moon house – was initiated in August 2002 a number of enthusiastic friends gathered around the idea. If Woodpecker meant that a number of friends offered their help in building the tree cottage, and Woodpecker presupposed a close cooperation with the municipalities' technical workshop, Luna Resort implied mobilizing a network of a whole other kind. No one puts a house on the moon by oneself. Well, perhaps that would be an assignment for the old Phantom, helping others by making the impossible possible. But, when it comes to the new version of the Phantom it is more about getting people to realize their own potential in making the impossible possible.

Mobilizing a network of different actors and organizations has been crucial in keeping the project alive and on the move. All the people who have taken an active part in the project, telling others about it on different occasions and establishing connections, have in social interactions shaped and formed 'the Moon House' as an opportunity, a possibility that has practically been an impossibility without all the people who have taken action and become involved in the project. At a cocktail party arranged by the non-profit association the Friends of the Moon House, 70 to 80 people were gathered to celebrate the success of the project so far, in the 600 square metre art studio close to ABB's headquarters:

> People are mingling with a glass in their hand establishing new relations. Greetings and laughter give the murmur a warm and friendly tone. Expectations are in the air. Suddenly someone is calling for attention. It is the county governor of Västmanland Mats Svegfors, and also the chairman of 'the Friends of the Moon House', who takes the opportunity to welcome everyone. Incidentally he mentions that this is a historic occurrence. It is probably easy to think of this event as an information event among others than as a historic occurrence. A happening that, together with all other episodes in the project, makes up chains of reactions and relations that bring forth creativity as well as scope of action and power of initiative of substantial importance for moving the project another step forward. It is here and now that opportunities are made as people get to know each other, tell about their relation to the project and perhaps find common interest to start to work from. As Mikael says a while after the chairman of Luna Resort made his speech, it would not be possible to carry through without all the people who for a while have been ready to let go of the commitments of everyday life and engage in the project. 'This project is not foremost about technology, economy or art, it is about people', he continues. (Field notes, 9 January 2007)

Obviously the work on moving Luna Resort one step further involves a large number of actors who can take the initiative and open doors; at least in comparison to Genberg's previously conducted projects. Some have come and gone, but many have faithfully stayed and participated as much as they have been able to. In moving the moon house one step further, traditional borders have been crossed which makes the distinction between private, public and non-profit organizations as well as to policy quite fuzzy. There are several examples where competitors have come to work together when they see a common goal and realize that the project is truly non-profit and benefits from their cooperation, and not from a deadlocked competitive position. In one of the installations – two moon house hills built near through-route E18 – two contractors that usually compete to get commissions were cooperating.

The vision on putting a house on the moon seems indeed to have created an arena where people are invited to take part in, stage and complete the work of art. But by completing this work of art, another process is continued by the House of the Moon Foundation for Mankind, which in different ways aims to provoke people into questioning what it means to shape a better world. It is thus not only about putting a house on the moon. It is about changing the world.

In practice actors come together in another context than around the conventional conference table. The work on the moon house can arguably be said to have challenged established borders as links are created between institutions such as the cultural sector, technology, art, science and industry in new ways.

Crossing a boundary could also be to see something in a new way. How could we otherwise act in new ways? To sit in the red tree house makes us, quite obviously, see the surroundings with new eyes. Likewise, to sit in the underwater hotel in the muddy Lake Mälaren trying to figure out which fish that is swimming around. It changes perspectives. The houses could thus be looked upon as an art and cultural project that invites the observer to take part in the project, where he or she can discover new interfaces, new ways to look upon the world. For example we perhaps realize, after one night under a clear and starry night on the veranda in the old oak, that a hotel visit could offer so much more than convenience. It could also become a more sensuous experience. In this way Genberg is talking about how the moon house has the potential to widen our mental rooms in order to make the world 'bigger and smaller at the same time, it is about looking into another person's space but also to hook up to the larger Internet' (Interview note).

In many respects the alternative housing is about challenging traditional conceptions about the boundaries we have made up historically. The small cottages provoke questions such as: What is art? What is entrepreneurship? What is a company? Who takes part? Who observes? Who owns Woodpecker and Otter Inn? And, who cares? as Genberg himself puts it. The whole idea of proprietorship is at stake. So also is the question of who is allowed to take part in artistic processes. In short, boundaries are challenged, crossed and moved in the work of putting a red cottage on the surface of the moon.

In many cases roles have been switched in the project. For instance, Genberg claims that he has sometimes found himself thinking as a space engineer, and that space engineers sometimes think as an artist. Sometimes they become intermeshed. At a meeting, the idea of letting the Swedish astronaut, Christer Fuglesang, take a small red house with him on the next space trip to the International Space Station (ISS) was born. No one protested, but instead the immediate response by a powerful space engineer was to send a phone message to Fuglesang, who gave a positive response. According to Genberg they, the space engineers, saw the picture of the house 'floating' in space as well as he did. And that is what artistry is all about, he commented.

What kind of function does Genberg then have? First and foremost he has become a symbol for the project, the one who appears in the limelight, but also the potential villain and loser if the project fails. One could then think that he is the one who is risking his image, at least as an artist and an entrepreneur, the most. This could be so, but another reading can be made as well, considering that Genberg always can claim his artistic legitimacy which gives him an emergency exit. However as a symbol his identity becomes fuzzy, always on the move, which forces involved actors to be clearer in their contours. As Genberg does not view himself to be the one who has the answers – to where the project is moving – he sometimes appears as a swing door which backlashes responsibility on those who are involved. Even if Genberg is the father of the idea, one important point about the whole process is that he has not done everything on his own. The project is a result of togetherness. Genberg's most essential assignment is arguably that he creates scope of action for the involved actors.

RESISTANCE SHAPING THE FUTURE

As we stated in the introduction the idea of the house on the moon, as well as some of the actions taken, has met both resistance and support. Previously we have tried to tell the story of the house on the moon and simultaneously give some glimpses of how the project has moved forward as action has met counteraction. We will now draw attention to how ideas and actions have met resistance, and to the idea that the process requires resistance to continue, as well as that entrepreneurial action is an act of resistance.

It is obvious that the idea of putting a house on the moon raises doubt, bewilderment and anger. Because: Why? Or, as Genberg regularly says in his presentations: 'Why on earth a house on the moon?' After he rhetorically answers: 'To make the world a better place', the next question is quite obvious: Then how? How can a house on the moon contribute to a better world? Why not use the money (that will possibly be made when the house stands there) and send it to the poor? Why not instead put the money the project will cost towards making the social national insurance system even better in Sweden? These questions are raised, but often at a distance, in debates in the local morning paper or in discussions in private rooms rather than in the public ones. On some occasions, however, voices have been raised in public which have significantly affected the way forward for the project. One of the incidents was a letter to the local morning paper that was so negative that one of the sponsors postponed contributing financially to the project. One could say that there is not an opposing team out there. There does not yet exist such a thing as a united front, or some kind of organized resistance. As the project expands, such resistance might develop. However, such incidents seldom become 'a threat' but they have instead made the involved actors think further, build arguments and express themselves more clearly. The following statements are 'typical' expressions used nowadays when the project is being described. Arguably, these expressions have been developed by the resistance that the idea has met:

> The project is not applying for funds in the social system, instead we want our Swedish big companies to let go of a fraction of their large marketing budgets that are spent on enormous advertising campaigns that vanish into thin air.

> The Foundation is not about extinguishing fires around the world, like the starvation in developing countries. Instead it is about making people in the Western world think about all the good we have in our world today and that the road ahead may not be to get more of that.

This kind of resistance has made visible the amount of money that companies spend on marketing, but also the possibility for Swedish companies to create a common symbol that will draw attention to Sweden as an entrepreneurial and technological nation, and that it should be something to be proud of. This resistance has also contributed to the idea of creating a Foundation which aims to lay the groundwork for discussions on whether our thoughts and actions lead towards a better world, or not. Resistance, in this shape, has forced thoughts to become clearer and more distinctly expressed. As Genberg said in one of the interviews: 'you look for resistance to be able to develop your thoughts'. In this vein resistance has made it possible for the people inside the project to find a greater feeling of 'togetherness' as they jointly articulate the answers, and thereby develop the idea of a house on the moon. A vocabulary develops by creative combinations of words. This formation brings about new webs of concepts that translate the world in new ways which works for all of those who relate to the idea of the house on the moon, moving the project in unexpected directions.

Another form of resistance is visible in some of the participators' organizations which have made it necessary to come up with some strategies in order to introduce the 'fantastic opportunity' in cooperating with a project such as the moon house. When Genberg talks about how he encounters organizations he says that: 'opponents must pass by in order to look for the delicious'. In a similar vein there have been a number of people who have come and gone in the project. Some of them have had the ambition to 'fix things' and see things through: simply to run the project according to dominating management logic in which financial gains, for instance, constitute a main motive. However if they have persisted in this they have not remained in the project, which constitutes a form of resistance from the project in staying vague and 'movable'. It seems that the project needs this kind of resistance in order to build the agenda that governs activities in a certain direction.

Do all of those who are involved know that they are involved in the same project that Genberg is thinking about? And does it matter? There are obviously several reasons for being involved. According to the first preliminary report five purposes were stated, which have attracted and filled a lot of actors with enthusiasm, for different reasons. This arguably created a breeding ground of fuzziness, but also for scope of action. Both Genberg and the project become incomprehensible, indeterminable and ambiguous at the same time. It becomes both fascinating and intriguing, which makes it hard to dismiss either the whole idea, or Genberg himself for that matter. Our argument is that the situation of 'fuzziness' requires resistance in order to move on.

We can also see resistance in conceiving things differently; the moon house is only a first step on the road that opens up new paths which makes old borders woolly. One could certainly ask: Is Genberg is embedded or not? Is he an effect or is he the effectuator? Has he become accepted by the establishment as the 'clown' that legitimates the idea, the court jester who makes it possible for interested people to create scope of actions for their purposes? Or could it be the other way around? That is: who is fooling whom? Is Genberg actually playing the game the way Foucault proposed artists to do in order to change structures? We can interpret Genberg as a change-maker who has ingratiated himself with the establishment, making not only himself but also his allies to play with the structure. Following this line of thought the project has created an amoeba-like creature aiming to transfigure and transform the limits of existing boundaries, that works from within.

Perhaps it is the border-crossing actions that are threatening; perhaps both the artist Genberg and County Governor Svegfors are making a threat as well as mobilizing resistance. They are partners in crime, but odd partners as the Swedish artist Thomas diLeva and Prime Minister Fredrik Reinfeldt would be, or to look for a similar 'international couple', Marilyn Manson and George Bush. They, one could argue, make up nice couples if one is interested in irritating the artistic establishment. Resistance, as shown by the examples, is linked to predominant truths that hold up the established, prevailing structures, and thus boundaries between art and entrepreneurship, the court jester and the establishment, the earth and the moon, art and money, and so forth. These boundaries are negotiated and provoked by the moon house idea and activities.

The very idea of the impossible seeks resistance; it also constitutes a motive force and moves the project in different directions. The movement of the project depends on how people, both 'inside' and 'outside', translate the idea and what actions they initiate and connect to it. The unthinkable is thus as much resistance as it is a motive force. Innovations both drive and seek resistance, and motivate people to take initiatives. It is obviously not realistic just to come up with any idea, but as Genberg shows, with a history and with connections in 'the system', it is possible to balance between provoking art and contributing to public welfare.

To sum up, the idea of the moon house and the actions taken provoke, irritate and question prevailing assumptions which make up acts of resistance towards certain establishments. These acts meet resistance as they raise doubt, bewilderment and anger. In short, acts of resistance are met by resistance, which releases new acts, and so forth. The process could be pictured as a spiral that makes the project move on. Simply, the spiral-like movement requires resistance in order for thoughts, togetherness and vocabulary to develop.

RESISTANCE CHANGING AND SHAPING IDENTITIES

In the opening of this chapter we discussed that entrepreneurship is linked to both Schumpeterian materialistic change and Spinosa et al.'s discussions about changing thought structures. Later on when we introduced the case we argued that the moon house story could be read in two different versions, which can be linked to both types of structural change. In the first Schumpeterian 'capitalistic' entrepreneurship version, radical innovations are emphasized. And, for sure, the moon house can be described as a radical innovation that could change the market structure in many unexpected ways. In the second version our eyes are instead directed at how the idea of the house on the moon could make us reconsider in everyday life our thoughts on our time, as well as the future, which comes close to history-making. By thinking differently, we can act differently, whereby new practices and thus structures become established. Looking at the moon house it is easy to get caught up by the white and black pictures of a phenomenon, without searching for grey shades. It is however not the grey shades that have been of interest here. Our intention has not been to deny, or rewrite, either one of these two versions but to highlight how resistance plays a part in organizing entrepreneurial endeavours which relates to both perspectives. What both perspectives have in common, though, is that resistance plays a part in changing structures. And what Foucault adds to that is that changing structures deals with provoking identities.

Hence, we believe that resistance is important for the entrepreneurship discourse in many ways that go beyond the notion of resistance as something that should be handled or something that is a response to destructive powers in society. What we have tried to show in this chapter is that resistance is an inherent part of entrepreneurial activity; a constructive part, and thus not something managers must overcome or something subtle that can be criticized. In the house on the moon project, resistance has played an important part in moving not only the project, but also actors' identities. The movement should not be described in terms of progress, or as deadlocking. Rather we should talk about friction, a movement back and forth, as well as here and there, which has created new paths both in material practice and in people's minds. As Wittgenstein once wrote:

> [we] have got on to the slippery ice where there is no friction and so in a certain sense the conditions are ideal, but also, just because of that, we are unable to walk: so we need friction. Back to the rough ground. (Wittgenstein, 1958, p. 46)

What is mainly challenged in the moon house project is the notion of the Self. The project creeps upon each and everyone, not only on Genberg but on all those involved, actors as well as spectators. And regardless if they are in, that is, positive, or out, that is, negative creating resistance. This project touches upon people which affect our identities. As the project moves, changes and makes up a new shape, it makes new identities possible. However, it contributes also to fear and resistance as it changes 'who one is'. In some way, perhaps, this project makes us aware of not only 'who we are', but also 'what we could become'. And precisely that was Foucault's life quest. To summarize: entrepreneurship challenges our identities in some way. Otherwise it would not be entrepreneurship.

In this chapter we have argued that resistance is an inherent part of an entrepreneurial process. By discussing the house on the moon project we have tried to show how resistance has worked to move the project in certain unexpected directions. In this last section we have returned to Foucault's idea that freedom is always yours to play with. And the game deals not with staying alive, but with having the courage to live to the full by allowing oneself to desire, create and transcend. Thereby the 'game' can be won and, as we have understood it, structures can be changed.

9. The spectacle of entrepreneurship: a duality of flamboyance and activity

Frederic Bill, Andreas Jansson and Lena Olaison

INTRODUCTION

Introducing a Spectacle

This chapter argues that entrepreneurship can be seen as comprising both spectacular and mundane aspects, and that entrepreneurship discourse, both popular and academic, tends to emphasize the spectacular while concealing the mundane aspects of entrepreneurship. A socially productive entrepreneurship, we argue, must however balance both spectacular and mundane aspects and always risks turning into a mere spectacle of entrepreneurship.

The argument takes its starting point in two different, albeit related, events. The first one is the European Commission's initiative to create 'the most competitive and dynamic knowledge-driven economy by 2010', the so-called Lisbon Agenda/Process/Strategy/Initiative. Entrepreneurship is defined as: 'the mindset and process to create and develop economic activity by blending risk-taking, creativity and/or innovation with sound management, within a new or an existing organisation' (European Commission, 2003, p. 7; see also Bill and Olaison, 2006).

In a recent attempt to operationalize the strategy, the Commission designated the year 2009 to be the 'Creativity and Innovation European Year 2009' (European Commission, 2009). The slogan for this initiative was: 'Creativity is a driver for innovation and a key factor for the development of personal, occupational, entrepreneurial and social competences and the well-being of all individuals in society' (ibid.). The motto of this initiative was: 'Imagine. Create. Innovate.' (ibid.). On the website for the initiative one can read that: 'the financial and economic crisis that came to light late in 2008 is the kind of extreme development that calls for one essential quality when seeking solutions: creativity. We need creativity to find the best answers' (ibid.) All in all, during 2009, immeasurable resources and energy were spent on support programmes, education and, not least, on concrete innovation and entrepreneurship projects (ibid.).

While the first event exemplifies the entrepreneurial discourse on the level of policymaking, the second event depicts the discourse on the level of individuals. Here, individuals – often named entrepreneurs – are believed to embody imagination, creation and the capacity for innovation. The event, or story of the entrepreneur, begins, as they often do, with a young man and his intentions to change the conditions of his life:

> We should go back to the early 1990s, when the 25-year old Stein Bagger worked his way into the inner circles of Copenhagen with a gold Rolex, white shirt, tie and cufflinks, driving a Porsche or Audi with Swedish plates. The young Mr Bagger hung out in Nyhavn hunting for the fat golden calf, which would secure his power and wealth for the rest of his life. (Andersen, 2009)

A few years later, the same hungry man wins several awards, among them Ernst & Young's Entrepreneur of the Year award which he should have received at Ernst & Young's yearly entrepreneurship gala in Denmark. And it is here, on this public stage, that the manifestation of the entrepreneurship tale – including flowers, the big cheque, the journalists, the women and men in suits, all prepared to celebrate the success not only of the Man himself, but of society as a whole – that the tale was supposed to reach its climax. But the most important component, however, is missing: the man himself, Stein Bagger, was nowhere to be found.

So, the gala ends without its grand finale – in fact, Ernst & Young would later announce that they had cancelled the award – and during the following weeks we could follow the worldwide search for the crook and fraud Mr Bagger, the villain of the tale, via Dubai to the US, where he finally surrenders. During the second half of 2009, as we write this chapter, the trial is taking place. Every day we can follow the story of the now not so celebrated Mr Bagger in various media. Six books have been written since that Gala in November 2008. Yet, the mystery is not solved. How could this happen? Crimes take place every day, for sure, but this? A renowned and celebrated entrepreneur has turned out to have been a fake. Mr Bagger never was an entrepreneur after all; he was rather an imposter who played the part of an entrepreneur. A part that was so convincingly validated by the 'best of the best' of Nordic business life that no one would think of calling his bluff.

Problematizing this Spectacle

Juxtaposing these two examples, these two sides of the same story of creativity, of entrepreneurship and innovation, one could argue that the very same creativity that we wish will save us is the same that caused the Bagger debacle and the financial and economic crisis. Mr Bagger's enterprise, similar to imaginative and creative innovations such as subprime, Enron or the imaginative business of Bernard L. Madoff Investment Securities LLC, are all examples of events seemingly trustworthy and tangible, that turned out not to be real; but they were certainly full of imagination, creativity and innovation. In fact these enterprises were so imaginative, creative and innovative that they could market products or stocks that were something other than what they appeared to be, while producing an aura of success attached to the enterprise. It almost seems that anyone learning to 'play the role' of an entrepreneur can be perceived as an entrepreneur, even without any tangible artefacts in the world that we perceive as real; and if done well enough, the imagery of success will appear, even though the enterprise evidently is, in a sense, 'incomplete'. We shall argue in this chapter that this can in part be traced back to a tendency in the entrepreneurship discourse, both popular and academic, to emphasize the spectacular aspect of entrepreneurship at the expense of its mundane aspects. This tendency, reinforced by initiatives such as the European Commission's, arguably made, among other things, Mr Bagger's enterprise possible.

The tendency to make creativity the saviour in the knowledge economy has been problematized by Sørensen (2008), who argues that this turning to something to save us has religious connotations. In entrepreneurship research, these concerns have mainly been put forward as a critique of the promotion of a hero imagery of entrepreneurship (Johansson, 2008b; Olaison, 2008; Berglund, 2004, 2007; Nicholson and Anderson, 2005; Ahl, 2002) that excludes and silences aspects of the entrepreneurial process pivotal to a socially productive entrepreneurship. However, even though it has become increasingly popular to apply a process perspective to entrepreneurship, as illustrated for instance by the attempts to promote the concept of 'entrepreneuring' (for example, Chell, 2007; Steyaert, 2007), the hero imagery is still very palpable in the popular and academic entrepreneurship discourse.

We use conceptual ideas originating in the works of Debord (1967, 1990) with the purpose of forming a critique against this tendency, and to suggest an alternative view of entrepreneurship that puts the spotlight on the mundane aspects of entrepreneurship and its interrelatedness to the spectacular aspects of the phenomenon. There are to our knowledge no attempts to adopt Debord's concept of societal phenomena being spectacles in entrepreneurship research, albeit that recent research does hint towards this (for example, Styhre, 2008b; Sørensen, 2008). Debord was a founder and seminal theoretician in the situationist movement who argued that the everyday society in which we live and dwell constitutes a spectacle of a society rather than a real society. He argued that: 'In societies where modern conditions of production prevail, all of life presents itself as an immense accumulation of spectacles. Everything that was directly lived has moved away into a representation' (Debord, 1967, p. §1).

We argue, analogously, that what we normally perceive as entrepreneurship amounts to a spectacle of entrepreneurship played out according to an underlying script (by 'script' we imply that a person, if he or she behaves in a certain way, will be perceived as an entrepreneur). Efforts of promoting entrepreneurship and indeed the entrepreneuring activities themselves may be, intentionally or not, a promotion or enactment of a spectacle of entrepreneurship; the becoming of a ceremonial and glamorous image of entrepreneurship; a script offered by the spectacle that indeed is considered more real than its non-spectacle counterpart, but which is not sustainable on its own.

The issue is certainly serious enough. It is no controversial statement to claim that entrepreneurship has joined with those ideas that, like success, are rich in self-proclaimed friends and helpers. Vast sums of money are spent on fostering growth and venture prosperity and this is true on all levels from local municipal steering groups to the European Union (EU) and numerous non-governmental organizations (NGOs) (cf. Bill and Olaison, 2006; European Commission, 2003, p. 7; Lambrecht and Pirnay, 2005). In Sweden, as well as in other member states, this has given rise to various regional and national programmes, for example, 'NUTEK's national entrepreneurship program 2005–2007' and 'Innovative Sweden: a strategy for growth through renewal' (Ministry of Enterprise, Energy and Communications/Ministry of Education, 2004, p. 36). Discussions on the national level encourage regional and local programmes aiming at supporting entrepreneurship in general, mainly through counselling to and networking between small and medium-sized enterprises (SMEs) (for example, Rylander, 2004; NUTEK, 2004, p. 10) and lately there has been an increased focus on entrepreneurship in the educational system (cf. Holmgren, 2005, VA-rapport, 2005, p. 2). A fair share of these resources may actually be spent on promoting a spectacle of entrepreneurship, dislocated from the mundane everydayness also characterizing entrepreneurial processes.

Outline of the Chapter

The remainder of this chapter is organized as follows. In the next section we will explore conceptually the prosaic and spectacular dimension of previous treatments of entrepreneurship. In the final section we then develop our conceptual ideas about how entrepreneurship, as a necessity, should be seen as both spectacle and mundane – both telling and doing – and the application of this idea to entrepreneurship and especially the mobilization of entrepreneurial energy.

ENTREPRENEURSHIP: SPECTACULAR RATHER THAN MUNDANE, AN OVERVIEW

Two Dominant Approaches to Entrepreneurship

The increasing demand for entrepreneurship and knowledge on this phenomenon has propelled the amount of academic research on the topic. Entrepreneurship as a field of research is now established, comprising a multitude of studies of various aspects of entrepreneurship. The field also encompasses a wide range of ontological, epistemological, methodological, theoretical and empirical variations (Steyaert, 2007; Shane and Venkataraman, 2000), which may be one indicator suggesting the elusiveness and impossibility to once and for all conceptualize entrepreneurship, or describe it in a definite model. In this great variety of studies, two basic perspectives are nonetheless often distinguished: entrepreneurship as a special kind of management, an approach exemplified by Mintzberg (1973) and Shane (2003), and entrepreneurship as forms of social creativity, an approach exemplified by Hjorth et al. (2003) and Gartner et al. (2003); see also Johannisson and Olaison, 2007, 2008.[1]

The perspective seeing entrepreneurship as a special kind of management, which can be termed the 'opportunity-driven perspective', situates entrepreneurship within a framework of economic rationality and efficient resource allocation. Entrepreneurship is regarded as a strategy 'concerned with the discovery and exploitation of profitable opportunities' (Shane and Venkataraman, 2000, p. 217) appearing in markets. Entrepreneurship implies, from this perspective, proactive allocation of resources to exploit such opportunities efficiently, making entrepreneurship 'the nexus of two phenomena: the presence of lucrative opportunities and the presence of enterprising individuals' (ibid., p. 218). Entrepreneurship is, however, always associated with risk, which is an effect of, among other things, incomplete information. Thus viewed, entrepreneurship research means: 'the scholarly examination of how, by whom, and with what effects opportunities to create future goods and services are discovered, evaluated, and exploited' (Venkataraman, 1997).

As a result, the research field consists of 'the study of sources of opportunities; the processes of discovery, evaluation, and exploitation of opportunities; and the set of individuals who discover, evaluate, and exploit them' (Shane and Venkataraman, 2000, p. 218). This stream of entrepreneurship research, endorsed by researchers working within what has been referred to as an American tradition, emphasizes systematic change and renewal, which is understood in a means–ends framework (Shane, 2003). Entrepreneurship thus viewed is very specific and strategic, and is unable to comprise much creativity and everyday practices (see also Johannisson and Olaison, 2007, 2008).

The perspective seeing entrepreneurship as forms of social creativity, which can be termed the 'creative process view', tends to associate entrepreneurship with social creativity in a more inclusive way. This way of understanding entrepreneurship, which is endorsed by researchers working with what has been referred to as a European tradition (Gartner et al., 2008), tends to:

> prefer to refer to entrepreneurship as forms of social creativity, taking place primarily in societal rather than in business contexts. Entrepreneurship is a societal force: it changes our daily practices and the way we live; it invents futures in populating histories of the present, here and now. In such processes, entrepreneurial processes, the present and the future is [*sic*] organized in stories and conversations, the primary form of knowledge used in everyday practices. (Hjorth and Steyaert, 2004, pp. 3–4)

Thus viewed, the market is only one arena in which entrepreneurship can take place. Neither is entrepreneurship always strategic and rational: chance, coincidences, and flukes may result in the enactment of new opportunities, leading ultimately to the creation of new worlds (Spinosa et al., 1997). Entrepreneurship, from this perspective, is playful adventuring, which is different in nature from management (which implies a willingness to control). This perspective thus calls for studies of entrepreneurial processes open to the creative/imaginative, aided by a language to handle such issues; a language that can relate to diversity and change in an adequate and affirmative manner (Hjorth, 2003; Gartner et al., 2003; Steyaert, 2004).

The imagery of a creative process view, it has been argued (Johannisson and Olaison, 2007, 2008), has taken two, slightly different directions: one that emphasizes the relation to art and aesthetics rather than model-building strategies and business plans, as associated with the opportunity-driven approach; and the other calling for a 'prosaics of entrepreneurship', the everydayness, what people are doing when they are doing entrepreneurship.

We will explore the prosaics of entrepreneurship in the next section, but already here point out that both the instrumental, model-building approaches and the creative process views seem to struggle with, if not neglect, explaining or understanding the mundane and boring aspect of the entrepreneurial process. However different the 'opportunity-driven' and the 'creative process' views are, they thus share a dilemma in that they, intentionally or not, risk overemphasizing the spectacular aspects of entrepreneurship, although in different ways. The 'opportunity-based' approach has focused on finding alert individuals who 'discover opportunities', which has led to a search for certain traits and certain individuals. When analysing texts from this tradition, it has been shown that the texts describe a hero-like individual, often a male (Johansson, 2008b; Olaison, 2008; Berglund, 2007; Ahl, 2002) who is even messianic to his character (Sørensen, 2008). It is the quest for the Entrepreneur with a capital E, a spectacular man indeed.

The imagery of the hero-like Entrepreneur is problematized in the creative process approach, making it what could be called a post-heroic approach. Entrepreneurship in this tradition is described as a process, entrepreneuring, and this makes the entrepreneur not an alert individual, but rather a subject position, a predescribed role, a performance to be performed. Such entrepreneurships 'call for a vocabulary that acknowledges the affinity between entrepreneurship and emotions and aesthetics rather than with cognitive facts alone' (Johannisson and Olaison, 2007, p. 58). The vocabulary has been drawn from organization theory and the humanities, and is accompanied by a methodology that focuses on storytelling and narratives (see for example Steyaert and Hjorth, 2003, 2006; Hjorth and Steyaert, 2004, 2009).

However necessary and successful the creative process approach has been in the problematization of the opportunity-driven approach, there are reasons to believe that it, too, to some extent promotes a hero-imagery; not the least when conceptual work becomes translated into policies and practice. One reason for this might be the state of methodological development (see further Steyaert, 1997). Few studies depict these 'daily practices and the way we live' (Hjorth and Steyaert, 2004, p. 3). A storytelling approach, thus, might rather enhance the spectacular and ceremonial dimensions of the entrepreneurial process, since it makes for 'better stories'. This tendency could also be reinforced because the entrepreneurs themselves have been taught to present themselves in a particular way when talking to researchers, to be such a 'great storyteller' (cf. Smith and Anderson, 2004). Indeed, the media we have to tell stories of entrepreneurships (for example, talking, writing, showing) plainly work better when reporting something spectacular rather than something ordinary and boring. Another reason might be intrinsic to the theoretical project of rewriting entrepreneurship and thus differentiating entrepreneurship from the managerial discourse (Hjorth, 2003). The call for finding the entrepreneurial in entrepreneurship, 'initiated by curiosity, organized by spontaneity and intrinsically driven by passion and joy' (Johannisson and Olaison, 2007, p. 58), and the search for entrepreneurial languages, might be running the risk of leading to a search for entrepreneurship in special places, putting forward the most spectacular and extraordinary cases, instead of the everydayness that initially was called upon.

The Boring Everydayness of a Creative Process

The creative process approach in contemporary entrepreneurship research, which builds on critical analysis and aims at renewing and rewriting entrepreneurship (cf. Johansson, 2008b; Sørensen, 2008; Bill, 2006; Hjorth, 2003; Steyaert and Hjorth, 2003; Gartner et al., 2003), supports the notion of broadening what is labelled 'entrepreneurship'. Based on a soft ontology, the creative process view denies the very idea of representation; every deliberation on a topic is therefore an act of creation rather than an act of representation: 'Reality is not only to be understood as that which must be represented, or as something of which one becomes conscious, but it assumes a series of possibilities. Every reality is active creation, and bears creativity in it, minimal as this may seem' (Steyaert, 1997, p. 21). To make sense of such a reality, Steyaert argues, we need to study the extreme or, even more preferably, the unexpected cases. As argued above, these are to be found in everyday practices (see also Steyaert, 2004).

However broad this call for alternative approaches has become (Gartner et al., 2008; Steyaert and Hjorth, 2003, 2006; Hjorth and Steyaert, 2004, 2009), research investigating the relationships between creativity/innovation and the prosaic/ordinary seems rather limited (see Kociatkiewicz, 2000 for one exception). That is, we easily assume that creative space is inherently linked with creative place. However, Steyaert (2004) proposes, that just as Bakhtin preferred:

> prose over the poem in writing a theory of literature . . . the prosaics of entrepreneurship thus combines this unique feature and association, namely that the everydayness of entrepreneurship refers as much to a mundane, and – why not – even a boring posture as to a literary connotation where a prosaics – as in the novel – addresses the actuality of becoming, its ongoing becoming effected through conversational processes. (Steyaert, 2004, p. 9)

Following Steyeart (2004), Johannisson and Olaison (2008, p. 246) argue that: 'all entrepreneurial processes certainly, however path breaking, include routine activities just as all human beings as adults occasionally engage in entrepreneurial processes'. Thus, it is reasonable to assume that creative space is as interlinked with prosaic places as with creative places, offering a perspective of the entrepreneurial as inherent in the seemingly mundane processes of everyday existence (for example, Hjorth, 2004, 2005; Johannisson and Olaison, 2007; Steyaert, 2004).

Steyeart (2004) and Johannisson and Olaison (2008) seem to be pointing towards the danger of only looking at one side of the story, and that we often prefer the shiny spectacle instead of the mundane and boring. In doing so, we risk missing out on the actual everyday processes of creating, capturing its mere (and often spectacular) representation. A prosaic perspective on entrepreneurship would acknowledge the importance of 'the everyday and the ordinary, the familiar and the frequent, the customary and the accustomed, the mediocre and the inferior' (Steyaert, 2004, p. 9).

We argue for a conceptualization of entrepreneurship as comprising both mundane and spectacular aspects – aspects that are interrelated and interdependent elements of the entrepreneurial process (see also Bill and Olaison, 2007). The spectacular dimension of entrepreneurship, which is often connected to the idea of creativeness and innovativeness, is also by necessity connected to the mundane and prosaic everydayness of this very creativeness and innovativeness. In the next section, this will be further conceptualized.

ENTREPRENEURSHIP: SPECTACULAR AND MUNDANE

Entrepreneurship in the Society of the Spectacle

The argument that contemporary society ought to be considered a spectacle of society was promoted by the political and artistic situationist movement during the 1960s and 1970s. Founded on a bricolage of ideas adopted from and critical of structuralism, situationist thinkers believed that real society was hidden behind an alluring spectacle staged primarily by modern capitalism. The theory of the spectacle was intended to be simultaneously descriptive and emancipatory since it offered insight into the foul play of capitalism while concurrently aspiring to be a tool created for aiding in the destruction of the spectacle (Debord, 1967, 1990).

We take the conceptual apparatus and revolutionary ideas of Guy Debord (1967), perhaps the most prominent thinker of the situationist movement, as our starting point, bringing his ideas to bear on entrepreneurship. His argument that society is increasingly turning into a spectacle of a society implies that life is increasingly taking place in a world of representations, rather than in a world of 'authentic' lived experiences. In this society that is increasingly becoming a spectacle of a society, the borderline between the mundane and the spectacular blurs. Everyday functions which are typically associated with function tend to seem dull and thus lose ground to the imagery of the spectacular world of representations. The ceremonial and symbolic lures spectators, causing the spectacle to define what is to be considered real and authentic. When confronted with manifestations of everyday functions we spectators consequently tend to perceive them as dull and mundane compared to the magnificent imagery of the spectacle.

Debord noted that:

> The image of blissful social unification through consumption merely postpones the consumer's awareness of the actual divisions until his next disillusionment with some particular commodity. Each new product is ceremoniously acclaimed as a unique creation offering a dramatic shortcut to the promised land of total consummation . . . But the object that was prestigious in the spectacle becomes mundane as soon as it is taken home by its consumer – and by all its other consumers. Too late, it reveals its central poverty, a poverty that inevitably reflects the poverty of its production. (Debord, 1967, p. 69)

In this way Debord points out one of the core characteristics of the spectacle. Since the phenomena, whatever their characteristics, which constitute the props of the spectacle have a mundane dimension, they will lose much of their allure as they are used or incorporated in everyday functions. They simply become dull as their spectacularity diminishes as they are exposed to the wear and tear of everyday use. However, in order for phenomena to be embedded in everyday activities in the first place they need to attract attention and are in that way dependent on the spectacle.

We need to point out that the theory of Debord (1967) is based on a clearly dichotomized opposition between real and false phenomena; with the underlying if often silent assumption that the former are superior to the later. Instead of arguing, as did Debord, in favour of the 'real' and against the spectacle, our framework is intended to illuminate the dynamics and reciprocity between the spectacular and that which come to be considered mundane. While using the terminology of Debord in this chapter, sometimes using 'pseudo-' and 'spectacle of' as denominators, we differ from him by not placing any evaluation in these epithets. From the horizon of the ontology of becoming, anything labelled 'entrepreneurship' is constantly in the process of becoming something else (Deleuze and Guattari, 1988). Situationism constitutes as much of an ideological as of a philosophical endeavour, and Debord (1967) consequently stated that his theory of the spectacle was intended to be useful in political struggle rather than merely correct in a representational sense. We bring the situationist distinction between spectacle and non-spectacle to bear on entrepreneurship not because we believe that the mundane, non-spectacular aspects of entrepreneurship are more of a 'real' entrepreneurship in any metaphysical sense, but because we believe that when focusing merely on the spectacular aspects of the phenomena, other, also important, aspects are neglected and overlooked.

In essence, it is the above-mentioned transformation of the spectacular into something mundane as the props lose their lure that is the core in the theory of Debord (1967). This sequence of something initially seeming to be grand and spectacular, to be over time diminished and dimmed into something mundane and unexciting, will mimic the view of entrepreneurship which we try to promote.

The Spectacular and the Mundane Side of Entrepreneurship

Our conceptualization relies on a fundamental distinction between the mundane and spectacular. We have argued above that every creative process necessarily involves both exciting and boring aspects. However, it simply does not make for an exciting image of entrepreneurship to consider, for example, waiting, routines, actual production, coffee-making, toilet visits, meetings and similar activities typically necessary for a viable entrepreneuring process. Entrepreneurship is more often associated with a superhuman character, the Entrepreneur, who is doing visionary work and is, for example, inventing interesting things that turn up on the market. Nicholson and Anderson shows for example, that the British press in 2000 represented the entrepreneur, among other things, as an: 'aggressive protagonist in battle . . . [who] remains royal magician, but is also portrayed as wizard, iconic legend, master of universe, giant tree, and bearded shadow. Mythological images surge as the entrepreneur is portrayed as God himself rather than just blessed by God' (Nicholson and Anderson, 2005, p. 161). This spectacle of entrepreneurship arguably dominates representations of entrepreneurship and entrepreneurs in a society that is turning into a spectacle of a society.

Early writers on entrepreneurship (Schumpeter, 1934/1968; Kirzner, 1973) understood entrepreneurs and entrepreneurship from the perspective of their/its function in the economic system, with a focus on what consequences entrepreneurship had rather than who the entrepreneur is and how entrepreneurship is done. This view implies, however, a perspective of the entrepreneur as someone with above-average qualities, and subsequent research has often developed this notion of the entrepreneur as a (male) hero figure with a more or less superior set of traits. Portrayed as a saviour who creates growth and prosperity, the anonymous functions in the writings of Schumpeter and Kirzner are to some extent individualized (cf. Sørensen, 2008). In the discussions of creative space, creative economy and creative individuals, the mundane and boring is arguably forgotten. The representation of entrepreneurship and the entrepreneur is arguably the hero-image of the entrepreneur, which thereby is further entrenched.

This is also true for the non-academic discourse on entrepreneurship. Using our example of the Lisbon strategy, although the goal is to accomplish the 'fostering artistic and other forms of creativity through preschool, primary and secondary education including vocational streams, as well as non-formal and informal education', when operationalizing the strategy, creativity is mainly looked for in the 'cultural and creative industries including design – where the aesthetic and the economic coincide', from where experiences can be drawn to 'contribute to economic prosperity as well as to social and individual wellbeing' (European Commission, 2009). That is, we tend to look for creativity in certain creative places associated with glamour and visionary work. Although one of the other goals is to develop 'a wider understanding of the innovation process and a more entrepreneurial attitude as prerequisites for continued prosperity' (European Commission, 2009), it is difficult to get a sense of how the programme statement relates to such processes, apart from being creative and innovative, and as such productive.

The spectacular imagery used for representing and delimiting entrepreneurship certainly applies also to how individual entrepreneurs are thought about. In fact, Stein Bagger, before being revealed as an impostor, is a good example of the imagery invoked by the word 'entrepreneurship'. He led an information technology (IT) company and was considered very charismatic and a saviour of the company he led, which was represented as fast-growing. This fits right in with the argument that entrepreneurs are represented as heroes and entrepreneurship as exciting, fast-paced and non-routine. In fact, as will be explored next, Mr Bagger's degree of entrepreneurial script-following could be gauged as very high.

The Scripted Spectacle of Entrepreneurship

There is thus a preoccupation with the spectacular side of entrepreneurship in the popular and academic discourse that has created a strong preconception of what it means to be an entrepreneur. A hunt for the ideal entrepreneur, the 'real' entrepreneur (see for example Johansson, Chapter 7 in this book) able to save us all in the new economy (Sørensen, 2008), has led to a powerful script of how to be entrepreneurial, a guide to how the spectacle of entrepreneurship should be played. This script is spectacular in nature, promoting the image of a male hero-like character who is different and thinks differently. The spectacular nature of this script is reflective of society becoming more spectacularized (Debord, 1967, 1990).

The script, when viewed from the perspective of representativeness, is a kind of pseudo-entrepreneurship, identifiable and possible to enact but not necessarily with much connection to the mundane everydayness of entrepreneuring processes.

Our example of the Lisbon Strategy is a good example of the scripted nature of entrepreneurship as expressed in the non-academic discourse. The process indicated through the motto 'Imagine. Create. Innovate' (European Commission, 2009) is a sequential, linear process from idea to the market, oozing of exciting and sexy creativity. The slogan also implicitly seems to indicate a tolerance towards a somewhat unconventional behaviour on the part of the entrepreneur, as someone thinking and acting differently. Of course, imagining and creating are not deviant behaviours by definition, but do seem to represent someone thinking differently and acting differently from those who are non-imaginative and non-creative. The Entrepreneur can use his and others' imagination as long as it is for the art of creation (after all, 'We need creativity to find the best answers'; European Commission, 2009). Yet creativity cannot be just any kind of creation – it must always be steered towards the market (the widely used definition of innovation is 'commercialization on the market'); it is part of the script of what being a 'real' entrepreneur is.

This celebration of creativity and innovation has moral and political implications (see further Jones and Spicer, 2009) and presents a ready-made script for individuals to enact. As long as the entrepreneur keeps him- or herself inside the fuzzy outer lines of morals and law, and as long as he or she acts in the best interest of society and as long as he or she is aiming to reach the market, he or she is encouraged to overact, even deceive to a limited extent. Popular belief would, for example, have it that entrepreneurs are supposed to be overly optimistic about their enterprises and, as a consequence, may be 'deceiving' investors to some extent. Gartner (1989), in a seminal contribution to the creative process approach, argued that entrepreneurial firms are different from established firms, in that the entrepreneur is 'acting as if' there were, for example, an organization, while he or she is working towards establishing an organization. Although Gartner may not be representative of mainstream academic thought on entrepreneurship, his idea is reflective of the wide acceptance of the view that entrepreneurs may 'break with the rules', even pretend in the beginning of the process – always following the underlying assumption that the entrepreneur does it not to deceive, but to make 'it' happen.

Stein Bagger is, against this background, an extreme example of someone following the script of entrepreneurship, differing only in degree from those passing as 'real' entrepreneurs in the sense that the deceit was taken a bit too far. As an entrepreneur he was 'supposed' to be imaginative and creative, be in a creative place (such as an IT company), and to some extent deceive; it is all part of the script. Because he played it so well, he was even appointed Entrepreneur of the Year. Apparently, nobody – not even an audit firm like Ernst & Yong – cared about the boring and mundane details of Mr Bagger's day-to-day activities that certainly were necessary for his spectacular performance, but were instead enchanted by the glorious spectacle of an entrepreneur enacted, creating the representation of a seemingly perfect entrepreneur. Why, one might ask, are the mundane aspects of the entrepreneurial process not a strong part of what is intuitively considered as 'entrepreneurship' when they occupy a large portion of the time of those who are typically considered 'entrepreneurs', not to speak of all other silent actors making the organized efforts termed 'entrepreneurial' possible?

Producing Entrepreneurs

The consequence stemming from a strong script of entrepreneurship in an increasingly spectacularized society is that would-be entrepreneurs must follow the script; they must star in the spectacle of entrepreneurship in order to be considered 'real' entrepreneurs, with all that this entails. The irony of this is that following a script is not, in a sense, very entrepreneurial. If we just perform the script, we are not creating anything, merely playing out a prewritten script (albeit well, of course). A suitable metaphor may be a song: 'The verses of entrepreneurship are not reproducible, the only reoccurring [sic] part is the refrain. Verse, success, verse, success, verse, success or perhaps verse, growth, verse, growth, verse, growth' (Bill and Olaison, 2006, pp. 12–13). To do entrepreneurship in the sense of dealing with dull and mundane everyday activities, one has to balance between reproducing the refrain (the spectacle of entrepreneurship) and creating a verse of one's own; one has to become an entrepreneur in the twofold sense of becoming simultaneously an entrepreneur and a pseudo-entrepreneur, that is, a representation of the Entrepreneur. When expecting, and receiving, a spectacle of entrepreneurship to consider someone an Entrepreneur, we are not creating more entrepreneurs, but rather the opposite: we are creating more of the same, just another refrain of entrepreneurship. If success and prosperity, as is proposed by much entrepreneurship research (for example, Schumpeter, 1934/1968; Shane and Venkatraman, 2000), is about doing the unique and thus breaking with the taken-for-granted and given ideas of the economy, 'there is an entrepreneurship and an entrepreneurship and an entrepreneurship' (Bill and Olaison, 2006, p. 13), none the same.

Yet policy-makers do not seem to want this pluralism; they want the scripted spectacle of entrepreneurship. The Lisbon Initiative, accordingly, looks for entrepreneurs who are supposedly imaginative, creative and innovative in specific senses and in specific places. In fact, advocators of entrepreneurship often fall into the rhetoric of entrepreneurship education or SME support where entrepreneurship is undoubtedly good and what is needed is simply to teach people what entrepreneurship really is and how it is to be carried out (cf. Wigren and Melin, 2009; Bill and Olaison, 2009). Neither is this unique for entrepreneurship, as could be expected in an increasingly spectacular society. Johansson and Kociatkiewicz (2008) demonstrate for instance how city planners use festivals to produce ideal images and scripts that stage spectacles of urban space. By copying and enacting existing scripts, phenomena are reproduced as spectacles of the phenomenon originally intended. Thus a city is manifested as a city, for instance, through the staged spectacle of itself taking place in accordance with the preset script. The spectacle of entrepreneurship tends to be seen as the script for entrepreneurship, and as it is reproduced in various settings the script becomes more real than the everyday activities being carried out as people are entrepreneuring.

While such initiatives often may have the best of intentions, what we want to bring attention to is that we might fall into teaching an ideal image of what we think entrepreneurship is, or should be, so as to promote a certain script of entrepreneurship that is used when performing the spectacle of entrepreneurship; a performance that has little to do with the boring and mundane realities of actual entrepreneuring activities. Our example of the 'European Year of Creativity and Innovation 2009' has been, for example, looking for 'good examples', but our examples of individuals that have played the part of the entrepreneur so well as to become celebrated as super-entrepreneurs – Stein Bagger and Bernard L. Madoff – show that discriminating between good and bad is not a straightforward task. Maybe that is why entrepreneurs are assessed according to their similarity to a script for playing out a spectacle of entrepreneurship, rather than according to their actions, boring and mundane as they may be. There is a risk that all the efforts spent on 'lifelong learning' – a concept taken from the goals of the initiative (European Commission, 2009) – teach how to play the role efficiently rather than doing actual innovation, entrepreneurship or creativity. Making actors play the script increases the chances of immediate gratification for policy-makers – more Entrepreneurs are seemingly created – and has few negative short-term consequences, making it treacherous.

The Spectacle and the Mundane: Interplay rather than Dichotomy

Our argument thus far suggests that the mundane aspects of entrepreneuring are concealed to the benefit of the spectacular side of this phenomenon, and actors wishing to be perceived as real entrepreneurs must engage in a scripted spectacle of entrepreneurship, applauded and celebrated. By implication our argument, at least on a rhetorical level, seem to be taking a stand against this tendency, trying to mobilize interest also in the mundane aspects of the entrepreneuring process that, though unglamorous, are essential for a socially productive entrepreneurship. However, the spectacular is a part of the inescapable reality faced by entrepreneurs who must balance these two aspects: performing the scripted spectacle of entrepreneurship, and mundane and boring work. Would-be entrepreneurs, we argue, need to direct their attention to both these sides of entrepreneurship: entrepreneurs must simultaneously become entrepreneurs and pseudo-entrepreneurs. Neglecting the script may very well cause the entrepreneur to lose esteem with important actors in his or her surroundings, while missing out on creating market sustainability will in the end destroy any endeavour. We explore, in this last section of our conceptualization, this interplay between the spectacular and the mundane in the entrepreneuring process.

The scripted spectacle of entrepreneurship represents an imagery that spectators are attracted to. We want superhuman entrepreneurs to save us (Sørensen, 2008). Charismatic individuals are allowed to amass vast amounts of resources for apparently splendid corporate projects, with the expressed purpose of changing the world, if they adhere to the script of entrepreneurship well enough. It is the renowned co-founder of Apple, Steve Jobs, who attracts attention, can raise countless dollars on the stock market, and is seen as a role model for entrepreneurs to be; not the taciturn engineer, who can be seen doing more routine work. And stories of successful entrepreneurs – Steve Jobs included – often emphasize that the individuals were once (while still being unsuccessful) a 'nobody' (just like everybody else). As our examples show, it may be enough to play the script well enough; whether the glorious representation that becomes the result has only a limited relation to the often mundane entrepreneuring process is irrelevant. Only after a significant time lag does this dissonance become obvious, as was the case with Stein Bagger and with Bernard L. Madoff Investment Securities LLC. Just as organizations incorporate formal structural elements for gaining legitimacy but decouple activities from them for efficiency (Meyer and Rowan, 1977), so entrepreneurs wishing to be seen as real entrepreneurs with all the benefits this entails must thus perform a spectacle of entrepreneurship to become a 'real' entrepreneur, while simultaneously engaging in the mundane and dull aspects of entrepreneuring in order to secure the long-term soundness of their endeavour.

Constant and balanced oscillation between performing the spectacular script of entrepreneurship and the dull and mundane aspects of entrepreneuring is thus likely to benefit the growth and success of a venture. Flashing the spectacular aspects of entrepreneurship may attract resources to entrepreneurial processes, but employing these resources in productive endeavours involves a large element of activities that are perceived as dull and mundane. Thus, ironically, the combination of a dull and down-to-earth entrepreneuring process and a flamboyant act of spectacular entrepreneurship may well be extremely productive, seen from an instrumental point of view. Furthermore, since there is often a more or less significant time elapsing between when these two defining character-istics are instrumentally useful (that is, an entrepreneurial project needs to mobilize resources before these can be managed), entrepreneurship becomes fiddly to pin down. Playing the spectacle of entrepreneurship is fun and glamorous; the spectacle produces a desire to become engaged in its activities and disengage from the dullness of mundane everydayness. Yet, the spectacle's image of entrepreneurship cannot sustain without prosaic and mundane activities.

CONCLUDING REMARKS

We have argued that entrepreneurship has both a spectacular and a mundane side, and that entrepreneurship discourse, popular and aca-demic, tends to emphasize the former at the expense of the latter. The search for the real and ideal entrepreneur has created a strong script for how to be an entrepreneur, and actors playing this spectacle are applauded and celebrated as real entrepreneurs by policy-makers and spectators alike, regardless of whether the act has any connection to the largely mundane entrepreneuring activities taking place. Entrepreneurs' spec-tacular performances are attractive to spectators and hold the promise of attracting resources of different kinds to the actor, which can be employed in furthering the entrepreneuring process. Our inquiry indicates the need for entrepreneurs to navigate carefully between handling the boring eve-rydayness of building a business, and staging the alluring spectacle of entrepreneurship. Attracting resources requires the entrepreneur to offer excitement, greatness and all the other paraphernalia associated with the rise of great men and women. At the same time, in the hidden background of the entrepreneurial venture, an increasing number of people partake in the mundane actions that taken together make up the prosaic processes of growing the venture.

The initiatives emanating from policy-makers such as the European Commission are played out in a lofty setting, far from the ordinary enterprise, and might serve just to strengthen the rigidity of the scripted spectacle of entrepreneurship, despite all the good intentions. The general notions of creativity and innovation expressed in statements and on home pages are of course very general, but the point is that they are also alluring. We are drawn like moths towards the beautiful concepts and the staging of growth and development they offer, far from the dull activities being carried out in our own working life. Or in most owner-managers' working lives, for that matter. Our example of someone playing the script almost perfectly but simultaneously engaging in unsustainable activities with little relation to the glorious image of the Entrepreneur, Stein Bagger, is not used to demonstrate the deficiencies of the scripted spectacle of entrepreneurship – in fact, if anything, he illustrates the opposite. There are numerous examples of entrepreneurs like Bill Gates, Steve Jobs and Richard Branson who have managed to create imagery that has drawn attention to themselves and their ventures, which seem viable and sound from an economic perspective. The example is rather intended to illustrate the danger of overemphasizing playing the spectacle of entrepreneurship without catering to the everyday activities of entrepreneuring. The spectacle can be productive, but its sustainability requires mundane activities to be carried out.

The script to which we refer is, however, not written in stone. Debord (1967) has argued that anyone wanting to change the predominant order of things needs a theory: one that, regardless of its truth value, points to the existing order as something bad, and one that can not readily be discarded as wrong. That is, there exists a need for another script to the spectacle if the current one is to be transformed. As soon as mundane everyday actions are acknowledged as entrepreneurship, they gain a spectacular lure, attracting the resources and attention that foster growth and development. Within organizations, this has been addressed by Hjorth (2004), who argues that creating spaces for play, rather than supporting specific entrepreneurship activities, is one way of creating development. A new theory is not enough, however, because there is also a need for a second element if the forces of change are to prevail. Debord (1967) argues that this second element is the proletarian manifesting the revolt. Thus, not only a grand theory of change is required, but also the mundane and often boring tasks of performing a revolution that tear the old spectacle and its beneficiaries to pieces.

NOTE

1. The following sections build on literature reviews that can also be found in Johannisson and Olaison (2007, 2008).

PART III

. . . Something Else . . .

10. Constellations of another other: the case of Aquarian Nation

Daniel Ericsson

PROLOGUE

In *A Thousand Plateaus*, Gilles Deleuze and Félix Guattari (1988) outline their nomadology and introduce the concept of the war machine. Although it is essentially seen as an abstract machine – an assemblage of points, lines, speeds, objects and flows existing in the virtual realm – Deleuze and Guattari (ibid., p. 230) highlight the war machine's historical origins, thereby connecting it with ancient nomadism's transition to an itinerant territoriality and differentiating it from the State and its apparatus. The war machine, they argue, represents a kind of self-organizing, decentralized and non-disciplinary force of aggression directed against the State apparatus in order to preserve the heterogeneity of the smooth space. The State, on the other hand, which strives for homogeneity and centralized control, seeks to appropriate the war machine for its own uses, thereby making it a piece, a plug-in, in its own apparatus and striating the space over which it reigns (ibid., p. 385). It is important to note, however, that the war machine does not have war as its objective. It only has war as potential:

> To the extent that war . . . aims for the annihilation or capitulation of enemy forces, the war machine does not necessarily have war as its object . . . But more generally, we have seen that the war machine was the invention of the nomad, because it is in its essence the constitutive element of smooth space: this is its sole and veritable positive object . . . If war necessarily results, it is because the war machine collides with States and cities, as forces (of striation) opposing its positive object: from then on, the war machine has as its enemy the State, the city, the State and urban phenomenon, and adopts its objective their annihilation . . . speaking like Derrida, we would say that war is the 'supplement' of the war machine . . . It is precisely after the war machine has been appropriated by the State in this way that it tends to take war for its direct and primary object. (Ibid., pp. 417–18)

Moreover, once war has broken out, the war machine unifies its resources and becomes a mission machine, 'a machine rooted to *centralized* resistance . . . 'a movement' in the sense of a vanguard' (Marzec, 2001).

In Search of Disargument on Disarmament

The discourse on entrepreneurship could, with reference to Deleuze and Guattari (1988), very well be depicted as a nomadic war machine appropriated by the State apparatus. Not only is it a machine with a wide territorial range, reaching into almost every corner of the Western world, but it is also a machine with a great missionary capacity for colonizing all that stands in its way. Opposing world-views, differing ethos, and other subjective dispositions and positions aside from the entrepreneurial one are all conquered and subsumed under a regime of truth that is composed of a set of binary oppositions that produces – and breathes upon – a number of hierarchical 'either–or' positions. According to this discourse, actors are either entrepreneurial or not, for or against, and the world is either good or evil from an entrepreneurial perspective. And, in relation to the present volume, the machine produces human activity as a case of either mobility or immobility.

This chapter attempts to disarm this war machine in order to bring about alternative constellations of entrepreneurship. This is done in two interrelated steps. On the one hand, in the first section, a demobilizing deconstruction of the discourse on entrepreneurship is carried out, with a special focus on other constructions of entrepreneurship aside from the dominating ones. How is this specific war machine assembled? What is the output of this specific assemblage? What subject (dis)positions does the war machine produce, and what (dis)positions does it not produce? In line with Derrida (1976/1998) and Braidotti (2005), it will be argued that the discourse on entrepreneurship could be understood as a phallogocentric war machine, a machine set up to produce (more of) the Same and (less of) the Other. And, in doing this, it is bound to (re)produce and perpetuate opposition between the two, by the provision of discursive plug-in devices to the war machine. All in all, therefore, the discourse on entrepreneurship could be conceptualized as a *perpetuum mobile* of conflict.

On the other hand, in the second section, an empirical case – Aquarian Nation – is presented, in which alternative constellations of entrepreneurship are brought to the fore. Being an independent actor within the music industry, the people of Aquarian Nation have created an artistic community in which music is produced, distributed and consumed in ways that break with the routines of both major(itan) and minor(itan) record companies. Under the motto 'A Sanctuary for Musicianship', the artists of Aquarian Nation, for instance, work with their audience in such a way that traditional practices of production, consumption and distribution – as well as traditional boundaries between producer, consumer and distributor – are transcended and altered in a 'both–and' manner.

In contrast to the prevailing discourse on entrepreneurship, it will be argued that Aquarian Nation could be understood as a machine that not only produces (more of) the Other and (less of) the Same, but also produces the other of the Other. In this sense it will be argued that Aquarian Nation could be conceptualized not as a war machine, but as 'something else'.

Configuring the Cartography of Interpretation

A key starting point for this text is that discourses are in no way objective or neutral. They are the resulting practices of social interaction – 'talk, text, writing, cognition, argumentation, and representation generally' (Clegg, 1989 – p. 151), and as such they 'systematically form the object of which they speak' (Foucault, 1969/1972, p. 49). Discourses are thus believed to stand in a dialectical relationship with their users: on the one hand they convey socially constructed regimes of truths that affect both the social world and its artifacts; and on the other hand they construct the social in such a way that they can be said to 'configure' the users (cf. Woolgar, 1991) in terms of the subjective and objective meanings that are made available to them by the discourses.

Trying to chisel out the different analytic approaches to discourse, Alvesson and Kärreman (2000) distinguish between two different understandings of discourse. On the one hand, they argue, there is a Teflon-like understanding of discourse, a transient and myopic approach in which discourses are not considered to 'stick on' to people. On the other hand, there is a Foucauldian version, a more categorical and deterministic approach in which, in principle, all aspects of human activity, by various types of technologies of power, are subjugated by the discourse in a clear-cut and specific manner. Alvesson and Kärreman (ibid.) thus give the Foucauldian discourses a much longer range, both in time and space, and they understand them as 'sticking' to people in a grandiose and muscular way.

Setting the problems associated with this typology (cf. Ericsson, 2007) aside for a while, in this text discourse is to be approached in a rather muscular manner. And in order to highlight even further the muscular aspect of discourses, Madeleine Akrich's (1992) concept of 'scripts' will be used to describe the deterministic functions of discourse. Akrich's idea is that all artefacts entail schemes of action, scripts, which determine how the 'thing' should be used, the framework into which it should be put, and who should handle it; here, this idea is translated into a notion of discourse as both script and scripter.

To emphasize further the discourses' gendered dimensions and consequences, the term 'gender scripts' (cf. Berg and Lie, 1993; Grahn, 2006) will be used to describe norms and values that, conveyed by discourses, are inscribed into artefact and humans and stipulate how men and women should relate to the world and to each other. A key aspect in this perspective is that different gender scripts may differ fundamentally in the way they standardize and regulate men's and women's relationships to each other and the world. For instance, if the gender scripts are categorized based on the extent to which they reproduce or violate the phallogocentric (cf. Derrida, 1976/1998) system that defines the male subject as the 'natural' centre of the symbolic universe, its ultimate goal and meaning, in accordance with Grahn (2006), it is fruitful to talk about the Same, the Other of the Same, the other of the Same and the other of the Other.

The gender script the Same reproduces phallogocentrism; it is a script that places the white, heterosexual man in the centre. The gender script the Other of the Same, however, reproduces the binary opposition to phallogocentrism, the female; while the other of the Same refers to men who, for one reason or another, can be considered to represent the phallogocentric man's male antipode. This other of the Same may, for example, be represented by other masculinities and ethnicities than the phallogocentric one.

The other of the Other, in turn, is constituted by gender scripts that represent women and men in alternative ways and/or 'on their own terms' (ibid., p. 133) – and which fill out the empty spaces of the binary system of 'either–or' positions created and maintained by (and within) the phallogocentric regime. In contrast to the Other and the other of the Same, scripts which are produced within the boundaries of phallogocentrism – the script of the other of the Other – go beyond the binary system. Thus, it breaks with mainstream as well as 'malestream' scripts.

As this cartography of different subject positions breaks with conventional constructions of the Same and the Other within feminist theory, and as the Same and the Other have different meanings, politically as well as theoretically, for different interpreters (see for example, de Beauvoir, 1949/1997; Irigaray, 1974/1985, 1977/1985; Braidotti, 2003, 2005), a note on the ontological and epistemological position here taken might be appropriate. As the goal in this text is to describe how different subject (dis)positions are expressed in the discourse on entrepreneurship, no other position is taken except for the assumption that the Same and the Other are socially constructed in a context of a phallogocentric regime in which a distinction is made between men and women. What the basis is for these construction processes, what alternative constructions are desirable and how these alternative structures are to be achieved are questions left unanswered. It is the cartography of different positions (cf. Braidotti, 2005) that is of interest as a theory of interpretation.

SECTION ONE: DEMOBILIZING THE DISCOURSE ON ENTREPRENEURSHIP

The discourse on entrepreneurship, also often conceptualized in terms of enterprise discourse (cf. du Gay, 1991, 2004; Berglund and Johansson, 2007a), has been a lively discussion topic in recent years (cf. Ogbor, 2000; Ahl, 2004; Jones and Spicer, 2005; Perren and Jennings, 2005; Parkinson and Howorth, 2008). The perspective most frequently taken has been Foucauldian, and attempts have been made to deconstruct the discourses in order to highlight taken-for-granted assumptions and practices experienced to be troublesome. In this vein, among others, John O. Ogbor (2000) has interpreted the discourse on entrepreneurship in terms of ideological control, arguing that entrepreneurship is 'discriminatory, gender-biased, ethnocentrically determined and ideologically controlled' (ibid., p. 605); Lew Perren and Peter L. Jennings (2005) have approached government discourses on entrepreneurship as issues of subjugation; Karin Berglund and Anders W. Johansson (2007a) have focused upon the discourse's suppression of equality; and Helene Ahl (2004) has questioned the discourse's underlying assumptions leading to gendered practices.

Summarizing the arguments presented so far within the confinements of this Foucauldian turn, the discourse on entrepreneurship could be said to consist of an array of binary constructs. For instance, Ahl (2004) – having studied research texts on entrepreneurship – shows how the words of the discourse encircle entrepreneurs and their non-entrepreneurial opposites in a bipolar fashion, in which the entrepreneurs are described in positive terms such as 'able', 'astute', 'foresighted' and 'visionary', and their opposites are portrayed with negating words such as 'unable', 'gullible', 'short-sighted' and 'pragmatist'. According to Ahl (2004, p. 54) this bipolarity could be interpreted in terms of the strong versus the weak, the active versus the passive, and the leader versus the follower, which in turn could be interpreted as a polarity between the masculine versus the feminine.

These bipolarities, argues Ahl (2004, p. 161), could be understood as effects of the discourse's basic assumption, which she identifies in terms of four different but interrelated constructs: 'entrepreneurship is good', 'men and women are different', 'the division between a public and a private sphere' and 'individualism'. To this complex package of constructs one could also add constructs such as 'white Anglo-Saxon Protestant' and 'bourgeoisie' in order to address the discourse's ethnical, racial and class demarcations (cf. Ogbor, 2000), as well as the construct of 'free will', which highlights the discourse's political foundation (cf. Perren and Jennings, 2005).

This array of constructs, the argument goes (cf. Ogbor, 2000), establishes entrepreneurship in a hegemonic way in society: on the one hand the discourse on entrepreneurship (re)produces, reinforces and enhances differences among people; and on the other hand it provides a ready-made hierarchical order and value structure to encompass these differences. The discourse on entrepreneurship is thus like any other discourse, in that it does not convey an 'innocent' representation of the social world (cf. Ahl, 2004, p. 161). On the contrary, it is guilty of creating the social world in a biased way: it draws upon and enhances existing power relationship in society, and mediates subjectivity by including some at the expense of excluded others. Within 'the Parsonian economic machine' (cf. Lipset, 2000), the discourse on entrepreneurship thus appears to function as a binary machine – it seems to be the discursive machine within the machine. Moreover, given the gendering aspects of the discourse, it could also – in terms of the cartography of different gender (dis)positions and their accompanying gender scripts outlined above – be (re)presented as a phallogocentric machine, designed and adjusted to produce more and more of the Same.

This phallogocentric machine has, however, not stood uncontested. Given the hegemony of the discourse on entrepreneurship many voices have tried to alter the discourse by way of different rewriting and reclaiming strategies (cf. Hjorth, 2003; Steyaert and Katz, 2004; Hjorth and Steyaert, 2004; Ahl, 2004). For example, feminist researchers have elaborated upon expanding the range of the discourse and shifting the epistemological position in such way that the Other of the Same, as well as other subject (dis)positions, is also included (cf. Ahl, 2004; Bruni et al., 2004). Constructionist writers have tried acting and talking about entrepreneurship differently, opening up for other (dis)positions than the dominating ones (cf. Bill, 2006). Lastly, critical theorists have sought emancipation from the binary logic of the discourse by highlighting its core of 'intellectual authoritarianism and intellectual Catholicism' (Ogbor, 2000, p. 630).

Despite the intentions behind the rewriting and reclaiming strategies, some of these efforts have tended to increase the binary output of the discursive machine, rather than to limit its supply; whereas other efforts have tended to increase the working range of the machine rather than to limit its discursive capacity. Instead of filling out the empty spaces in between the (dis)positions of the binary system of 'either–or', by inscribing the other of the Other, the reclaiming and rewriting efforts have simply reinforced the phallogocentric regime and its accompanying gender scripts of the Same, the Other of the Same and the other of the Same. That is, the only thing that has been reclaimed and rewritten is the hegemony of the discourse on entrepreneurship: the machine runs without any breaks in the routine.

To highlight how this is being accomplished, two examples of criticism regarding the discourse on entrepreneurship will be elaborated upon and deconstructed. In the first example, it is revealed how emancipation from the discursive subjugation is offset by an eristic stance, which not only feeds the binary machine, but also turns it into a phallogocentric machine of conflict. In the second example, how the gender script of the Same is erected despite a majestic stance is highlighted, as is how this erection colonizes everyday life.

Government Discourses on Entrepreneurship

To make it clear from the outset: Lew Perren and Peter L. Jennings (2005) do not deal with the phallogocentric discourse on entrepreneurship, at least not explicitly. Their interest is primarily directed towards government discourses on entrepreneurship as they are externalized on different governmental websites around the world, and therefore they do not recognize the discourse on entrepreneurship as a discourse in its own right. Nonetheless, their critical discourse analysis is of relevance in this context, not primarily because the authors, inspired by Fairclough (1995) and Ogbor (2000), challenge the official rhetoric on entrepreneurship out of emancipatory reasons and reclaiming ambitions, but because they implicitly approach the government discourses on entrepreneurship as if these were part of a greater functionalist discourse on entrepreneurship – 'a structural grand narrative of entrepreneurs and small business', as they call it (Perren and Jennings, 2005, p. 177). It is a discourse that might very well be interpreted as *the* discourse on entrepreneurship.

Perren and Jennings's (2005) point of departure is that entrepreneurship has been embedded into political discourse by a belief in market ideology coupled with the assumption that entrepreneurs function as some kind of motor of the economic machine. And, from their point of view, this embeddedness also characterizes many of the academic efforts attempting to say something about the abundant entrepreneurial policies issued by various governments all over the world. When it comes to critical analysis of discourses, Perren and Jennings conclude that there is a 'dearth' within entrepreneurship studies (ibid., p. 174), and by using critical discourse analysis on empirical material consisting of texts (all in English) taken from governmental websites in Australia, Hong Kong, Japan, Korea, Thailand, the USA and the UK, they seek to fill this 'gap' by exploring 'how political agendas dominate governmental discourse on entrepreneurship and lead to an assumed "taken for granted" convention of the subordination of entrepreneurial freedom to the will of government' (ibid., p. 174).

The study uncovers three different discursive issues and corresponding arguments, the first of which concern the discourses of power. Perren and Jennings (2005, p. 177) argue that entrepreneurs are captured in a narrative of progression, encircled by economic accounts on how important it is to provide economic returns, to grow, to help with employment, and so on. These accounts are frequently emotional in nature, applying pressure on the entrepreneurs to act in the interests of the nation, and they never need to be explained or corroborated. They are simply taken for granted, just as the relationship between the governmental and the entrepreneurial subjects is. On the one hand the government appropriates the right to 'impose its wishes and desires upon others' (ibid., p. 177), and on the other hand the entrepreneur is given the (dis)position of being such an other.

The second issue that Perren and Jennings (ibid., p. 178) deal with concerns discourses of legitimization. Entrepreneurship, they state, is called for by the ideology of 'economic man', and like a Trojan horse, they see the notion of entrepreneurship in disguise being linked to the 'facticity' of this ideology in terms of functionality, rationality and competition. Supporting this linkage is, according to the authors, a 'macho-driven discourse of scale' (ibid., p. 178): numbers and figures abound describing the value and contribution of entrepreneurship, as well as creating a cause-and-effect relationship between the size of governmental investments and the level of entrepreneurial activity.

The third and final issue addressed by Perren and Jennings (ibid., p. 179), revolves around the ironic contradiction found in the notion of entrepreneurs as being the active component of the economic machine, yet at the same time being in severe need of governmental assistance to be able to function within this machine. Interpreting this contradiction as an example of a collocated discourse, Perren and Jennings (ibid., p. 179) conclude that it establishes an:

> iniquitous melodrama as it subsumes the aspirations of entrepreneur's life-world into the machine and then removes the possibility of entrepreneurs creating personal agency . . . Rhetorically, the entrepreneurs' life-worlds are banished to oscillating contradictory discourses of important function and dependency – a rhetorical loop of perpetual domination. (Ibid., p. 179)

This domination is further enhanced by certain rhetorical devices, such as the abundant phrase 'voice of small business', a phrase which, according to the authors, not only indicates that the entrepreneurs need to be spoken for, but also subjugates them into muteness.

Summarizing their arguments, Perren and Jennings (ibid., p. 181) address the issue of emancipation, and they direct their messages to both academics and policy-makers. Academics are recommended to 'step outside the functionalist paradigm', whereas policy-makers are challenged to (re)consider their dominating and colonizing positions. In these addresses, however, Perren and Jennings submit to a discourse that is as macho-driven as the governmental discourses on entrepreneurship they criticize, although it is of a slightly different nature. Instead of legitimizing their arguments with 'facts and figures' they frame their opponents by using patronizing irony, indignation and emotive language. The article, they write, 'is a call to arms', and it is their hope to 'encourage a wave of academic indignation' (ibid., p. 181) at this state of affairs.

Now, the end might sometimes justify the means, at least to some extent. The drawback of this kind of discursive 'machismo', however, is that it enacts conflict – in this case between the dominating and the subjugated – which in turn reinforces the binary opposition between the two. The purpose of the authors' 'machismo' could indeed very well be seen as an attempt to destabilize governmental phallogocentrism; but since the object of their emancipative desire – the entrepreneur – is made up of the very same array of binary constructs that establish the hegemonic discourse on entrepreneurship, the outcome of their undertaking is reversed. It goes without saying in Perren and Jennings's (ibid.) text that entrepreneurship is something that is inherently good; the design of the study rests upon a hidden assumption of a division between the public and the small business sector; the selection of empirical material reveals an Anglo-Saxon bias; and the authors repeatedly return to the notion of the entrepreneur as a strong individual acting with 'free will' (were it not for the evil governments, that is). Moreover, as for the gendering aspects of entrepreneurship, it becomes all too clear in the last section of the article that the entrepreneur is assumed to be a man: 'This analysis has shown', Perren and Jennings (ibid., p. 181) conclude, 'that entrepreneurial life-worlds may be subjugated by an official discourse of domination and control that hinders personal agency and contributes significantly to the emasculation of entrepreneurs.'

Perren and Jennings's emancipatory project could thus be seen as a simultaneous masculation of entrepreneurship and emasculation of officialdom. The Same is written into the entrepreneurial subject, whereas the other of the Same – or is it the Other of the Same? (cf. discussion of the gendering mythology of bureaucrats and heretics in Ericsson and Nilsson, 2008) – is bluntly written off.

Reclaiming the Space of Entrepreneurship in Society

Far from writing in a 'machismo' style, Chris Steyaert and Jerome Katz (2004) present strong arguments for a different and wider understanding and conception of entrepreneurship as a societal rather than (merely) an economic phenomenon in their editorial for the special issue of *Entrepreneurship and Regional Development* titled *Entrepreneurship in Society: Exploring and Theorizing New Forms and Practices of Entrepreneurship*. By bringing entrepreneurship into its societal context, they argue, not only is focus shifted from 'singular entrepreneurs to the everyday processes where multiple actors and stakeholders are made visible as related to entrepreneurship' (ibid., p. 182), but previously neglected entrepreneurial scenes, spaces and 'travel destinations' may also come into focus (ibid. p. 183). With the aim of outlining 'a geopolitics of everyday entrepreneurship', Steyaert and Katz (ibid.) consequently bring attention to the dominant entrepreneurial practices, and they question the spaces, the discourses and the actors that are being privileged. They wonder: What other alternatives are there?

As regards the privileged spaces of entrepreneurship, Steyaert and Katz conclude that the focus seems to be where the light is. Unarguably, nations, industrial regions and business clusters have been the main units of attention, and for good reasons has Silicon Valley stood out as the leading symbol of the discourse on entrepreneurship. But entrepreneurship does not have to be encircled this way. Boundaries are social constructions and therefore the entrepreneurial searchlight could also be shed upon other social and spatial objects, such as households, communities and circles. On the one hand they claim that 'There is no need for installing an "either–or" logic in the field of entrepreneurship studies' (ibid., p. 183), stating that: 'there is nothing wrong with an interest in Silicon Valley' (ibid.). On the other hand, however, they explicitly look for entrepreneurial sites in the periphery of the discourse, abandoning the 'valleys' in favour of the 'alleys'.

As regards the discursive spaces of entrepreneurship, Steyaert and Katz identify the economic discourse as the privileged one par excellence. This discourse, they argue, does not only lead to a uni-dimensional (and thereby flawed) conception of entrepreneurship; there is also a danger that this discourse, due to efforts of certain power elites to harness entrepreneurship for their own ends, becomes even more dominant as it spreads beyond the business economy. Therefore, to promote a multidimensional understanding of entrepreneurship, it becomes crucial for Steyaert and Katz (ibid., pp. 188 ff) to counterbalance, destabilize and decentre the economic discourse with the help of other kinds of discourse, preferably theoretical discourses in between the social sciences and the humanities, or even new discourses.

Finally, as regards the privileged actors of entrepreneurship, the authors explicitly strive to break with the taken-for-granted notion of the entrepreneur as something extraordinary, be it an overachieving individual, or one with a special competence, will or motivation, or in a unique situation. Instead of reproducing the notion(s) of 'an elite group of entrepreneurs', Steyaert and Katz talk about the possibility, not to say the desirability, of decentring this elite by focusing on the 'everydayness' of entrepreneurship. They state that: 'There are many behaviours that display the elements of entrepreneurship' (ibid., p. 191), and continue with examples: 'the pursuit of the new, better or innovative; the identification of market needs or opportunities; the pursuit of gain or improvement of situation; and the use of exchange with others as a basis for all of the above.' By highlighting the everydayness of entrepreneurship, according to Steyaert and Katz (ibid.) the perspective is altered from an elitist one to a democratic one; on the one hand, entrepreneurship becomes encompassing, turning all kind of people into participants, and on the other hand it turns into a 'tactic on the public scene' (ibid., p. 192). The advantages of perceiving entrepreneurship this way, according to Steyaert and Katz (ibid.), is that entrepreneurship can promote democratic transformation of society in the sense that, as previously unseen entrepreneurial actors are identified, privileges might be renegotiated as actors are (re)connected and (re)positioned in new and different ways.

Indeed, Steyaert and Katz (ibid.) present some very compelling arguments in favour of their geopolitics of everyday entrepreneurship. And, as for their rhetoric, it certainly does not convey the kind of eristic attitude found elsewhere among the critics of the discourse on entrepreneurship. The authors are duly critical towards the discourse on entrepreneurship and they raise some provocative questions, but they do not take a stand against either the dominant economic discourse or privileged interest groups. Rather than trying to exclude any opponents from the research agenda, they are trying to incorporate their arguments within the existing body of research in an explorative, not to say majestic, 'both–and' manner. Steyaert and Katz thus not only subscribe to the Same, the Other of the Same and the other of the Same; they also open up the discourse on entrepreneurship for the other of the Other: gender scripts that break with the phallogocentric regime's binary system.

From a non-phallogocentric perspective such encompassing explorations are surely welcome, although they do also pose the problem of mixed discourses (cf. Giorgi, 1994) – a problem which could very well have been downplayed, if not overcome, were it not for the binary bias that is shown and the totalitarian knowledge claims that the authors make at the end of the article. Here they first reveal some sort of entrepreneurial blueprint that is believed to determine the 'elements of entrepreneurship' and sift the entrepreneurial wheat from the non-entrepreneurial chaff, so to speak. These elements are given some sort of universal status, since it is argued that entrepreneurship can potentially be found in 'almost any interaction we see' (Steyaert and Katz, 2004, p. 194). 'There is a saying that all the beauty of winter can be found in any single snowflake', Steyaert and Katz write, and then go on to bring the analogy home: 'Indeed, the space of entrepreneurship in society is about nothing less than beauty' (ibid., p. 194).

The Same is thus not abandoned after all. It is still erected and, through the concept of 'everydayness', it penetrates and colonizes every corner of the social world.

Discursive Plug-In Devices for the War Machine

From the perspective of the nomadology of Deleuze and Guattari (1988), both Perren and Jennings's (2005) account of 'Government discourses on entrepreneurship' and Steyaert and Katz's (2004) plea for 'reclaiming the space of entrepreneurship in society' could be conceptualized as discursive plug-in devices for the war machine. In both texts, entrepreneurship is not only given the nomadic connotations, but is also construed as being in opposition to the State apparatus.

The oppositional character of the discourse on entrepreneurship is most compelling in the eristic phallogocentric setting created by Perren and Jennings (2005). Here the war machine is experienced to have been appropriated, not to say captured, by the State apparatus, imposing 'its wishes and desires' upon the entrepreneur; consequently war has become its primary objective. In this sense Perren and Jennings's (ibid.) 'call to arms' represents nothing but the war machine's assembling of troops in order to go on a mission against the State oppressor.

If war already has broken out in the 'Government discourses on entrepreneurship', then this does not seem to be the case in the majestic erection offered by Steyaert and Katz (2004). The State apparatus here is not explicitly singled out as the opponent ('the enemy') and the discourse on entrepreneurship is not portrayed as being under the forces of State appropriation. Nevertheless, reading between the lines, their case is the war machine's case: the striated national and regional spaces are abandoned in favour of smooth ones, and the geopolitics of everyday entrepreneurship is a call for a new entrepreneurial becoming – a nomadic territorialization in, and of, the periphery, in opposition to the State's deterritorialization in, and of, the centre.

In line with Derrida (1976/1998), Braidotti (2005) and Deleuze and Guattari (1988), it could thus be argued that the discourse on entrepreneurship functions, on the one hand as a discursive machine set up to produce (more of) the Same and (less of) the Other, and on the other hand functions as a war machine which feeds itself with discursive plug-in devices. Moreover, in doing this, the discourse is bound to (re)produce and perpetuate opposition between the Same and the Other, as well as between nomadism and the State. All in all, the discourse on entrepreneurship could therefore be conceptualized as a *perpetuum mobile* of conflict.

SECTION TWO: THE CASE OF AQUARIAN NATION

In contrast to the prevalent discourse on entrepreneurship, the independent record company Aquarian Nation seems neither to advocate binary opposition nor to have conflict as its primary objective. Instead the people of Aquarian Nation, under the motto 'A Sanctuary for Musicianship', have created an artistic community in which music is produced, distributed and consumed in such a way that traditional boundaries are transcended and binary oppositions are altered in a 'both–and' manner.

Could it be that Aquarian Nation represents a nomadic war machine, but without the war? Could it be that Aquarian Nation does not embrace war, either as its potential or as its supplement? And could it be that Aquarian Nation represents movement, but not in the sense of a military vanguard, but in the sense of a creative avant-garde?

In the following section a short glimpse of Aquarian Nation is given in order to tentatively answer questions like these, and in order to inquire whether Aquarian Nation brings other constellations of subject (dis)positions to the fore besides those being enacted within the discourse on entrepreneurship. The case is based on an ongoing ethnographic study of the company and its founder Francis Dunnery, previously partly reported in Ericsson (2007).

A Sanctuary for Musicianship

Aquarian Nation is presented on its website as: '*an independent Multi Media Company created to help support and promote artistic integrity*'. The company started out around 1998 when Francis Dunnery, former member and front man of the progressive rock band It Bites and guitarist for Robert Plant, Santana and Lauryn Hill amongst others, was unable to pursue his burgeoning solo career within the established music industry in the way that he wanted to. In 1991 he had left Virgin Records in disappointment over the company's negative attitude towards his debut solo album *Welcome to the Wild Country*, which was only released in Japan at the time, and his comeback with Atlantic Records in 1994, which produced two major successes, *Fearless* (1994) and *Tall Blonde Helicopter* (1995), ended in 1996 with him having a grievance with the record industry's managers, their greediness and their attempt to control the artistic production processes in order to produce hits. The sleeve of *Fearless* boldly stated that: 'This record was made in an A+R free zone', but this might have been more an ironic statement, rather than a reflection of what actually took place. Either way, *Fearless* stands out as a symbolic inscription of a man in an ambivalent position towards the industry, and it can be interpreted as a sign of things to come (cf. Ericsson, 2007). Later, Francis Dunnery would comment on his strained relationship with the music industry in the essay 'The golden castle' (Dunnery, 2005).

In Francis Dunnery's official biography, presented on the Aquarian Nation website, it says that in 1998 he was no longer able to 'sustain his enthusiasm for the music industry' and therefore decided to release the next CD, *Man* (2000), on his own label. The name of the label, Aquarian Nation, was well chosen. On the one hand it reflected Francis Dunnery's deep interest in astrology, and on the other it reflected the intention of creating something more than just a label – and something greater than just being the outlet of yet another singer-songwriter having trouble finding a place in the field of music.

As the label became a company, the communitarian side of Aquarian Nation was accentuated, creating a repertoire of different activities. As regards music production and distribution, the backbone of the company, Francis Dunnery continued his solo career by selling his new CD exclusively from his own website (www.francisdunnery.com), as well as at live shows, and he acquired the proprietary rights to his 'forgotten' CD, *Welcome to the Wild Country*, which was re-released under the Aquarian Nation label. At the same time he started a career as a producer, specializing in working with artists in search of a 'voice'. In 2002 he co-wrote and produced former Squeeze member Chris Difford's long-awaited solo debut, *I Didn't Get Where I Am*, the Cumbrian duo John & Wayne's debut *Nearly Killed Keith*, and former The Cult member and studio technician Stephen Harris's (aka Kid Chaos, aka Haggis) *Songs From the Mission of Hope*. More recently he has produced Dorie Jackson's *The Courting Ground* (2007) and James Sonenfeld's *Snowman Melting* (2008). All of these CDs are mainly distributed through the Aquarian Nation website.

Besides music production and distribution, Aquarian Nation and its signed artists engage in various projects. First of all, they are mutually helping each other out, on and off stage, in different constellations of people. For example, John & Wayne and Dorie Jackson back up Francis Dunnery at times, and at other times it is the other way around. Secondly, every year in October all of the Aquarian Nation artists gather in Francis Dunnery's catholic hometown Egremont, Cumbria, to raise money for charity. This event is staged by the non-profit organization the Charlie and

Kathleen Dunnery's Children's Fund, founded by Francis Dunnery, and involves concerts, happenings, special guest performances and auctions, and ends with a group Sunday walk around one of the many lakes of the Lake District.

House Concerts and the New Progressives

Special invitations to this event are sent to all individuals around the world who have organized a so-called 'house concert' with Francis Dunnery. As described on www.francisdunnery.com, a 'house concert' is 'a completely unique experience combining Music, Personal Stories, Psychology, Philosophy and Astrology, all in the comfort of your own home. The House Concerts are very easy to Host and our tremendous experience virtually guarantees a fantastic evening for both you and your guests.' The story behind the 'house concert' is that Francis Dunnery was once asked to perform at a friend's house for a one-time-only occasion. However, after experiencing the sheer joy of performing in the living-room of his friend, meeting his audience in an intimate atmosphere and interacting with them face to face, Francis Dunnery decided to hold another house concert, and yet another, and another. The positive experiences of these concerts eventually led him to take the house concerts concept on the road in a more elaborated fashion, announcing the possibility of hosting a concert in your own living room on his website. It was an immediate success, with over 2000 requests, leading Francis Dunnery to embark on a series of 'house concert world tours'.

The 'house concerts' are now in their sixth year, and reflecting upon his invention Francis Dunnery is quoted on his website:

> I think the success of the House Concerts is mainly due to the uplifting nature of the evenings. Even if people hated my music there is still enough positive energy in the dialogue to engage even the most difficult of people.
>
> I think it is incredible . . . I never in a million years thought I would be doing this. Whatever is going on is a phenomenon, it just keeps on getting bigger every year. I have a great bunch of people around me organizing the events and I'm just gonna keep rolling with the flow until it stops . . . if it ever does.

When a house concert is requested and booked, a contract is made between the host and Francis Dunnery. In this contract the host takes on the responsibility of hosting and arranging a concert with Francis Dunnery on a specified date and agrees to adhere to 'the Francis Dunnery House Concert Guidelines'. Besides providing information on Francis Dunnery's fee, the guidelines outline that the host is asked to see that there are to be no children under 12 years of age at the concert (due to explicit language) or any pets; it is also suggested what admission to the concert could be and that the number of audience members should be no less that 25 paying attendees and no more than 50 paying attendees. The guidelines further state that the concert will start at 8.30 p.m. and last for approximately 90 minutes. Most important, however, is the non-alcohol policy: the host is required to provide an alcohol-free environment before and during the performance. Stressing the communitarian sense of the evening, the host is also encouraged to gather the guests an hour or so before the performance to mingle, to invite their guests to bring finger food as a way of contributing to the atmosphere.

In order to help new hosts organize the concert, a number of names and e-mail addresses of people who have previously hosted a house concert are attached to the contract and guidelines. These individuals are however not only made available to help and support new hosts; they are also available for networking, thus fulfilling the communitarian intention of Aquarian Nation.

On the evening of the concert Francis Dunnery arrives with his guitar some 20 minutes before the start of his performance. Accompanying him is a 'merchandise person', who most of the time is his girlfriend Erica Brilhart who, apart from administering and running the operations of Aquarian Nation, also plays the keyboard in the Francis Dunnery Band. While Francis Dunnery withdraws to a private room for a warm-up, the merchandise person quickly arranges for CDs and T-shirts to be sold, and the show begins thereafter.

Near the end of the concert, which blends music, philosophy and astrology into a humourous 'stand-up' kind of performance, Francis Dunnery picks up a video camera in order to document his audience. He talks into the camera, contextualizes the concert, and then directs the camera towards the audience asking the people to say hello to the world. After the show, and sometimes also before the show, the host is interviewed in front of the camera. Together with commentaries from Francis Dunnery, these documents are then edited into a House Concert Tour Video Diary, which is published on both YouTube and the Aquarian Nation/Francis Dunnery websites. After the house concert, the host is encouraged to write about the experience – to testify about the event. These texts are later published on Francis Dunnery's website under the vignette 'Testimonials'.

On his website, as well as on AquarianNation.com, Francis Dunnery in turn communicates with his audience in many different ways. For instance, he has his own blog, he announces concerts and other events on a bulletin board, he publishes songs, videos and interviews for free download, he offers to draw astrology charts and he airs radio shows on Aquarian Nation Radio. Besides these activities, he also posts links to Umbrello

TV, presented as a broadcasting alternative to mainstream video that airs the making of the album *Big Sky*, a joint recording and filming venture between Francis Dunnery and Syn's Steve Nardelli. On Umbrello TV the viewer gets to experience *Big Sky* as it is being developed, from the first jam sessions to the finished product.

In line with this project Francis Dunnery has recently announced the coming of the 'new progressives', a remake of classic progressive songs using new technology together with Joel Veatch, President of the Flying Spot Entertainment Group:

> 'We are going to develop some new and exciting projects to serve the Progressive Rock Medium.' Explains Dunnery, 'Joel and I both feel that it is one area of music that has been ignored by the mainstream media for such a long time that it deserves a larger audience. There are so many really cool new progressive bands beginning to appear that we wanted to create a central hub for Promotion, Video, News and Sales of New Progressive Rock'. Dunnery joked 'We are going to make Progressive Rock so cool that even your girlfriend might like it! (www.francisdunnery.com)

Constellations of Another other?

In many regards the evidence speaks against Aquarian Nation as representing something else than the discourse on entrepreneurship and the *perpetuum mobile* of conflict – the phallogocentric discursive war machine – plugged into it.

On the one hand the company comes into existence in harsh opposition to, if not a State apparatus, then an industry apparatus that is trying to plug artistic integrity into its own capitalist machinery. This opposition in many senses resembles the 'logic' of the war machine: not only does it offer a smooth space in terms of 'a sanctuary for musicianship' devoid of any (e)motional infringements on the artists, but it also embraces the self-organizing and itinerary aspects of the nomad. In this respect the house concerts represent nothing but the becoming of a nomadic war machine. On the other hand, Aquarian Nation, as a gender script and scripter, reproduces phallogocentrism in a striking manner. Francis Dunnery takes the stand as a solid representation of the Same, whereas the Other of the Same – in terms of an opposing 'girlfriend' – is inscribed into 'the new progressives', as a kind of 'necessary periphery' (cf. Holgersson, 1998). Yet at the same time two pieces of evidence point in opposite directions, making Aquarian Nation stand in sharp contrast to the prevalent discourse on entrepreneurship.

The first piece of evidence is that the people of Aquarian Nation seem to break with the binary logic and hegemony of the discourse on entrepreneurship. Of the complex package of binary constructs identified as the discourse's basic assumption, all but one are refuted. 'The division between a public and a private sphere' is offset by the house concerts' inherently boundary-breaking character; 'individualism' is replaced by the strong communitarian sense; 'white Anglo-Saxon Protestant' and 'bourgeoisie' are broken by the fact that many of the people of Aquarian Nation are Catholics and belong to the working class; and 'entrepreneurship is good' seems to be substituted for the quite different construct: 'charity is good'.

As for the binary construct 'men and women are different', this is not questioned by the people of Aquarian Nation. But it might very well be countered by another kind of construct, which not only replaces sex as the main differentiator between people but also breaks with the binary and hegemonic logic of the sexes. This construct is 'astrology', and with it comes a twelvefold non-hierarchical typology of signs, which could be conceptualized as a machine set up to increase heterogeneity instead of to nourish homogeneity.

The 'astrology' construct is part of the second piece of evidence, as it is a supplement to the circumstantial evidence established by the many different voices of Aquarian Nation. Mainstream and 'malestream' gender scripts are indeed enacted by the Aquarian Nation machinery, but working with artists in search of a 'voice', and encouraging the house concert hosts to write about their own experiences also promotes the enactment of the other of the Other. In this sense, Aquarian Nation not only breaks with traditional scripts of 'either–or' regarding the production, consumption and distribution of music, but also goes beyond the confinements of phallogocentrism, transcending and altering it in a 'both–and' manner. In analogy with the reasoning of Steyaert and Katz (2004), one could argue that Aquarian Nation is reclaiming the space of men and women in society, without installing an 'either–or' logic. The privileged spaces of entrepreneurship are temporarily, not entirely, abandoned in favour of the alleys of Egremont and the living-rooms of ordinary people all over the world. The privileged economic discourse on entrepreneurship is counterbalanced, not outweighed, by alternative and communitarian discourses, and the privileged actors of entrepreneurship are decentred and challenged by a non-elite notion of agency, although from an elite centre of the Same.

In the final analysis, given the non-binary and communitarian character of Aquarian Nation, the very idea of conflict and opposition – the idea built into Deleuze and Guattari's (1988) war machine, into phallogocentrism, and into the discourse on entrepreneurship – thus becomes somewhat out of place. The interpretative potential of 'either–or' seems to be close to nil, and the case for Aquarian Nation as a discursive plug-in device for the war machine becomes somewhat far-fetched. Aquarian Nation does not have war as its objective, it does not have war as a potential, and it is certainly not a phallogocentric machine 'rooted to centralized resistance'. Instead, Aquarian Nation presents itself as a *perpetuum mobile*, not of conflict, but of constellations of another other.

EPILOGUE

Aquarian Nation is not yet part of the discourse on entrepreneurship. The people of Aquarian Nation do not present themselves as entrepreneurs and others do not perceive them as entrepreneurs. So be it: there is no need for Aquarian Nation to feed the war machine with yet another discursive plug-in device. Nevertheless, the case of Aquarian Nation might have something to contribute to the discourse on entrepreneurship, unplugging some of its plugged-in discursive devices, disarming them and reconnecting them into constellations of another other.

PART IV

. . . Or None of It?

11. In the beginning was entrepreneuring

Bengt Johannisson

INTRODUCTION: WHETHER TO MOBILIZE OR DEMOBILIZE THE ENTREPRENEURSHIP DISCOURSE IS THE WRONG QUESTION

Entrepreneurship as an academic field of inquiry is quite young, becoming institutionalized as a generally researched phenomenon only in the 1980s. Since then entrepreneurship has evolved from signifying business start-ups to becoming associated with social forces which trigger societal change. This development gives us a reason to search for the origins of entrepreneurship far beyond contemporary discourses on entrepreneurship. Accordingly, I propose that entrepreneurship is a generic human characteristic that is intrinsically associated with human existence itself. Thus, as the entrepreneurship discourse is intimately related to entrepreneurship in action, the challenge is neither to mobilize the entrepreneurship discourse, since there is obviously no need if we acknowledge our humanity, nor to demobilize it, since that would make us non-human. Instead the right question to ask is: How can we prevent society from making its young citizens unlearn, even deny, their entrepreneurial selves? Answering this question is an intellectual challenge of great theoretical and practical, ethical relevance. If this challenge is successfully dealt with there will be no need to reintroduce entrepreneurship to adults as a generic way of approaching life.

In order to substantiate my frank statement I have to scrutinize how entrepreneurship – itself intrinsically associated with emergence and thus according to Steyaert (2007), rightfully addressed as 'entrepreneuring' – may be associated with man, from childhood to adulthood. Generally, it is easy today to draw parallels between entrepreneuring and children's curiosity, imagination and experimental approach to life. According to James et al. (1998, pp. 9–21), children have as human becomings been associated with many intrinsic features such as evil (according to Hobbes), innocence (Rousseau), immanence (Locke), cognitive maturing (Piaget) and unconsciousness (Freud). Among these thinkers we can track ideas about children as natural-born entrepreneurs, but also ideas that contradict that view. Only further theorizing and associated empirical inquiry can help us to test the basic proposition that children epitomize entrepreneuring as not only associated with the creative organizing of resources according to opportunity, but also as showing concern for others and society and taking the responsible action called for in order to make a better world; see Spinosa et al. (1997).

Next, I briefly reflect discursively upon how the proposed entrepreneurial features associated with childhood, such as playfulness and passions, have been dealt with in the literature on childhood. School, together with the family, then appears as the most influential institution in the making and maintaining of children as entrepreneurial selves. Accordingly, the following section reports two interrelated empirical studies whose original field research aimed at uncovering how entrepreneuring is embodied in children. In a third section the education system is researched – again in two empirical studies – with respect to how it may restrain and support children's enactment of their entrepreneurial identity. The concluding section discusses how children's aptitude for entrepreneuring may help us to break out of the iron cage that the many institutions in modern society build in order to discipline its citizens.

INQUIRING INTO CHILDHOOD: SOME ONTOLOGICAL, THEORETICAL AND METHODOLOGICAL REFLECTIONS

Presenting children as entrepreneurial selves invites generic tension. On the one hand, children are 'educated' by adults in general and by parents and teachers in particular. As incomplete human beings they are guided to become members of the world of grown-ups. On the other hand, children when among themselves spontaneously break out of the straitjacket that primary socialization puts on them as playful beings, as specimens of *Homo ludens* (Huizinga 1950). In accordance with their socio-biological development, children consider alternative world-views and identities and the associated need for change to be 'only' natural. Among younger children play provides this counterculture which among adolescents often appears as overt protest. The virtual realities that digital technology make possible provide children with further escape routes.

Children live an ontology of becoming, that is, they consider change as a natural state, implying that process and emergence prevail while structure only appears as (wishful) imagination and a social construct. This world-view, contrasting an ontology of being, has deep philosophical and theoretical origins. They go back to the Greek philosopher Heraclitus, while more recent, twentieth-century contributors were Bergson, Whitehead and Deleuze. Chia (1995) has proposed an ontology of becoming as a basis for organization studies and Steyaert (1997) has introduced it in the field of entrepreneurship. Accordingly, Steyaert (2007), as indicated, a decade later suggested 'entrepreneuring' as a more appropriate presentation of the phenomenon than the noun 'entrepreneurship'. Even if *Homo economicus* does not reign unrestricted, *Homo traditionalis* certainly rules in a(n adult) world dominated by management (Hjorth et al., 2003). In such a world control supersedes creativity and stability rules over change, which means that children are dominated by and dependent upon adults. Children's immediacy and experiential approach to life are not weaknesses, as Lee (2001) indicates, but represent assets when environments are turbulent. Chronological time, *chronos*, as the basic temporal order then has to be replaced by *kairos*, that is 'timing' or 'catching the right moment', reflected in entrepreneuring as turning coincidences into opportunities.

Whether we associate entrepreneuring with imitation or creativity, attentiveness or reflexivity, general curiosity or dedicated focus, (young) children thus outperform adults simply because their world and their existence in it are genuinely emerging. The linguistic turn in social research, and its practice in different settings, tells us that we (as adults) are caught in the web of meaning that the vocabulary in use provides. Consequently, a change in language is needed to see the world differently. Children appropriate language along with their ongoing experimentation (also with language itself) and world-making, their everyday practice. Children do not have to be told or trained to be creative and to play; they always create space for that, whatever the circumstances.

Children thus appear as bicultural, since they inhabit two worlds, one dominated by adults where socialization means dependence and subordination, and one governed by the children themselves together with peers, the world of play. Sometimes these worlds connect, for example when adults are invited to participate in playing activities. Children's constant experimentation when young is conditioned by trustful dependence on adults (Winnicott, 1971) as well as on peers, as pointed out by Vygotskij (see Corsaro, 2005, p. 15). However, just as history is written by the victors, the stories about children and their approach to life are written by adults. Rather than discursively trying to imagine what the creation of a framework for entrepreneuring as a genuinely human practice carried by the young would call for in terms of philosophical speculation and analytical theorizing, we should consult the children themselves and reflect upon the life of children as it evolves in different settings. This provides a more direct and promising road to insight.

Certainly, renowned thinkers such as John Dewey (1902/1990) and Lev S. Vygotskij (1995) have recognized children as playful and creative beings. Nevertheless, their writings remain impregnated by ambitious attempts to educate young people to become what in their minds appears as able and responsible citizens. These scholars' minds, naturally disciplined by their own education, are prejudiced as much as those of any adults towards certain mental mapping. Thereby their ideas run an obvious risk of choking rather than enforcing the entrepreneurial potential of the children they wish to guide. What is more, Dewey's and Vygotskij's ideas were created in times and settings when it was taken for granted that adult men knew what was in the interest of children (and women). In those days industrialism was at its zenith and humans were thus expected to submit to technological rationales, that is, being considered at an early age as cheap labour only to later be disciplined by authoritarian schooling in the name of progress and modernity (Lee, 2001).

Well over a century ago there were also voices that questioned the potential of the school system to provide insights of relevance for (entrepreneurial) life. The Irish writer Oscar Wilde plainly stated: 'Nothing that is worth knowing can be taught'. Much later, others have brought to our attention that we as adults may learn from children as much as the other way around (March, 1976). Proposing (four) different discourses on childhood, James et al. (1998, p. 214) introduced the notion of 'the tribal child'. This discourse suggests that the 'child is voluntaristic and particularistic; it exercises a strong sense of self-determinacy and is finitely located in specific terms and spaces' (James et al., 1998, p. 216). Such a conceptualization of childhood appears as an appropriate departure for bridging between the bicultural child and the different understandings of entrepreneuring.

Studying children as not only independent but also entrepreneurial selves calls for research methodologies which do not make themselves dependent upon contexts dominated by adults and the institutions they construct. Most studies of children are done in institutional contexts such as schools and homes, which also make ethnographic studies biased. For practical reasons this is, however, a problem that is difficult to escape and therefore the alternative is to accept this context for empirical research and look for ingenious approaches to apply there. Accordingly, I report research into child creativity as an entrepreneurial quality where the instrument is adapted to the 'language' (drawings) of children – although the study is carried out in a school setting. I then scrutinize the educational system itself as a context for learning for and in entrepreneuring. In combination these two studies will inform us both about children as entrepreneurial selves and about the possibilities for children to enact such an identity.

THE ENTERPRISING WORLD OF CHILDREN: DRAWINGS ARE DEEDS

Recognizing human beings as entrepreneurial selves means assuming that all children are equally entrepreneurial. Just as the inducement structure, and the institutional setting in general, will direct whether the entrepreneurial energy of a nation or culture is used in a productive, unproductive or even destructive way (Baumol, 1990), so socialization will direct children's entrepreneuring practices. In order to find out about the possible impact of different socio-cultural contexts on the crafting of entrepreneuring, I will, as indicated, reflect upon the findings of two of my own empirical studies of child creativity. The first was carried out in the mid-1980s and the second in the beginning of the new millennium. The specific question addressed was whether the entrepreneurial identity of children represents a power that can withstand the pressure towards homogeneity that culture as social life (Berger and Luckmann, 1967) and societal institutions (DiMaggio and Powell, 1983) exert.

Inspired by the British creative-management guru Edward de Bono and his book *The Dog-Exercising Machine* (1970), I designed and carried out in the autumn of 1984 a study of child creativity in its (regional) sociocultural context.[1] The basic proposition was that if entrepreneurial orientation, an enterprising attitude to life and the practice of entrepreneuring is a social construct and not an inherently human gift, its impressions on 'local' entrepreneurial practices among adults and children alike should reveal themselves. Accordingly I selected two contrasting Swedish regions as regards entrepreneuring dressed as independent business activity. One of the regions is known in Sweden as 'the Mecca of small business', being the country's only fully fledged industrial district (Davidsson, 1995; Johannisson, 2009). The other region is dominated by one-company towns where centuries of a paternalistic culture have pushed its inhabitants into perceived helplessness.

In each region I approached children in their 'lateral age', that is between nine and 12 years old. At that age creativity is assumed to peak because then the children balance self-centredness and social curiosity. That is, children at that age have both the self-confidence needed to stand up for their own ideas and the ability to open up and listen to others, a combination that Koestler (1964) sees as the source of creativity. Besides, children at that age are still able spontaneously to tell stories in drawing while beginning to organize their thoughts in writing; see Vygotskij (1995). The experiment was thus designed in a mode of reflecting upon the world that is natural to children. This seems to be a necessary and sufficient condition for providing a context that enables children to inform us about how their entrepreneurial selves or identities are construed.

In two municipalities in each region I invited myself to two classes, one with junior-level students aged nine and one with intermediate-level students aged 12. There, drawing upon de Bono's study, I personally presented the challenge which basically read as follows (the original story was told in about 150 words): 'Imagine an old disabled lady living alone with her dog in the middle of a large forest. How will she walk her dog considering that she cannot do it herself? Create and draw an arrangement that will help her to give the dog exercise and add on the drawing some comments in writing how the device will work.' The elaborated text was in addition handed over to each child in writing.

Without any questions or protests all the children within five minutes had started to make a drawing and about an hour later the majority had completed their assignment and handed it over to the teacher. On my behalf the teacher copied all the drawings and gave the copies to the children the next day, offering them the possibility to take them home for a couple of days and possibly revise or improve, them. My (naive?) assumption was that the children in the industrious small-business region would bring their drawings to one of the many local inventors and ask for advice. However, most of the children declined the offer to revise their drawing altogether, arguing that the original was good enough. The small minority that took the opportunity to improve their creation never reached beyond their primary family context (and then mainly asking their mother or an older sister). Obviously most children have self-respect, the strength and conviction needed to stand up for what they do. The children may also have considered the proposition to revise the drawings as an act of distrust which, if accepted, would make the children degenerate into needing selves. Living, embodying and practising an ontology of becoming, children are more concerned about projecting as time goes by than about reflecting upon mistakes they might have made, let alone correcting them. Revisions do not make sense in a world that is constantly changing.

When the field research was completed the original drawings were anonymously presented class by class to teachers and students at teachers' colleges, as well as to practitioners representing artistry and product development, for example, designers and product developers. These evaluators were asked to rank order the class sets of drawings along the three dimensions of creativity: imagination, ingenuity and realism. Controlling for grade and age, the statistical analysis, however, on all three dimensions of creativity revealed only small differences between the two contrasting regional settings. The main conclusion from this study is thus that not even an everyday-life context that denies entrepreneuring and is impregnated by a culture of learned helplessness can degrade children as entrepreneurial selves.

Children obviously keep their alertness and curiosity when confronted with new challenges, whatever the societal context. Actually the intermediate-level students from the municipality with the biggest structural problems turned out to be the most creative class of all in the study. The only available explanation is that this municipality, at the time of the study, was involved in a local development programme, also engaging the local school teachers. The teacher in the class concerned joined an evening class in technology. Resignedly, but also proudly, she told me that when she on the day following the course brought the challenges that she had experienced as a learner to her own students, they dealt with the exercises much faster than she did herself.

The original study of child creativity thus tells us that all children are not only creative, but also self-confident enough to act spontaneously on their own. However, entrepreneuring is not just about individually coping with technical issues but about social projecting, about creative organizing. One may even argue that the original child study only reproduces a world consisting of many small and young heroes. In order to get beyond this image I carried out, almost two decades after the first study, another investigation of child creativity, this time in a collective setting. The aim was to find out about how children organize venturing activities between themselves, as a mode of learning (see Corsaro, 2005). Again I staged the experiment in a school context since this appears as a comfort zone to most children. However, in order to break out of the traditional school context, which at lower levels in Sweden still is dominated by individualistic pedagogy, I collaborated with the local culture school. Its afternoon classes attract students with a special interest in artistry and generally adopt an experimental pedagogy that acknowledges child interactivity; in a setting, it is true, staged by adults.

Again I approached students aged nine and 12. The younger group of students included two girls and three boys, while the group with older children comprised of six girls. Each group got the same assignment: to create an Easter present for their art teacher in terms of an illustrated story by making a drawing, and jointly to narrate an accompanying story orally to her. The children were brought to a table, a square metre large, that was covered in white drawing paper and provided with drawing-pens. Soon enough the children started to overlay this *tabula rasa* with their imaginations. Within 40 minutes both groups had provided the illustrations needed to make a story.

The two groups approached the challenge quite differently. The younger children each took a firm position at the table and started to draw their favourite characters: princesses, knights, animals and monsters, castles, obviously originating in their own minds. Few connections were made to the teacher and her story or to the co-creators around the table. The children's self-centredness and disconnection from the local context were equally salient. The older children, in contrast, started off by jointly deciding to recreate and expand upon a story told by their charismatic teacher. Mobilizing their most immediate personal memory of the story, the girls positioned themselves around the table and started to draw. Step by step the individual memories and creations were organized into a creative imitation of the original story. Down the road the emerging shared narrative – the girls continuously created conversations while drawing – was completed with details in order to make it into a consistent whole. The ongoing sense-making included inserting further characters and events in order to make a complete narrative. Rural and urban local characters, events and landscapes, presumably reflecting the children's everyday settings, were concretely linked by a road that ran along the edge of the drawing (the table).

Obviously only the older children could use the collaborative setting to break out of both their own personal worlds and the (cultural) school setting as a framing context. The younger children only reproduced their individual habits, still not able to imaginize, let alone enact, shared storytelling. The older group, both individually and collectively, soon enough turned the assignment into joint world-making guided by spontaneous organizing. The girls were captured by each others' contributions to the drawing, which was reflected in their ongoing dialogue, typically including comments such as: 'If you do that I will do this', 'Great, if you draw that I will draw this', but also a constant search for spaces to insert favourite details which would add the overall picture without disturbing the basic message of the story they wanted to tell: 'Fine, there is an empty spot, there I will put my deer'.

The ongoing conversation in the older group included both rationalizations of own contributions to the overall drawing and repeating, retelling or recreating of the overall story as it emerged – spontaneous action (rationality) inviting improvisations combined with reflected decision (rationality); see Brunsson (1985). The girls obviously realized that the making of a coherent illustrated story called for the inclusion of further characters, artefacts and events. What is more, the older girl group also practised a 'caring' rationality. Thus, when they realized that one of them had been absent when the original story was delivered by the teacher, the other girls in the group allocated one among themselves to act as a counseller while the others went on working. Hereby the girls co-created the very context of their learning, emerging as much as the very storytelling project itself.

Purposefulness and seriousness characterized the drawing venture itself but both its realization and its enthusiastic presentation to the teacher were accompanied by lots of wordy elaborations and giggling. The girls were both attached to and distanced from an exercise that obviously only represented a temporary commitment in their evolving lives. Accordingly, immediately after my exercise the girls became equally deeply involved in another challenge. In a world of becoming there is no time for rest.

The individual and collective drawing exercises demonstrate that children experience the practice of creativity and entrepreneuring as closely associated with their general coping in the world. Learning and entrepreneuring thus appear as two sides of the same coin conditioning each other. On the one hand, entrepreneuring calls for attentiveness and consideration. Reflecting different modes of learning, these coping tactics sometimes imply the assimilation of new experiences in established mental structures, sometimes accommodating new ways of behaviour. On the other hand, only if learning is practised as an entrepreneurial process including continuous experimentation and creative enactment of a learning context will it be able to cope with a world of becoming; see Hjorth and Johannisson (2007). The field research has thus not only supported the original argument put forward here – that children are original entrepreneurial selves – but also revealed how their spontaneous entrepreneuring is reflected in learning processes.

A tentative conclusion is that in order to promote entrepreneuring in society, the challenge is not to make (young) people more entrepreneurial. It is rather about protecting their original entrepreneurial selves as adult human beings in the making. Children's attentiveness includes socializing with other children – soon enough two children who meet by coincidence start to interact and play, whether the setting is a designed playground, an airport transit hall or a church. Obviously children (girls) aged 12 can already cope with ambiguity without the presence of an adult or a 'transitional object' that provides the feeling of security that is needed to release entrepreneurial capabilities (compare Winnicott, 1971). By jointly creating a world of their own when playing, children can overcome both their marginalization in society and adults' attempts to control them; see Prout and James (1997/2008). As pointed out by the Swedish sociologist Johan Asplund, children in their everyday play demonstrate that as human beings we are genuinely social animals (Asplund, 1987).

Children's entrepreneuring approach to life reveal them as talented bricoleurs, who are able to create, or rather recompose, new artefacts out of resources that have lost their original use, or enact new social structures by creatively imitating adult behaviour and talk while playing (see, for example, Baker and Nelson, 2005). Children construct a reality of their own by appropriating bits and pieces of practices in their (adult) social context. While pre-modernity and proto-industrial times made the children use, or rather recontextualize, natural objects in their play, modernity and industrialization structured play as much as work by offering technical devices such as Meccano and later Lego, where standardized components both encouraged and tamed children's imagination. In present postmodern digitalized times, interactive videos provide enormous potential spaces for creative organising. Games open up to unbounded virtual realities and potential bridges to everyday social life. For the first time in history children are ahead of adult human beings when it comes to dealing with ambiguous environments. A simple explanation in the perspective of what has been argued above is that digital information technology has brought us a huge step closer to a world of becoming, not just as an ontological positioning but as a materialized reality.

The School as an Obstacle to or an Amplifier of Entrepreneuring

As indicated, a generic question is whether the compulsory school as a major institution in children's life encourages, remains indifferent to or even counteracts the entrepreneurial force that children obviously possess. In order to answer that question I will again draw upon two empirical studies. The first one, presented in this section, is a report on the development and application of a test of 'entrepreneurial action capability' in different educational contexts in order to diagnose and position the knowledge about and attitudes to 'hard core' entrepreneuring – that is, business venturing – in the Swedish education system. The second empirical study reported in the second section is a broad regional project aiming at introducing entrepreneuring in the Swedish youth school.

The writer and philosopher Johann Wolfgang von Goethe succinctly stated: 'It is not enough to know, it also has to be used; it is not enough to desire, it also has to be done.' Learning from this and more recent discourses on entrepreneuring, it is obvious that new ventures have to be literally and relationally enacted or actualized. Accordingly, studies of attitudes and value preferences give little guidance when inquiring into the concrete making of entrepreneurial events; see Davidsson (1995). Instead we have to look into what concrete actions people take, that is, what they do hands-on, during their (potential) business venturing career (Carter et al., 1996). The conclusive finding of the ongoing Global Entrepreneurship Monitor (GEM) is that the major determinant of venturing realization and success is how active the founders are (Reynolds, 2007). Certainly, in a world of becoming, ongoing improvisation is the only coping tactic that works, whether we have the market or any other arena for the entrepreneurial processes in mind.

Ideally then, in order to find out how the school relates to entrepreneuring, ethnographic research including (participant) observation is called for. Lacking such qualitative studies of what characterizes schools as contexts for entrepreneuring, we have to rely on methods which identify attitudes to entrepreneuring as concrete creative organizing.

The Teachers' Dilemma: Knowing but not Practising Entrepreneuring

In order to capture what I associate with propensity to engage in new business events we have introduced and applied the 'entrepreneurial action capability test' to university students and practising small-business owner-managers (Johannisson et al., 1998). The test, which was developed at Växjö University, consists of four brief stories (about 120 words each) from business settings which communicate the need for creative and resolute (inter)action. The respondent is asked to live the part of the chief executive officer (CEOs), presumably an entrepreneurial person, in each small independent firm concerned and to take the action needed. In the test context this means marking, for each case, either of four optional ways to cope with the challenge that each story narrates. The optional responses are rank-ordered and ascribed values (0–3) making 12 the maximum score. For details as regards the generation of the scale, see Johannisson et al. (1998).

In order to encourage intuitive and spontaneous responses, a kind of action bias in itself, the respondents are given a (very) limited time to read the cases and make their choices. While the original study concerned groups of university students (as well as small-business owner-managers), follow-up empirical research in 2005–06 (also) included different groups of stakeholders within and around the compulsory educational system.

Table 11.1 shows that university students according to the original inquiry in the mid-1990s score higher than practising businesspeople and that business students come out more favourably than engineering students on the action capability test. These findings as regards different students groups make sense – according to my experience it is difficult to foster entrepreneurship inside the academic system – but the fact that the business students score considerably higher than active businesspeople on the action capability test is quite surprising. A possible explanation is that

Table 11.1   The action capability test: findings across different educational
settings (maximum score 12; respondent groups varying
between 30 and 300)

Respondent category	Score	
	1994/95	2005/06
University		
Students in Business Management	7.11	7.85
Students in Small Business Management/	8.47	
Entrepreneurship (with internships)		
Business students in Project Management		7.74
Engineering students	6.18	
Engineering students studying Product Development	6.38	
and Innovation (enacting own projects)		
Design students		8.06
Senior high school		
Educationalists (teachers, leaders, administrators)		8.62
Study counsellors		7.82
Junior Achievement coaches		8.07
Small business owner-managers	6.03	

while the testing procedure – typical formal 'paperwork' – possibly makes
the inexperienced students act on impulse (or see through the construction
of the cases), practitioners experience the test on the one hand as awkward
in their hands-on, oral setting, but on the other hand as an opportunity,
albeit brief, for reflection. Then they are made aware of risks associated
with radical actions such as those proposed in the cases, risks that they
would not consider in their 'real' business life.

Accordingly, practitioners make conservative choices. Engineering students are closer than business students to the reality (of owner-managers)
in the manufacturing industry (which was the empirical context of the
stories being told in the cases) and therefore may have concerns similar
to those of the active businesspeople as regards the realism of the cases
making the test. A second interesting finding is that students who join
programmes that offer company-based internships or own venturing in
the (business) context score higher than traditional business or engineering students with little or no experience of the professional world. Both
the boundary-crossing itself and the acquaintance with concrete business
events presumably encourage entrepreneuring. The findings also suggest

that entrepreneurship 15 years ago in Sweden was associated with doing business rather than with technological change.

Well after a decade after the original study, the test was used to discriminate between different characters on the educational scene who were tested with respect to their entrepreneurial action capability. The respondents belong to convenience samples from different regions of Sweden, all associated with the compulsory educational system. First, the replicated study of university business students indicates that general understanding of what it takes to run a business has increased since the mid-1990s in Sweden. Second, 'educationalists', here referring to teachers (who dominate the group), school leaders and municipal school administrators, score higher than university students, even students joining the special programme on project management (including internships) at Växjö University. A possible explanation is that the educationalists, at the time of the test, were involved in regional programmes aiming at communicating an enterprising attitude – rather than promoting hard-core (business) venturing. Further, for the same reasons as students rate higher than owner-managers, teachers may score well because they are, on one hand, detached from any business practice with all its detailed considerations and, on the other hand, they have been manipulated by the rhetoric of the public discourse that has in the Swedish context over the first decade of the new millennium strongly favoured entrepreneurship. This discourse has also broadened the notion of entrepreneuring beyond the business arena to the public and voluntary sectors. This cultural impact may explain why none of the groups according to Table 11.1 report any differences between women and men.

The findings suggest that Swedish teachers can easily imagine what venturing on the market calls for. However, this insight in a national culture that is still dominated by wage-earners' values and ambivalence vis-à-vis a business career may rather increase the scepticism against entrepreneuring and blindfold teachers against the broader understandings of the concept. The overall effect of different efforts to enlighten the teachers about entrepreneuring may thus have mobilized resistance rather than encouraged hands-on initiatives in the educational system.

A Quest for Entrepreneuring in the Swedish Education System[2]

During the period between the two action capability tests reported above there was an intense debate in Sweden in general and in the educational system in particular on entrepreneuring as an end or a means for societal development. This debate created two contrasting understandings of entrepreneuring: one associating it with creative business venturing; another with a mode of learning, a pedagogy. Either interpretation created resistance among practising teachers and, especially, the staff at teachers' colleges. Some wondered whether the introduction of entrepreneuring in the schools meant submitting to market values and norms, and market practices. Others feared that entrepreneuring would threaten the professional identity of the teachers in the general education system. Teachers' colleges in particular, which had recently become members of the Swedish academic community, proudly and eagerly defended their internally generated theories and practices.

During the time period concerned, international and national pressure to encourage entrepreneurship as an engine in national and regional growth has, however, equally intensely forced itself upon the education system. Several projects have been launched, including one aiming to 'actively contribute to changes in attitudes and to integrate entrepreneurial thinking in schools and in teacher education' in Sweden's northernmost region. I was asked to evaluate the project with respect to teaching practices concerning entrepreneuring in the compulsory school (mainly) and at university level. Teachers and school administrators were interviewed, the majority of them in focus groups, in order to find out about their practices as regards educating in and for entrepreneuring.[3] The teachers and leaders who were approached had participated in a regional development programme aiming at making visible and enforcing entrepreneurial practices in the educational system.

The basic lesson from the conversations in the focus groups is that the higher the level in the education system, the more difficult it becomes to make the teachers accept the world-view that entrepreneuring involves communication in general and a generic approach to teaching in particular. Thus, although the university in the region had declared itself to be an 'entrepreneurial university' the general awareness of, and accordingly interest in, the programme and its message was negligible. Within the teachers' college the indifference appeared almost as a protest. The inclusion of an optional course on entrepreneuring in their general programme at the college was negotiated, only to be more or less boycotted by the students.

The reception of the project at the lower levels in the youth school, especially in pre-school, was in sharp contrast to how it was received at the university. The aim and vocabulary of the proposed programmes aiming at an 'entrepreneurial pedagogy' were sincerely welcomed since it legitimized the existing practice to enforce the children's experiential approach to life. The connotation 'pre-school' and even more its synonym 'kindergarten' (although there definitely are different kinds of gardens) communicate that children are invited to maintain their natural talent for entrepreneuring as play in a permissive environment before they become disciplined by the 'real' school. At lower levels the children are (still) offered a world where they can make their own discoveries while adults limit their interference to mentoring moves and providing protective boundaries. The voices in a focus group of teachers at a pre-school in the region reveal what kind of learning processes are set free once the children's gift for entrepreneuring has been acknowledged. On my invitation, some teachers early in the interview stated their understanding of entrepreneuring and how they designed a supportive educational setting:

> Teacher's voice 1: Every day I reflect upon what they (the children) are capable of, what they know, what they want to find out about and how to go ahead. For me it is important to preserve these capabilities.

> Teacher's voice 2: In order to be able to finally launch a venture you must experience the freedom, strength and self-confidence needed to try things out, to claim space for action, to challenge what is taken for granted. This feeling emerges if you have been allowed to try something new without first being told what to do. Be surprised, bring that experience somewhere else and do something with it.

> Teacher's voice 3: If the children get access to their own creativity they become more entrepreneurial. Then it is very important that the school and the pre-school offer a learning context where the children can develop. It is a matter of attitude but also of how this attitude is reflected in how the schoolday and the physical context are organised and how the output from the [childrens'] projects are taken care of.

One of the projects concerned inquiry into the phenomenon of light, especially relevant in the region since it is crossed by the Arctic circle. This 'light' project not only framed experimenting inside the school but created bridges to the community as well, including an exhibition of children's creations at the House of Culture in the regional centre. The development programme wherein the teachers participated provided a vocabulary that made them realize the potential for entrepreneuring that the children have:

> Teacher's voice 4: You try to coach the children, to make them proud of what they have done so that they show it to others and tell others about it. You do not only bring it to your mum and dad but also to class mates and others outside school.

It is important to underline that what the children do is neither a random activity, nor (creative) imitation of what adults do. Children also reflect, even theorize, on their own:

Teacher's voice 3: Children have fantastic theories but they have to be listened to. You have to inquire about their theories and give them the opportunity to practise them. You should not think that children are children who only have fantasies. Their theories have to become important.

The conversation with the teachers revealed that, for example, the light project has inspired them to search out and enforce children's entrepreneurial capabilities. What is more, the teachers themselves have been motivated as entrepreneurial selves. The interaction that the project initiated has given them the experience needed to deal with indifference and resistance within and outside the school setting, as mentioned above. The tactics used, all calling for commitment and persistence, include both action and open confrontation with opponents, and reflection in order to identify and practice alternative ways of reaching the objectives aimed at. One teacher has even been inspired to launch an own business venture but has in addition developed an even broader outlook that includes a special concern for the children:

Teacher's voice 3: During the project I have become an owner-manager. It has pushed me to take action and to market courses in my own business. I have gained the courage and strength to go ahead. We have to give the children the same kind of support. Self-confidence is needed to take further steps. Our role is to promote children's rights in society, give them a voice and make them visible.

The experiences gained in the development project for entrepreneuring have also made the teachers reflect upon how to make an impact on coming generations of teachers. It took them years of persuasion to convince the university's school of education and teachers' college to invite practising teachers to meet with students in order to communicate their experiential knowledge. The general experience from Sweden is that the universities and their schools of education represent a major obstacle to the making of an entrepreneurial school. Their so far hegemonic position is being challenged because an entrepreneurial outlook means a radical shift in the basic pedagogy being practiced:

Teacher's voice 4: When I got my professional training the children were approached as a group. Now we deal with them as individuals and take their interests as a point of departure for different activities. This means that we have to change what we do from one group of children to the next. This view existed before the development programme but the programme has enforced this kind of thinking.

Junior-level teachers also do not have any problems accommodating the message of learning as entrepreneurship since it again mainly recognizes ongoing practices. A tight financial budget and a professional training that is more focused on 'how' rather than 'what' to teach, inviting the children themselves to co-construct their own learning processes:

> Teacher's voice 5: With the six year old kids we are planning to make a newspaper. We have been talking about its contents and the children are invited to propose contributions. The day before yesterday a girl approached me and said: 'We want to investigate the top ten dishes. What food is the most popular one.' 'Well', I said, 'how do you plan to bring that about?' 'We are going to ask everybody' she said. They had written the questions on pieces of paper. Their ideas were certainly different to mine. But it is important not to put on a brake or monitor them. You ask yourself: 'How are you going to put all this together?' But you have to hold such thoughts back and let the children go on. Problems have to be dealt with afterwards when we can ask ourselves why things went the way they did.

This teacher who at the beginning of the development programme had serious doubts about entrepreneuring when presented as business venturing, soon enough became enthusiastic about the approach. It confirmed and legitimized the kind of pedagogy that is in use and, what is more, is proposed in the national curriculum. Obviously there is no problem to bridging the suggested approach to educating for entrepreneuring to the contemporary research frontier in entrepreneurship. Sarasvathy (2001) with her logic of effectuation proposes that business venturing advances along the same learning track as the one practised by this enlightened teacher when she leaves it to the children to find the proper way to craft the venture.

At higher school levels, where content seems to dominate form in teaching, entrepreneuring usually becomes an alien phenomenon that occupies special spaces. In senior high school entrepreneuring is officially associated with business venturing as in junior achievement projects with few connections to regular school work. Less obvious is the role of the entrepreneurial pedagogy at the so-called 'individual programmes' in senior high school. These programmes are designed to help students who have difficulties in participating in regular teaching programmes. Both the teachers and the students on these individual programmes appreciated the view that entrepreneuring is about making sense of one's own life, starting off with whatever personal interest and dreams you may have. The entrepreneurial approach made the self-confidence of the students as well as the teachers on the individual programme increase considerably.

> Teacher's voice 6: Many of our students lack their own engine. It disappeared somewhere down the road. We try to find it and restart it, create more enterprising individuals who can do something creative on their own. Start something, carry something out. It does not mean that they have to start their own

company. To launch and finalize a project is enough. This programme aiming at entrepreneurship means that we help them to get in touch with the world outside the classroom. In the school but also in the community. We leave it to themselves to make that contact.

At the university level the border between traditional academic teaching and education in and for entrepreneurship is further enforced. Entrepreneuring is restricted to special zones dominated by programmes on management and technology. The extraordinary resistance to entrepreneuring at universities' schools of education thus did not come as a surprise. The staff at the school of education defended their moderate interest in entrepreneurship education with the argument that students are not interested since the subject is vague, and that an entrepreneurial mode of teaching will not be very much in demand at their future places of work. They also argued that the entrepreneurial objectives according to the national curriculum are anyway considered to be unrealistic by the general Swedish teaching community. This indifference at the academic teaching level means that the responsibility for the practice of entrepreneuring is handed over to the local school leaders. The irony is that this view, throwing the blame on somebody else and submitting to external forces when searching for local solutions, contradicts the very idea of entrepreneuring as a (teaching) practice.

There are different ways to interpret the insight gained by studying how the school system deals with entrepreneuring. One way to argue is that young children are naive and immature, unable to absorb any kind of education (for/in entrepreneuring) but pedagogy based on play as integrated with everyday (school) activities. Only older children, and certainly university students, are able to deal with 'true facts' and formal knowledge. Such analytical skills can only be acquired if the educational system has closed its boundaries and refrains from interacting with other communities of practice. This view certainly dominates the public discourse where university and senior-level teachers look down on the staff at kindergartens and junior-level schools. This is only an educational system that produces a society populated by *Homo traditionalis* and *Homo economicus*. However, the stories told by pre-school teachers above announce another potential discourse. This states that younger children invite their teachers to join in the co-creation of reality where playfulness and spontaneity rule and where interaction with the local community in which the school is embedded is taken for granted. This is a productive context for learning where new things, factual as well as imaginary, are enacted every day. Here children are taught to discipline their egoistic impulses and instead learn how to interact and collaborate in settings which are close to everyday life. This is a world populated by *Homo ludens* and *Homo curans*.

CONCLUSIONS: CHILDHOOD AS A DIFFERENT AND ENTREPRENEURIAL WORLD-MAKING

The discourse above suggests that children's ongoing entrepreneurial way of approaching life may be encouraged and can only temporarily be held back by the education system as a major institution. Adults, in contrast, constantly have to fight to restore and secure their entrepreneurial identity. Considering the emerging digitalized knowledge economy, this for the first time makes adults dependent on children, rather than the other way around. Reflecting upon an ontology of becoming, Lee (2001), however, does not draw the conclusion that only if man considers himself as a human becoming, and not as a human being, will he be able to cope with upcoming challenges in increasingly ambiguous environments. Our view is that children's curiosity, their concern for details as the origin of potentiality, should be encouraged so that, once life experience has made them trust their intuition, they can spontaneously turn coincidences into opportunities. Only then will a much-needed diverse and sustainable society emerge. This can only be accomplished if childhood is reconstructed from being a process of formation to become an adult to an existence in its own right (Prout and James, 1997/2008). The present educational system is too oriented towards 'professionalism', which means teaching a particular vocabulary that by definition brackets, categorizes and generalizes a given part of the world. As pointed out by Asplund (1987), Huizinga (1950), when identifying *Homo ludens,* missed the point on the one hand by seeing play as a voluntary activity, and on the other hand by excluding profane playing. But this everyday experimenting is what guides (all) children and (some) adults in being socially responsive to their environments. This is what entrepreneuring in a generic sense is all about. And some educational philosophies such as those provided by Reggio Emilia and Montessori bridge what we associate with entrepreneuring as learning and becoming.

As long as children are allowed to play (around) with words and deeds their inexorable socialization into adult life will be accompanied by entrepreneuring. Then 'education', whether associated with 'raising' as the core of primary socialization or formal training, does not (only) impose discipline. Prohibitions and reprimands as much as guidance and instructions in words or action or role modelling provide the experience that the child or the young person lacks. The transformative years between childhood and adulthood make the real challenge. As much as adolescents, due to group pressure and opposition, neither listen to nor imitate adults, their entrepreneurial capabilities become locked in and are only partially released in management programmes for business venturing such as Young Enterprise. Senior high school students with a need for testing the boundaries of the adult world, that is, practising entrepreneuring, are considered to have 'problems' and are accordingly dealt with in 'individual' programmes in the Swedish school. The turbulent times of adolescence, when children position themselves against their parents, is also reflected in how they relate to a business career. In a study a decade after my original child study, Davidsson (1995) examined regional variations in attitudes to and values associated with entrepreneurship. His studies included, for example, a municipality in each of the two regions dealt with by me. Davidsson found that in the locality with a favourable business climate and many role models the adolescents had a less favourable attitude to entrepreneurship than in the one-company town in the region in decline.

The playing child and the protesting adolescent are not the only ones opposing being thrown into irons by a powerful (adult) majority. What adults are to children, institutions are to (collective) adults in terms of providing rules of the game. Although Schumpeter associated entrepreneurship with radical innovation, its effect was challenging the ruling industrial logic, not the societal order. What is more, what in retrospect is narrated as a dramatic change, in its becoming may have been quite a smooth process produced by infinitesimal changes. Sweden's most successful (market) entrepreneur, IKEA's founder Ingvar Kamprad, is well known for his concern for detail in everyday practices and spontaneity in social relations, both child-like features for sure. Some entrepreneurs rather appear as adolescents, practising civil disobedience, and questioning regulative, normative or cognitive institutions; see Johannisson and Wigren, (2004). To some of these 'extreme' entrepreneurs, the questioning of institutions is only a means of paving the road for business activities. Other extreme entrepreneurs in the same way as artists make the provocation of what is taken for granted – that is, institutions – the very objective of their venturing in society. Then they act on behalf of a silent majority since provocation as a mode of testing the boundaries of what is possible is used by every child and adolescent.

So, if adults/parents and children can learn from each other, what should children be taught that on the one hand helps them in exploring new worlds, and on the other hand does not hinder them once they embark upon such journeys? The limit, including the responsibility, seems to be to teach them reading, writing and doing arithmetic. According to the exiled Somalian author Nurruddin Farah, illiteracy is the major threat to development in Africa (*Aftonbladet*, 2009). Only when given access to the written language are the children able to bridge between their everyday life and the potentialities of the world. If children are left to make a short-cut between an oral tradition and the digitalized world of the television and computer games with its focus on violence, the road to what Baumol labels destructive entrepreneurship becomes wide open to the next generation.

NOTES

1. The study has previously been reported (in Swedish) in Johannisson (1985/1999, 2004).
2. This section heavily draws upon Johannisson (2008).
3. For a review on literature on the 'focus group' technique, see Bill et al. (2008) and Johannisson (2008).

References

Acs, Z.J. (2002), *Innovation and the Growth of Cities*, Cheltenham, UK and Northampton, MA, USA: Edward Elgar.

Aftonbladet (2009), Interview with Nuruddin Farah, 22 February.

Agnew, J. (1987), *The United States in the World Economy*, Cambridge: Cambridge University Press.

Ahl, H.J. (2002), 'The making of the female entrepreneur: a discourse analysis of research texts on women's entrepreneurship', Doctoral dissertation, Jönköping International Business School.

Ahl, H.J. (2004), *The Scientific Reproduction of Gender Inequality: A Discourse Analysis of Research Texts on Women's Entrepreneurship*, Copenhagen/Malmö/Oslo: CBS Press/Liber/Abstrakt.

Akrich, M. (1992), 'The description of technical objects', in B. Wiebe and J. Law (eds), *Shaping Technology/Building Society*, Cambridge, MA: MIT Press.

Akrich, M., M. Callon and B. Latour (1988/2002a), 'The key to success in innovation part I: the art of interessement', *International Journal of Innovation Management*, **6**(2), translated by A. Monaghan. Originally published in French in 1988 as 'A quoi tient le success de innovations? 1. L'art de l'intéressement, *Annales des Mines, Gérer et Comprendre*, **11**, 4–17.

Akrich, M., M. Callon and B. Latour (1988/2002b), 'The key to success in innovation part II: the art of choosing good spokespersons', *International Journal of Innovation Management*, **6**(2), 207–25, translated by A. Monaghan. Originally published in French 1988 as 'A quoi tient le succès des innovations? 2. L'art de choisir les bons porte-parole', *Annales des Mines, Gérer et Comprendre*, **12**, 14–29.

Alberti, F. (2003), 'What makes it an industrial district? A cognitive perspective', *Uddevalla Symposium*.

Allen, T. (2007), 'A toy store(y)', *Journal of Business Venturing*, **22**(5), 628–36.

Althusser, L. (1970/1971), 'Ideology and ideological state apparatuses (notes towards an investigation)', *Lenin and Philosophy and Other Essays*, New York: Monthly Review Press.

Altman, I. and S.M. Low (eds) (1992), *Place Attachment*, New York and London: Plenum Press.

Alvesson, M. (2002), 'Identity regulation as organizational control: producing the appropriate individual', *Journal of Management Studies*, **39**(5), 619–44.

Alvesson, M. and D. Kärreman (2000), 'Varieties of discourse: on the study of organizations through discourse analysis', *Human Relations*, **53**(9), 1125–49.

Alvesson, M. and H. Willmott (1996), *Making Sense of Management*, London: Sage.

Andér, B. (2003), 'Låt Tensta Konsthall leva! Rapport från utredning om Tensta Konsthalls Framtid' (*Let Tensta Konsthall live! Report from a Study on the Future of Tensta Konsthall*), Stockholms stads kulturförvaltning (Culture Committee of the City of Stockholm).

Andersen, J. (2009), 'Stein Bagger-bøger: Dansen om guldkalven' ('Stein Bagger books: the dance around the golden calf'), available at http://www.business.dk/article/20090327/nyhedsmagasin/90326080/ (accessed 30 December 2009).

Anderson, R.B., B. Honig and A.M. Peredo (2006), 'Communities in the global economy: where social and indigenous entrepreneurship meet', in C. Steyaert and D. Hjorth (eds), *Entrepreneurship as Social Change*, Cheltenham, UK and Northampton, MA, USA: Edward Elgar.

Andersson, N. (2001), 'The power of thought? The philosophical politics of Louis Althusser 1960–1978', Doctoral dissertation, Lund University.

Apel, K.-O. (1984), *Understanding and Explanation*, Cambridge, MA: MIT Press.

Arbnor, I. (2004), *Vägen från Klockrike* (*The Road from the Industrial Clockdom*), Stockholm: SNS Förlag.

Asplund. J. (1987), *Det sociala livets elementära former* (*Elementary Forms of Social Life*), Göteborg: Korpen.

Audretsch, D.B. and R. Thurik (1999), 'Capitalism and democracy in the 21st century: from the managed to the entrepreneurial economy', *Journal of Evolutionary Economics*, **10**, 17–34.

Augé, M. (1995), *Non-Places: Introduction to an Anthropology of Supermodernity*, London: Verso.

Austin, J.L. (1962), *How to Do Things with Words*, London: London University Press.

Badham, R., K. Garrety, V. Morrigan, M. Zanko and P. Dawson (2003), 'Designer deviance: enterprise and deviance in culture change programmes', *Organization*, **10**(4), 707–30.

Baker, T. and R. Nelson (2005), 'Creating something from nothing: resource construction through entrepreneurial bricolage', *Administrative Science Quarterly*, **50**(3), 329–66.

Barabási, A.-L. (2002), *Linked: The New Science of Networks*, New York: Perseus Publishing.

Baron, J., M. Hannan and D. Burton (1999), 'Building the iron cage: determinants of managerial intensity in the early years of organizations', *American Sociological Review*, **64**(4), 527–47.

Baron, R.A. (1998), 'Cognitive mechanisms in entrepreneurship: why and when entrepreneurs think differently than other people', *Journal of Business Venturing*, **12**, 275–94.

Barry, A. and N. Thrift (2007), 'Gabriel Tarde: imitation, invention and economy', *Economy and Society*, **36**(4), 509–25.

Baumol, W.J. (1990), 'Entrepreneurship: productive, unproductive, and destructive', *Journal of Political Economy*, **98**(5), 893–921.

Beckard, R. and W. Dyer (1983), 'Managing continuity in the family-owned business', *Organizational Dynamics*, Summer, 5–12.

Becker, H.S. (1982), *Art Worlds*, Berkeley, CA: University of California Press.

Becker, M.D., T. Knudsen and J.G. March (2006), 'Schumpeter, Winter, and the sources of novelty', *Industrial and Corporate Change*, **15**(2), 353–71.

Berg, A.-J. and M. Lie (1993), 'Feminism and constructivism: do artefacts have gender?' *Science, Technology and Human Values*, **20**, 332–51.

Berg, P.-O. (2001), 'The summoning of the Øresund region', in B. Czarniawska and R. Solli (eds), *Organizing Metropolitan Space and Discourse*, Solna: Liber.

Berger, P.L. and T. Luckmann (1967), *The Social Construction of Reality*, London: Allen- Lane.

Berglund, K. (2004), 'Discursive diversity in fashioning entrepreneurial identity', in D. Hjorth and C. Steyaert (eds), *Narrative and discursive approaches in entrepreneurship*, Cheltenham, UK and Northampton, MA, USA: Edward Elgar.

Berglund, K. (2007), 'Jakten på entreprenörer. Om öppningar och låsningar i entreprenörskapsdiskursen' (*Hunting Entrepreneurs. About Openings and Gridlocks in the Entrepreneurial Discourse*), Doctoral dissertation, Mälardalens högskola.

Berglund, K. and A.W. Johansson (2007a), 'Entrepreneurship, discourses and conscientization in processes of regional development', *Entrepreneurship and Regional Development*, **19**(November), 499–525.

Berglund, K. and A.W. Johansson (2007b), 'Constructions of entrepreneurship: a discourse analysis of academic publications', *Journal of Enterprising Communities*, **1**(1), 77–102.

Berglund, K., M. Dahlin and A.W. Johansson (2007), 'Walking the tightrope between artistry and entrepreneurship: the stories of the Hotel Woodpecker, Otter Inn and the Luna Resort', *Journal of Enterprising Communities: People and Places in the Global Economy*, **1**(3), 268–84.

Berglund, K. and A.W. Johansson (eds) (2008), *Arenor för entreprenörskap* (*Arenas for Entrepreneurship*), Örebro: Swedish Foundation for Small Business Research.

Beyes, T. (2006), 'City of enterprise, city as prey? On urban entrepreneurial spaces', in C. Steyaert and D. Hjorth (eds), *Entrepreneurship as Social Change*, Cheltenham, UK and Northampton, MA, USA: Edward Elgar.

Bill, F. (2006), *The Apocalypse of Entrepreneurship*, Växjö: Växjö University Press.

Bill, F., B. Johannisson and L. Olaison (2008), 'The Incubus paradox: attempts at foundational rethinking of the "SME support genre"', in B. Johannisson and Å. Lindholm Dahlstrand (eds), *Bridging the Functional and Territorial Views on Regional Entrepreneurship and development*, Örebro: Swedish Foundation for Small Business Research.

Bill, F. and L. Olaison (2006), 'Between a rock and smooth space: the hypocrisy of a striated refuge', paper presented at NCSB, Stockholm, Sweden, 11–13 May.

Bill, F. and L. Olaison (2007), 'The used-books store: a haven for prosaic creativity', paper presented at the 23rd EGOS Colloquium, Vienna, Austria, 5–7 July.

Bill, F. and L. Olaison (2009), 'The incubus paradox: attempts at foundational rethinking of the "SME support genre"', *European Planning Studies*, **17**(8), 1135–52.

Bjerke, B. (1999), *Business Leadership and Culture: National Management Styles in the Global Economy*, Cheltenham, UK and Northampton, MA, USA, Edward Elgar.

Bjerke, B. (2007), *Understanding Entrepreneurship*, Cheltenham, UK and Northampton, MA, USA: Edward Elgar.

Bjerke, B. and C. Hultman (2002), *Entrepreneurial Marketing: The Growth of Small Firms in the New Economic Era*, Cheltenham, UK and Northampton, MA, USA: Edward Elgar.

Block, S. and S. Rosenberg (2002), 'Toward an understanding of founder's syndrome: an assessment of power and privilege among founders of nonprofit organizations', *Nonprofit Management and Leadership*, **12**(4), 353–68.

Boeker, W. and R. Karichalil (2002), 'Entreprenurial transitions: factors influencing founder departure', *Academy of Management Journal*, **45**(4), 818–26.

Borgerson, J. (2005), 'On organizing subjectivities', *Sociological Review*, **53**(October), 63–79.

Bornstein, D. (1998), 'Changing the world on a shoestring', *Atlantic Monthly*, **281**(1), 34–9.

Boschee, J. (1998), 'What does it take to be a social entrepreneur?' www. socialentrepreneurs.org./whatdoes.html (17 March 2006).

Bourdieu, P. (1979), *La distinction: critique sociale du jugement*, Paris: Editions de Minuit.

Bourdieu, P. (1993), *The Field of Cultural Production: Essays on Art and Literature*, New York: Columbia University Press.

Braidotti, R. (2003), 'Becoming woman: or sexual difference revisited', *Theory, Culture and Society*, **20**(3), 43–64.

Braidotti, R. (2005), 'A critical cartography of feminist post-postmodernism', *Australian Feminist Studies*, **20**(47), 169–80.

Braunerhjelm, P., B. Carlsson and D. Johansson (1998), 'Industriella kluster, tillväxt och ekonomisk politik' ('Industrial clusters, growth and economic policy'), *Ekonomisk Debatt*, **26**(4), 419–30.

Brenner, N. (1997), 'Global, fragmented, hierarchical: Henri Lefebvre's geographies of globalization', *Public Culture*, **10**(1), 135–67.

Bridge, S., K. O'Neill and S. Cromie (2003), *Understanding Enterprise, Entrepreneurship and Small Business*, 2nd edn, New York: Palgrave Macmillan.

Brockner, J. (1992), 'The escalation of commitment to a failing course of action: towards theoretical progress', *Academy of Management Review*, **17**(1), 39–61.

Brown, A.D., G. Yiannis and G. Silvia (2009), 'Storytelling and change: An unfolding story', *Organization*, **16**(3), 323–33.

Bruni, A., S. Gherardi and B. Poggio (2004), 'Entrepreneur-mentality, gender and the study of women entrepreneurs', *Journal of Organizational Change Management*, **17**(3), 256–68.

Brunsson, N. (1985), *The Irrational Organization. Irrationality as a Basis for Organizational Action and Change*, New York: Wiley.

Burt, R.S. (1997), 'The contingent value of social capital', *Administrative Science Quarterly*, **42**, 339–65.

Butler, J. (1997a), *The Psychic Life of Power*, Stanford, CA: Stanford University Press.

Butler, J. (1997b), *Excitable Speech*, London: Routledge.

Butler, J. (2004), *Undoing Gender*, New York: Routledge.

Buttimer, A. and D. Seamon (eds) (1980), *The Human Experience of Space and Place*, New York: St Martin's Press.

Callon, M. (1986), 'Some elements of a sociology of translation: Domestication of the scallops and the fishermen of St Brieuc's bay', in

J. Law (ed.), *Power, Action And Belief. A New Sociology of Knowledge?*, London: Routledge & Kegan Paul.

Callon, M. and J. Law (1982), 'On interests and their transformation: enrolment and counter-enrolment', *Social Studies of Science*, **12**(4), 615–25.

Callon, M. and J. Law (1997), 'After the individual in society: lessons on collectivity from science, technology and society', *Canadian Journal of Sociology*, **22**(2), 165–82.

Cameron, D. (1996a), 'The language–gender interface: challenging co-optation', in V.L. Bergvall, J.M. Bing and A.F. Freed (eds), *Rethinking Language and Gender Research: Theory and Practice*, London: Addison Wesley Longman.

Cameron, D. (1996b), 'Verbal hygiene for women: constructing feminine speech', in Y. Hyrynen (ed.), *Voicing Gender*, Tampere: Tampere English Studies.

Carter, N.M, W.B. Gartner and P.D. Reynolds (1996), 'Exploring start-up event sequences', *Journal of Business Venturing*, **11**, 151–66.

Casey, E.S. (1993), *Getting Back into Place: Toward a Renewed Understanding of the Place-World*, Bloomington, IN: Indiana University Press.

Casey, E.S. (1997), *The Fate of Place: A Philosophical History*, Berkeley, CA: University of California Press.

Castells, M. (1998), *Nätverkssamhällets framväxt* (*The Growth of the Network Society*), Göteborg: Daidalos.

Chell, E. (2007), 'Social enterprise and entrepreneurship: towards a convergent theory of the entrepreneurial process', *International Small Business Journal*, **25**(1), 5–26.

Chia, R. (1995), 'From modern to postmodern organizational analysis', *Organization Studies*, **16**(4), 579–604.

Chiapello, E. (1994), 'Les modes de contrôle des organisations artistiques', unpublished Doctoral dissertation, Université Paris IX Dauphine.

Clark, T.N. (ed.) (1969), *Gabriel Tarde on Communication and Social Influence*, Chicago, IL: Chicago University Press.

Clegg, S.R. (1989), *Frameworks of Power*, London: Sage.

Cohen, S., W. Eimicke and M. Salazar (1999), 'Public ethics and public entrepreneurship', paper presented to the Annual Research Meeting of the Association of Public Policy Analysis and Management, Washington, DC, November.

Cooren, F. (2000), *The Organizing Property of Communication*, Philadelphia, PA: Amsterdam: John Benjamins Publishing Co.

Corsaro, W.A. (2005), *The Sociology of Childhood*, 2nd edn, London: Pine Forge.

Coulter, M. (2001), *Entrepreneurship in Action*, Upper Saddle River, NJ: Prentice Hall.

Cray, D. and L. Inglis (2007), 'Arts management issues in the 21st century', *21st Century Management: A Reference Handbook*, Sage e-reference, available at http://www.sage-ereference.com./management/Article_n97. html (accessed 15 March 2009).

Cresswell, T. (2004), *Place: A Short Introduction*, Oxford: Blackwell.

Cronon, W. (1992), 'Kennecott journey: the paths out of town', in W. Cronon, W. Miles and J. Gitlin (eds), *Under an Open Sky*, New York: Norton.

Curry, M.R. (2000), 'Wittgenstein and the fabric of everyday life', in N. Thrift and M. Crang (eds), *Thinking Space*, London: Routledge.

Curry, M.R. (2002), 'Discursive displacement and the seminal ambiguity of space and place', in L. Lievrouw and S. Livingstone (eds), *Handbook in New Media*, London: Sage Publications.

Czarniawska, B. (1997), *Narrating the Organization: Dramas of Institutional Identity*, Chicago, IL: University of Chicago Press.

Czarniawska, B. (2005), 'Karl Weick: concepts, style and reflection', *Sociological Review*, **53**(S1), 267–78.

Czarniawska, B. and B. Joerges (1996), 'Travels of ideas', in B. Czarniawska and G. Sevón (eds), *Translating Organizational Change*, Berlin and New York: De Gruyter.

Dalademokraten (DD) (2006), 'Dalhalla får nya ägare' ('Dalhalla gets new owners'), 1 December, available at http://www.dalademokraten. se/ArticlePages/200612/01/20061201103943_DD830/20061201103943_ DD830.dbp.asp (accessed 6 April 2009).

Dareblom, J. (2005), 'Prat, politik och praktik – Om individers möten med strukturer i en kommunal satsning på kvinnors företagande' ('Talk, politics and praxis – about individuals' meetings with structures in a local political region's investment in women's entrepreneurship'), Doctoral dissertation, Stockholm School of Economics.

Davidsson, P. (1995), 'Culture, structure and regional levels of entrepreneurship', *Entrepreneurship and Regional Development*, **7**(1), 41–62.

Davies, B. (2003), 'Death to critique and dissent? The policies and practices of New Managerialism and of "evidence-based practice"', *Gender and Education*, **15**(1), 91–103.

Davies, B. (2005), 'The (im)possibility of intellectual work in neoliberal regimes', *Discourse: Studies in the Cultural Politics of Education*, **26**(1), 1–14.

Davies, B. (2006), 'Subjectification: the relevance of Butler's analysis for education', *British Journal of Sociology of Education*, **27**(4), 425–38.

Davies, B., J. Browne, S. Gannon, L. Hopkins, H. McCann and M. Wihlborg (2006), 'Constituting the feminist subject in poststructuralist discourse', *Feminism and Psychology*, **16**(1), 87–103.

Dean, M. (1999), *Governmentality: Power and Rule in Modern Society*, London: Sage.

de Beauvoir, S. (1949/1997), *The Second Sex*, London: Vintage.

de Bono, E. (1970), *The Dog-Exercising Machine*, London: Cognitive Research Trust.

Debord, G. (1967), *Society of the Spectacle*, London: Rebel Press.

Debord, G. (1990), *Comments on the Society of the Spectacle*, London: Verso.

de Bruin, A. (2003), 'State entrepreneurship', in A. de Bruin and A. Dupuis (eds), *Entrepreneurship: New Perspectives in a Global Age*, Aldershot: Ashgate Publishing.

de Certeau, M. (1984), *The Practice of Everyday Life*, Berkeley, CA: University of California Press.

De Faoite, D., C. Henry, K. Johnston and P. van der Sijde (2004), 'Entrepreneurs' attitudes to training and support initiatives: evidence from Ireland and The Netherlands', *Journal of Small Business and Enterprise Development*, 11(4), 440–48.

Defourney, J. (2001), 'From third sector to social enterprise', in C. Borzaga and J. Defourney (eds), *The Emergence of Social Enterprise*, Oxford, UK and New York, USA: Routledge.

Deleuze, G. and F. Guattari (1988), *A Thousand Plateaus: Capitalism and Schizophrenia*, London: Athlone Press.

Dellefors, M. (2008), *Dalhalla. Kampen för ett brott* (*Dalhalla: Fighting for a Quarry*), Stockholm: Carlssons.

Derrida, J. (1976/1998), *Of Grammatology*, Baltimore, MD: John Hopkins University Press.

Devin, L. and R. Austin (2007), 'Artistic methods and business disorganization', *21st Century Management: A Reference Handbook*, Sage e-reference, available at http://www.sage-ereference.com./management/Article_n48.html (accessed 15 March 2009).

Dewey, J. (1902/1990), *The Child and the Curriculum*, Chicago, IL: University of Chicago Press.

DiMaggio, P.J. and W.W. Powell (1983), 'The iron cage revisited: institutional isomorphism and collective rationality in organizational fields', *American Sociological Review*, 48(April), 147–60.

Dimov, D. (2007), 'Beyond the single-person, single-insight attribution in understanding entrepreneurial opportunities', *Entrepreneurship Theory and Practice*, 31(5), 713–31.

Disch, L. (1999), 'Judith Butler and the politics of the performative', Review Essay, *Political Theory*, 27(4), 545–59.

Dreyfus, H.L. and P. Rabinow (eds) (1982), *Michel Foucault: Beyond Structuralism and Hermeneutics*, London: Harvester Wheatsheaf.

Droysen, J.G. (1858/1987), *Grundrisse der Historik*, published (1987) as *Outline of the Principles of History* (transl. E.B. Andrews), Boston, MA: Ginn & Co.

Drucker, P.F. (1986), *Innovation and Entrepreneurship: Practice and Principles*, New York: Harper & Row.

Due Billing, Y. and M. Alvesson (1994), *Gender, Managers and Organizations*, Berlin: Walter de Gruyter.

du Gay, P. (1991), 'Enterprise culture and the ideology of excellence, *New Formations*, **13**, 45–61.

du Gay, P. (2004), 'Against "Enterprise" (but not against "enterprise" for that would make no sense)', *Organization*, **11**(1), 37–57.

du Gay, P., G. Salaman and B. Rees (1996), 'The conduct of management and the management of conduct: contemporary managerial discourse and the constitution of the 'competent' manager', *Journal of Management Studies*, **33**(3), 263–82.

Dunnery, F. (2005), 'The golden castle', www.francisdunnery.com (accessed 8 September).

Dupuis, A., A. de Bruin and R.D. Cremer (2003), 'Municipal-community entrepreneurship', in A. de Bruin and A. Dupuis (eds), *Entrepreneurship: New Perspectives in a Global Age*, Aldershot: Ashgate Publishing.

Ehrlich, S. and R. King (1994), 'Feminist meanings and the (de)politization of the lexicon', *Language and Society*, **23**(1), 59–76.

Eikhof, D. and A. Haunschild (2006), 'Lifestyle meets market: bohemian entrepreneurs in creative industries', *Creativity and Innovation Management*, **15**(3), 234–41.

Ekman, R. and J. Hultman (2007), 'Produktgörandet av platser' (Manufacturing places), in R. Ekman and J. Hultman (eds), *Plats som produkt* (Place as a product), Lund: Studentlitteratur.

Eliasson, G. (2006), 'From employment to entrepreneurship: shifting perspectives in Europe and the US on knowledge creation and labour market competition', *Journal of Industrial Relations*, **48**(5), 633–56.

Englund, K. (2004), 'Eldsjälar, svartfötter och byråkrater. En undersökning av konflikten kring Tensta Konsthall' ('Champions, blackfeet and bureaucrats. A study of the conflict around Tensta Konsthall'), Bachelors thesis, Autumn Semester, Department of Art History, Södertörn University College, available at http://www.divaportal.org/diva/getDocument?urn_nbn_se_sh_diva-282-1__fulltext.pdf (accessed 19 February 2008).

Epstein, L. (2004), 'Chefen som försvann' ('The boss who disappeared'), *P1*, Sveriges Radio, documentary radio programme, 20 October.

Ericsson, D. (2007), *Musikmysteriet. Organiserade stämningar och motstämningar* (*The Music Mystery. Organized Moods and Anti-Moods*), Stockholm: EFI at Stockholm School of Economics.

Ericsson, D. and P. Nilsson (2008), 'Bureaucrats and heretics: gendering mythology', in M. Kostera (ed.), *Organizational Epics and Sagas: Tales of Organizations*, London: Palgrave Macmillan.

Ericsson, L.O. (2005), *Mordet på Tensta Konsthall. En anklagelseskrift (The Murder of Tensta Konsthall. An Accusation Document)*, Stockholm: Books-on-Demand.

European Commission (2003), *Green Paper: Entrepreneurship in Europe*, COM (2003) 27 final, 21 January, Brussels: Enterprise Publications, European Commission.

European Commission (2009), 'European Year of Creativity and Innovation 2009', available at http://www.create2009.europa.eu (accessed 30 December 2009).

Fairclough, N. (1992), *Discourse and Social Change*, Cambridge, UK and Cambridge, MA, USA: Polity Press and Blackwell Publishers.

Fairclough, N. (1995), *Critical Discourse Analysis: The Critical Study of Language*, London: Longman.

Fay, B. (1996), *Contemporary Philosophy of Social Science*, Oxford: Blackwell Publishers.

Feldman, M. (1994), *The Geography of Innovation*, Norwell, MA: Kluwer Academic Publishers.

Fleming, P. and A. Spicer (2003), 'Working at a cynical distance: implications for power, subjectivity and resistance', *Organization*, **10**(1), 157–79.

Fleming, P. and A. Spicer (2007), *Contesting the Corporation: Struggle, Power and Resistance in Organizations*, Cambridge: Cambridge University Press.

Florida, R. (2002), *The Rise of the Creative Class*, New York: Basic Books.

Foucault, M. (1969/1972), *The Archeology of Knowledge*, London: Tavistock.

Foucault, M. (1980), 'The eye of power: a conversation with Jean-Paul Barou and Michelle Perrot', in C. Gordon (ed.), *Power/Knowledge: Selected Interviews and Other Writings, 1972–1977 by Michel Foucault*, Hemel Hempstead: Harvester Press.

Foucault, M. (1990), *The History of Sexuality. Vol. 1, The Will to Knowledge*, Harmondsworth: Penguin.

Gaglio, C.M. (1997), 'Opportunity recognition: review, critique and suggested research directions', in J. Katz and R.H. Brockhaus (eds), *Advances in Entrepreneurship, Firm Emergence and Growth*, Greenwich, CT: JAI Press.

Gartner, B.W. (1989), '"Who is an entrepreneur?" is the wrong question', *Entrepreneurship Theory and Practice*, **13**(4), 47–69.

Gartner, B.W., N.M. Carter and G.E. Hills (2003), 'The language of opportunity', in C. Steyaert and D. Hjorth (eds), *New Movements in Entrepreneurship*, Cheltenham, UK and Northampton, MA, USA: Edward Elgar.

Gartner, B.W., D. Hjorth and C. Jones (2008), 'Recontextualizing/recreating Entrepreneurship', *Scandinavian Journal of Management*, **24**(2), 81–4.

Gilbertsson, K. (2008), 'Evenemangsmätning Dalhalla 2008. Region Siljan – Inom ramen för projekt 'Destination Siljan med Dalhalla som besöksmotor' (*Event Measurement Dalhalla 2008. Region Siljan – within the Framework of the Project 'Destination Siljan with Dalhalla as a visiting Attraction'*), report, Gothenburg: Turismens utredningsinstitut (TUI).

Giorgi, A. (1994), 'A phenomenological perspective on certain qualitative research methods', *Journal of Phenomenological Psychology*, **25**, 190–220.

Grabher, G. and D. Stark (1997), 'Organising diversity: evolutionary theory, network analysis, and post-socialism', in G. Grabher and D. Stark (eds), *Restructuring Networks in Post-Socialism: Legacies, Linkages, and Localities*, Oxford: Oxford University Press.

Grahn, V. (2006), '*Känn dig själf. Genus, historiekonstruktion och kulturhistoriska Museirepresentationer ('Know Your Self'. Gender, History Construction and Cultural Historical Representation at Museums*'), Doctoral dissertation, Linköping: Linköping University

Granovetter, M. (1985), 'Economic action and social structure: the problem of Embeddedness', *American Journal of Sociology*, **91**, 481–510.

Gratzer, K. (1996), 'Småföretagandets villkor. Automatrestauranger under 1900-talet' ('The conditions for small businesses. Automatic restaurants during the 1900s'), Doctoral dissertation, School of Business, Stockholm University.

Gratzer, K. (2009), 'Staten som företagare: från entreprenör ex ante till owner-of-last resort' ('The state as business venture: from entrepreneur ex ante to owner-of-last-resort'), unpublished material, personal discussions.

Greimas, A.J. (1971), 'Narrative grammar: units and levels', *MLN*, **86**(6), 793–806.

Guillet de Monthoux, P. (2004), *The Art Firm. Aesthetic Management and Metaphysical Marketing*, Stanford, CA: Stanford University Press.

Håkanson, L. (2003), 'Epistemic communities and cluster dynamics: on the role of knowledge in industrial districts', research paper, Copenhagen Business School.

Hall, E.T. (1959), *The Silent Language*, New York: Doubleday.

Hambrick, D., M. Geletkanycz and J. Fridrickson (1993), 'Top executive commitment to the status quo: some tests of its determinants', *Strategic Management Journal*, **14**(6), 401–18.

Harris, L. and E. Ogbonna (1999), 'The strategic legacy of company founders', *Long Range Planning*, **32**(3), 333–43.

Harvey, D. (1989), 'From managerialism to entrepreneurialism: the transformation of governance to late capitalism', *Geografiska Annaler*, **71B**, 3–17.

Hedfeldt, M. (2008), 'Företagande kvinnor i bruksort. Arbetsliv och vardagsliv i samspel' ('Venturing women at industrial communities. Working life and private life in interplay'), Doctoral dissertation, Örebro University.

Hedstrand, S. (2003), 'Vem ska styra Tensta Konsthall?' ('Who is to run Tensta Konsthall?'), *Dagens Nyheter*, 21 December.

Henton, D., J. Melville and K. Walesh (1997), *Grassroots Leaders for a New Economy: How Civic Entrepreneurs Are Building Prosperous Communities*, San Francisco, CA: Jossey-Bass.

Herbert, N. (2004), 'Maktkamp och avundsjuka bakom kulisserna på Tensta Konsthall' ('Power play and jealousy behind the scenes of Tensta Konsthall'), *Stockholms Fria Tidning*, 16 April.

Hernadi, A. and C. Poellinger (2005), 'Kulturkrocken i Tensta' ('The culture clash in Tensta'), *Svenska Dagbladet*, 15 July.

Hjalmarsson, D. and A.W. Johansson (2003), 'Public advisory services: theory and practice', *Entrepreneurship and Regional Development*, **15**(1), 83–98.

Hjorth, D. (2003), *Rewriting Entrepreneurship – For a New Perspective on Organisational Creativity,* Copenhagen/Malmö/Oslo: CBS Press/Liber/ Abstrakt.

Hjorth, D. (2004), 'Creating space for play/invention: concepts of space and organizational entrepreneurship', *Entrepreneurship and Regional Development*, **16**(September), 413–32.

Hjorth, D. (2005), 'Organizational entrepreneurship: with de Certeau on creating heterotopias (or spaces for play)', *Journal of Management Inquiry*, **14**, 386–98.

Hjorth, D. (2008), 'Nordic entrepreneurship research', *Entrepreneurship Theory and Practice*, **32**(2), 313–38.

Hjorth, D. and B. Bjerke (2006), 'Public entrepreneurship: moving from social/consumer to public/citizen', in C. Steyaert and D. Hjorth (eds), *Entrepreneurship as Social Change*, Cheltenham, UK and Northampton, MA, USA: Edward Elgar.

Hjorth, D. and B. Johannisson (2002), '"Conceptualizing": a "collective identity"', paper presented at 2nd Conference of the International Entrepreneurship Forum, Entrepreneurship and Regional Development, Beijing, 5–7 September.

Hjorth, D. and B. Johannisson (2007), 'Learning as an entrepreneurial process', in A. Fayolle (ed.), *Handbook of Research in Entrepreneurship Education, Volume 1. A General Perspective*, Cheltenham, UK and Northampton, MA, USA: Edward Elgar.

Hjorth, D., B. Johannisson and C. Steyaert (2003), 'Entrepreneurship as discourse and life style', in B. Czarniawska and G. Sevón (eds), *The Northern Lights: Organization Theory in Scandinavia*, Malmö, Copenhagen, Oslo: Liber/Copenhagen Business School Press, Abstrakt.

Hjorth, D., C. Jones and W.E. Gartner (2008), 'Recontextualizing/recreating entrepreneurship', *Scandinavian Journal of Management*, **24**(2), 81–4.

Hjorth, D. and C. Steyaert (eds) (2004), *Narrative and Discursive Approaches in Entrepreneurship*, Cheltenham, UK and Northampton, MA, USA: Edward Elgar.

Hjorth, D. and C. Steyaert (eds) (2009), *The Politics and Aesthetics of Entrepreneurship*, Cheltenham, UK and Northampton, MA, USA: Edward Elgar.

Hoggart, K. (1991), *People, Power and Place: Perspectives on Anglo-American Politics*, London: Routledge.

Holgersson, C. (1998), 'Den nödvändiga periferin' ('The necessary periphery'), in A. Wahl, C. Holgersson and P. Höök, (eds), *Ironi och sexualitet – om ledarskap och kön* (*Irony and Sexuality – About Leadership and Gender*), Stockholm: Carlssons.

Holmgren, C. (2005), 'The case of Sweden', in A. Lundström (ed.), *Creating Opportunities for Young Entrepreneurship, Nordic Examples and Experience*, Örebro: Swedish Foundation for Small Business Research.

Holmquist, C. and E. Sundin (1989), *Kvinnor som företagare. Osynlighet, mångfald, anpassning. En studie* (*Women as Business Venturers. Invisibility, Variety, Adaptation. A Study*), Malmö: Liber.

Hooper, K. and K. Kearins (2007), 'Looking for Joan of Arc: collaboration in the rise and fall of heroes', *Culture and Organization*, **13**(4), 297–312.

Hubbard, P. and T. Hall (1998), 'The entrepreneurial city and the "new urban politics"', in T. Hall and P. Hubbard (eds), *The Entrepreneurial City*, Chichester, John Wiley & Sons.

Hudson, R. (2001), *Producing Places*, London: Guildford Press.

Huizinga, J. (1950), *Homo Ludens: A Study of the Play Element in Culture*, Boston, MA: Beacon Press.

Irigaray, L. (1974/1985), *Speculum of the Other Woman*, New York: Cornell University Press.

Irigaray, L. (1977/1985), *This Sex Which Is Not One*, New York: Cornell University Press.

Jack, S.L. and A.R. Anderson (2002), 'The effects of embeddedness on the entrepreneurial process', *Journal of Business Venturing*, **17**, 467–87.

Jacobs, J. (1961), *The Death and Life of Great American Cities*, New York: Random House.

Jacobsson, C. (2008), 'Trappstäderskans nya uppdrag: ambassadör' ('The staircase cleaner's new task: ambassador'), *Dagens Nyheter*, 26 March.

James, A., C. Jenks and A. Prout (1998), *Theorizing Childhood*, Cambridge: Polity Press.

Jammer, M. (1982), *Concepts of Space. The History of Theories of Space in Physics*, 3rd edn, enlarged, New York: Dover Publications.

Jansson, E. (2008), 'Paradoxen (s)om entreprenörskap: en romantisk ironisk historia om ett av-vikande entreprenörskapande' ('The paradox as and about entrepreneurship: a romantic ironic story of di-verging entrepreneurial creativity'), Doctoral dissertation, Stockholm University School of Business.

Javefors Grauers, E. (2002), 'Profession, genus och företagarpar: en studie av advokater och köpmän' ('Profession, gender and business couples: a study of lawyers and business men'), Doctoral dissertation, Linköping University.

Jermier, J.M., D. Knights and W.R. Nord (eds) (1994), *Resistance and Power in Organizations*, London: Routledge.

Jessop, B. (1994), 'Post-Fordism and the state', in A. Amin (ed.), *Post-Fordism*, Blackwell: Oxford.

Jessop, B. (1997), 'The governance of complexity and the complexity of governance: preliminary remarks on some problems and limits of economic guidance', in A. Amin and J. Hausner (eds), *Beyond Markets and Hierarchy: Third Way Approaches to Transformation*, Cheltenham, UK and Northampton, MA, USA: Edward Elgar.

Johannisson, B. (1985/1999), 'Barnatro och företagaranda' ('Childrens' beliefs and venturing spirit'), Report from Östersund University 1985:11, Östersund: Östersund University. Reprinted at Växjö University 1999.

Johannisson, B. (1992), *Entreprenörskap på svenska* (*Entrepreneurship in Swedish*), Malmö: Almquist & Wiksell.

Johannisson, B. (2000), 'Networking and entrepreneurial growth', in D.L. Sexton and H. Landström (eds), *The Blackwell Handbook of Entrepreneurship*, Oxford: Blackwell Publishers.

Johannisson, B. (2004), 'Låt barnet komma till dig!' ('Let the children come to you'), in D. Ericsson (ed.), *Det o(av)sedda Entreprenörskapet* (*The Unintended Entrepreneurship*), Lund: Academia Adacta.

Johannisson, B. (2008), *Visst är du företagsam, lilla vän! – reflexioner kring ett projekt för skolning i entreprenörskap i Norrbottens län* (*You are venturesome, for sure, my little friend! – reflections around a Project for Training Entrepreneurship in One Northern Swedish Area*), Luleå: Luleå Tekniska Universitet.

Johannisson, B. (2009), 'Industrial districts in Scandinavia', in G. Becattini, M. Bellandi and L. De Propris (eds), *Handbook of Industrial Districts*, Cheltenham, UK and Northampton, MA, USA: Edgar Elgar.

Johannisson, B. and A. Abrahamsson (2004), 'Familjeföretagandets gaseller i Sverige, en inventering och hälsoundersökning av 2002 års bestånd' ('The gazelles among family firms in Sweden, one inventory and health study among the stock of 2002'), in F. Bill and B. Johannisson (eds), *Entreprenörskapets rationaliteter och irrationaliteter* (*The Rationalities and Irrationalities of Entrepreneurship*), Växjö: Växjö University Press.

Johannisson, B., H. Landström and J. Rosenberg (1998), 'University training for entrepreneurship: an action frame of reference', *European Journal of Engineering Education*, **23**(4), 477–96.

Johannisson, B., M. Ramirez-Passilas and G. Karlsson (2002), 'The institutional embeddedness of local inter-firm networks: a leverage for business creation', *Entrepreneurship and Regional Development*, **14**(4), 297–315.

Johannisson, B. and L. Olaison (2007), 'The moment of truth: reconstructing entrepreneurship and social capital in the eye of the storm', *Review of Social Economy*, **65**(1), 55–78.

Johannisson, B. and L. Olaison (2008), 'Emergency entrepreneurship: creative organizing in the eye of the storm', in H. Landström, H. Crijns, E. Laveren and D. Smallbone (eds), *Entrepreneurship, Sustainable Growth And Performance: Frontiers in European Entrepreneurship Research*, Cheltenham, UK and Northampton, MA, USA: Edward Elgar.

Johannisson, B. and C. Wigren (2004), 'Extreme entrepreneurs: challenging the institutional framework', in P.R. Christensen and F. Poulfeldt (eds), *Managing Complexity and Change in SMEs: Frontiers in European Research*, Cheltenham, UK and Northampton, MA, USA: Edward Elgar.

Johansson, A.W. (1997), 'Att förstå rådgivning till småföretagare' ('To understand giving advice to small business people'), Doctoral dissertation, Lund University.

Johansson, A.W. (2004a), 'Consulting as story-making', *Journal of Management Development*, **23**(4), 339–54.

Johansson, A.W. (2004b), 'Narrating the entrepreneur', *International Small Business Journal*, **22**(3), 273–93.

Johansson, A.W. (2008a), 'Nätverk och resurscentra som arena för entreprenörskap' ('Networks and resource centra as arena for entrepreneurship'), in K. Berglund and A.W. Johansson (eds), *Arenor för entreprenörskap* (*Arenas for Entrepreneurship*), Örebro: Forum för Småföretagsforskning.

Johansson, A.W. (2008b), 'Regional development by means of broadened entrepreneurship', in B. Johannisson and Å. Lindholm Dahlstrand (eds), *Bridging the Functional and Territorial Views on Regional Entrepreneurship and Development*, Örebro: Swedish Foundation for Small Business Research.

Johansson, M. and J. Kociatkiewicz (2008), 'Beyond bread and circuses: city festivals and transformation of urban space', paper presented at SCOS, Manchester, 1–4 July.

Johansson, U. (1998), *Om ansvar-ansvarsföreställningar och deras betydelse för den organisatoriska verkligheten* (*About Responsibility and Notions of Responsibility and their Importance for the Organizational Reality*), Lund: Lund University Press.

Johnstone, H. and D. Lionais (2004), 'Depleted communities and community business entrepreneurship: revaluing space through place', *Entrepreneurship and Regional Development*, **16**, May, 217–33.

Jones, C. and A. Spicer (2005), 'The sublime object of entrepreneurship', *Organization*, **12**(2), 223–46.

Jones, C. and A. Spicer (2009), *Unmasking the Entrepreneur*, Cheltenham, UK and Northampton, MA, USA: Edward Elgar.

Jones, J. (2008), 'Dalhallas betydelse som 'besöksmotor' för Siljansregionen – en förstudie' ('The importance of Dalhalla as a 'visiting engine' for the Siljan region – a pilot study'), press release, 26 November, available at http://www.regionsiljan.se/_webdoc/Data/6/Files/27/Pressmeddelande%2008-11-26.pdf (accessed 6 April 2009).

Karlsson, C., B. Johansson and R.R. Stough (2001), 'Introduction: endogenous regional growth and politics', in B. Johansson, C. Karlsson and R.R. Stough (eds), *Theories of Endogenous Regional Growth*, Berlin, Heidelberg and New York: Springer-Verlag.

Kelly, K. (1998), *New Rules for the New Economy*, New York: Viking.

Kihlström S. (2004), 'Bakgrund: styrelsen och Wroblewski rejält oense' ('Background: the board and Wroblewski disagreeing a lot'), *Dagens Nyheter*, 9 January.

Kirzner, I.M. (1973), *Competition and Entrepreneurship*, Chicago, IL: University of Chicago Press.

Kirzner, I.M. (1979), *Perception, Opportunity, and Profit*, Chicago, IL: University of Chicago Press.

Kociatkiewicz, J. (2000), 'Dreams of time, times of dreams: stories of creation from roleplaying game sessions', *Studies in Culture, Organizations and Societies*, **6**, 71–86.

Koestler, A. (1964), *The Act of Creation*, London: Hutchinson.

Kurvinen, J. (2009), 'Imitation och omtolkning. Entreprenörers identi-fieringsprocesser ur ett genusperspektiv' ('Imitation and reintrepre-tation. The entrepreneurial identification processes from a gender perspective'), Doctoral dissertation, Handelshögskolan, Umeå University.

Laitinen, A. (2002), 'Charles Taylor and Paul Ricoeur on self-interpretations and narrative identity', in R. Huttunen, H. Heikkinen and L. Syrjälä (eds), *Narrative Research: Voices of Teachers and Philosophers*. Jyväskylä: SoPhi.

Lambrecht, J. and F. Pirnay (2005), 'An evaluation of public support measures for private external consultancies to SMEs in the Walloon Region of Belgium', *Entrepreneurship and Regional Development*, **17**(2), 89–109.

Landström, H. (1999), *Entreprenörskapets rötter* (*The Roots of Entrepreneurship*). Lund: Studentlitteratur.

Larson, A. and J.A. Starr (1993), 'A network model of organization for-mation', *Entrepreneurship Theory and Practice*, **17**(2), 5–15.

Larsson Segerlind, T. (2009), 'Team entrepreneurship. A process analysis of the venture team roles in relation to the innovation process', Doctoral dissertation, School of Business: Stockholm University.

Latour, B. (1996), *Aramis or the Love of Technology*, Cambridge, MA: Harvard University Press.

Latour, B. (1998), *Artefaktens återkomst. Ett möte mellan organisationste-ori och tingens sociologi* (*The Return of the Artefact. A Meeting between Organizational Theory and the Sociology of Things*), Göteborg: Nerenius & Santérus AB.

Leana, C.R. and H.J. van Buren (1999), 'Organizational social capital and employment practices', *Academy of Management Review*, **24**, 538–54.

Lee, N. (2001), *Childhood and Society: Growing up in an Age of Uncertainty*, Maidenhead: Open University Press.

Lefebvre, H. (1991), *The Production of Space*, trans. Norman Kemp Smith, New York: St Martin's Press.

Lepinay, V.-A. (2007), 'Economy of the germ: capital accumulation and vibration', *Economy and Society*, **36**(4), 526–48.

Lévi-Strauss, C. (1945/1963), 'Structural analysis in lingustics and in anthropology', in *Structural Anthropology*, London: Penguin Press.

Liedman, S.-E. (2002), *Ett oändligt äventyr* (*An Eternal Adventure*), Stockholm: Albert Bonniers Förlag.

Lif, A. (2008), *Mångalen – Genberg och de tusen musketörerna* (*Moonstruck – Genberg and the Thousand Musketeers*), Västerås: Sportförlaget.

Lindgren, M. and J. Packendorff (2004), 'A project-based view of entre-preneurship: towards action-orientation, seriality and collectivity', in

C. Steyaert and D. Hjorth (eds), *New Movements in Entrepreneurship*, Cheltenham, UK and Northampton, MA, USA: Edward Elgar.

Lindqvist, K. (2007a), 'Eros and Apollo: The curator as pas-de-deux leader', in P. Guillet de Monthoux, C. Gustafsson and S.-E. Sjöstrand (eds), *Aesthetic Leadership: Managing Fields of Flow in Art and Business*, Basingstoke: Palgrave Macmillan.

Lindqvist, K. (2007b), 'Politik och konst – några ekonomiska konsekvenser' ('Politics and arts – some economic consequences'), in B. Ayata (ed.), *Kulturekonomi. Konsten att fånga osynliga värden* (*Cultural Economy. The Art of Catching Invisible Values*), Lund: Studentlitteratur.

Lipset, S.M. (2000), 'Values and Entrepreneurship in the Americas', in R. Swedberg (ed.), *Entrepreneurship: The Social Science View*, Oxford: Oxford University Press.

Lowe, A. (1995), 'The basic social processes of entrepreneurial innovation', *International Journal of Entrepreneurial Behavior and Research*, **1**(2), 54–76.

MacKinnon, D., A. Cumbers and K. Chapman (2002), 'Learning, innovation and regional development: a critical appraisal of recent debates', *Progress in Human Geography*, **26**(3), 293–311.

Maravellias, C. (2003), 'Post-bureaucracy: control through professional freedom', *Journal of Organizational Change Management*, **16**(5), 547–66.

March, J.G. (1976), 'The technology of foolishness', in J.G. March and J.P. Olsen (eds), *Ambiguity and Choice in Organizations*, Oslo: Universitetsförlaget.

Marshall, A. (1898), *Principles of Economics*, London: Macmillan.

Marzec, R.P. (2001), 'The War Machine and Capitalism', *Rhizomes*, **3**, Fall, available at http://www.rhizomes.net/issued/marzec/UnitedFrameset-14-html (accessed 10 August 2009).

Massey, D. (1995), 'The conceptualization of place', in D. Massey and P. Jess (eds), *A Place in the World*, Oxford: Oxford University Press.

McCarthy, A., F. Schoorman and A. Cooper (1993), 'Reinvestment decisions by entrepreneurs: rational decision-making or escalation of commitment', *Journal of Business Venturing*, **8**(1), 9–24.

Merrifield, A. (2000), 'Henri Lefebvre: a socialist in space', in M. Crang and N. Thrift (eds), *Thinking Space*, London and New York: Routledge.

Meyer, J.W. and B. Rowan (1977), 'Institutional organizations: formal structure as myth and ceremony', *American Journal of Sociology*, **83**(2), 340–63.

Miller, J. (1993/2000), *The Passion of Michel Foucault*, Cambridge, MA: Harvard University Press.

Ministry of Enterprise, Energy and Communication/Ministry of Education

(2004), *Innovative Sweden: A Strategy for Growth through Renewal*, Ds 2004:36, October, Stockholm: Ministry of Enterprise, Energy and Communications/Ministry of Education.

Mintzberg, H. (1973), *The Nature of Managerial Work*, New York: Harper & Row.

Molander, B. (1996), *Kunskap i handling* (*Knowledge in Action*), Göteborg: Daidalos.

Mossetto, G. (1993), *Aesthetics and Economics*, Dordrecht: Kluwer.

Motte, A. and F. Cajori (1934), *Sir Isaac Newton's Mathematical Principles of Natural Philosophy and his System of the World*, Berkeley, CA: University of California Press.

Mumby, D.K. (2005), 'Theorizing resistance in organization studies', *Management Communication Quarterly*, **19**(1), 19–44.

Nahapiet, J. and S. Ghoshal (1998), 'Social capital, intellectual capital and the organizational advantage', *Academy of Management Review*, **23**, 242–67.

Nicholson, L. and A.R. Anderson (2005), 'News and nuances of the entrepreneurial myth and metaphor: linguistic games in entrepreneurial sense-making and sense-giving', *Entrepreneurship Theory and Practice*, **29**(2), 153–72.

Nilsson, P. (1997), 'Business counselling services directed towards female entrepreneurs: some legitimacy dilemmas', *Entrepreneurship and Regional Development*, **9**(1), 239–58.

Nilsson, P. (2002), 'Reflektioner kring IT-entreprenörerns hjältespegel' ('Reflections around the hero mirror of the IT entrepreneur'), in C. Holmquist and E. Sundin (eds), *Företagerskan. Om Kvinnor och entre-prenörskap* (*The entrepreneuse. Women's Entrepreneurship*), Stockholm: SNS Förlag.

Nilsson, S.-E. (2006), 'Tecknande av aktier i Dalhalla Arena AB' ('Signed-up shares in Dalhalla Arena AB'), dated 20 September, available at http://www.mora.se/ArticlePages/200609/19/20060919173628_UK895/20060919173628_UK895.dbp.html (accessed 6 April 2009).

Nord, W.R. (2003), 'Core group theory and the emancipation agenda', *Journal of Organizational Change Management*, **16**(6), 684–90.

Normann, R. (2001), *Reframing Business: When the Map Changes the Landscape*, New York: John Wiley & Sons.

NUTEK (1996), *Affärsrådgivare för kvinnor. Att främja kvinnors före-tagande – Slutrapport* (*Women Business Advisors. Supporting Female Entrepreneurship – Final Report*), 1996: 55, Stockholm: NUTEK Förlag.

NUTEK (1998a), *Affärsrådgivare för kvinnor. Utvärdering del 1. Förutsättningar för Förändring* (*Women Business Advisors. Assessment Part I. Possibilities for Change*), 1998:4, Stockholm: NUTEK Förlag.

NUTEK (1998b), *Affärsrådgivare för kvinnor. Utvärdering del 2. Identitetsskapande inom lokalt näringslivsarbete* (*Women Business Advisors – Assessment Part II. Creating Identity in Local Business Work*), (1998:5), Stockholm: NUTEK Förlag.

NUTEK (2004), *Tio frågor och svar om samverkan i småföretag* (*Ten Questions and Answers about Cooperation in Small Firms*), Stockholm: NUTEK Förlag.

NUTEK (2006), *Verket för näringslivsutvecklings föreskrifter om statsbidrag till kooperativ utveckling* (*NUTEK's Directions to Public Support of Cooperative Development*), 2006:1, Stockholm: NUTEK Förlag.

Nyström, L. (2002), 'Det tredje Sverige' ('The third Sweden'), in P. Aronsson and B. Johannisson (eds), *Entreprenörskapets dynamik och regionala förankring* (*The Dynamism and Regional Roots of Entrepreneurship*), Växjö: Växjö University Press.

O'Connor, A. (2009), 'Enterprise, education and economic development: an exploration of entrepreneurship's economic function in the Australian government's education policy', Doctoral dissertation, Victoria, Australia: Swinburne University of Technology.

Ogbonna, E. and L. Harris (2001), 'The founder's legacy: hangover or inheritance?' *British Journal of Management*, **12**(1), 13–31.

Ogbor, J.O. (2000), 'Mythicizing and reification in entrepreneurial discourse: Ideology-critique of entrepreneurial studies', *Journal of Management Studies*, **37**(5), 605–35.

Oinas, P. (1999), 'Voices and silences: the problem of access to embeddedness', *Geoforum*, **30**, 351–61.

Olaison, L. (2008), 'An emerging legend of a Kosovar heroine: narrating female entrepreneurs', in M. Kostera (ed.), *Organizational Olympians: Heroes, Heroines and Villains of Organizational Myths*, London: Palgrave.

Osborne, D. and T. Gaebler (1992), *Reinventing Government: How the Entrepreneurial Spirit is Transforming the Public Sector*, Reading, MA: Addison-Wesley.

Osborne, D. and P. Plastrik (1997), *Banishing Bureaucracy: The Five Strategies for Reinventing Government*, Reading, MA: Addison Wesley.

Osborne, P. (1996), 'Gender as Performance', *A Critical Sense: Interviews with Intellectuals*, London: Routledge.

Ostgaard, T.A. and S. Birley (1994), 'Personal networks and firm competitive strategy: a strategic or coincidental match?' *Journal of Business Venturing*, **9**, 281–305.

Painter, J. (1998), 'Entrepreneurs are made, not born: learning and urban regimes in the production of entrepreneurial cities', in T. Hall and P. Hubbard (eds), *The Entrepreneurial City*, Chichester, John Wiley & Sons.

Parkinson, C. and C. Howorth (2008), 'The language of social entrepreneurs', *Entrepreneurship and Regional Development*, **20**(May), 285–309.

Pereira, A.A. (2004), 'State entrepreneurship and regional development: Singapore's industrial parks in Batam and Suzhou', *Entrepreneurship and Regional Development*, **16**(March), 129–44.

Perren, L. and P.L. Jennings (2005), 'Government discourses on entrepreneurship: issues of legitimization, subjugation, and power', *Entrepreneurship Theory and Practice*, **29**(2), 173–84.

Persson, A. (2003), 'Det blåser snåla vindar i Tensta' ('Skimpy winds are blowing in Tensta'), *Dagens Nyheter*, 15 November.

Petersen, A., I. Barns, J. Dudley and P. Harris (1999), *Poststructuralism, Citizenship and Social Policy*, London: Routledge.

Pettersson, K. (2002), 'Företagande män och osynliggjorda kvinnor' ('Business venturing men and invisible women'), Doctoral dissertation, Uppsala University.

Philo, C. (2000), 'Foucault's geography', in M. Crang and N. Thrift (eds), *Thinking Space*, London and New York: Routledge.

Piore, M.J. and C.F. Sabel (1984), *The Second Industrial Divide: Possibilities for Prosperity*, New York: Basic Books.

Pitt, M. (1998), 'A tale of two gladiators: "reading" entrepreneurs as texts', *Organization Studies*, **19**(3), 387–415.

Polanyi, M. (1966), *The Tacit Dimension*, London: Routledge & Kegan Paul.

Polkinghorne, D.E. (1988), *Narrative Knowing and the Human Sciences*, New York: State References.

Porter, M. (1990), *The Competitive Advantage of Nation*, New York: The Free Press.

Porter, M. (1998), 'The Adam Smith address: location, clusters, and the "new" microeconomics of competition', *Business Economics*, January, 7–13.

Portes, A. and J. Sensenbrenner (1993), 'Embeddedness and immigration: notes on the social determinants', *American Journal of Sociology*, **98**, 1320–50.

Powel, W. and P. DiMaggio (eds) (1991), *The New Institutionalism in Organizational Analysis*, Chicago, IL: University of Chicago Press.

Prout, A. and A. James (1997/2008), 'A new paradigm for the sociology of childhood? Prevenance, promise and problems', in A. James and A. Prout (eds), *Constructing and Reconstructing Childhood. Contemporary Issues in the Sociological Study of Childhood*, London: RoutledgeFalmer.

Pyke, F. and W. Sengenberger (eds) (1992), *Industrial Districts and Local Economic Regeneration*, Geneva: International Institute of Labour Studies.

Raz, J. (1999), *Emerging Reason. On the Theory of Value and Action*, Oxford: Oxford University Press.

Redding, G. (1993), *The Spirit of Chinese Capitalism*, Berlin: Walter de Gruyter.

Rehn, A. and S. Taalas (2004), 'Acquaintances and connections: *blat*, the Soviet Union, and mundane entrepreneurship', *Entrepreneurship and Regional Development*, **16**(May), 235–50.

Relph, E. (1976), *Place and Placelessness*, London: Pion.

Renstig, M., S. Fölster and J. Frycklund (2008), 'Anställningstrygghet stoppar kvinnorna' ('Employment security is stopping the women'), *Dagens Nyheter*, 27 February.

Reynolds, P. (2007), Personal communication.

Ricoeur, P. (1981), 'The model of the text: meaningful action considered as text', in J.B. Thompson (ed. and transl.), *Hermeneutics and the Human Science,* Cambridge: Cambridge University Press.

Ricoeur, P. (1984), *Time and Narrative Vol 1*, Chicago, IL: University of Chicago Press.

Robson, P.J.A. and R.J. Bennet (2000), 'The use and impact of business advice by SMEs in Britain: an empirical assessment using logit and ordered logit models', *Applied Economics*, **32**(13), 1675–89.

Rose, N. (1999), *Powers of Freedom: Reframing Political Thought*, Cambridge: Cambridge University.

Rylander, D. (2004), 'Nätverkan och regional utveckling' ('Networking and regional development'), Department of Geography, University of Gothenburg.

Rämö, H. (2000), 'The nexus of time and place in economical operations', Doctoral dissertation, Stockholm School of Business, Stockholm University.

Rämö, H. (2004), 'Spatio-temporal notions and organized environmental issues: an axiology of action', *Organization*, **11**(6), 849–72.

Sack, R. (1997), *Homo Geographicus*, Baltimore, MD: Johns Hopkins University Press.

Sahlin-Andersson, K. and G. Sévon (2003), 'Imitation and identification as performatives', in B. Czarniawska and G. Sévon (eds), *The Northern Lights: Organization Theory in Scandinavia*, Oslo: Liber.

Sanner, L. (1997), 'Trust between entrepreneurs and external actors: sensemaking in organizing new business ventures', Doctoral dissertation, Department of Business Administration: Uppsala University.

Sarasvathy, S.D. (2001), 'Causation and effectuation: toward a theoretical shift from economic inevitability to entrepreneurial contingency', *Academy of Management Review*, **26**(2), 243–63.

Sarasvathy, S.D. (2004), 'The questions we ask and the questions we care about: reformulating some problems in entrepreneurship research', *Journal of Business Venturing*, **19**(5), 707–17.

Saussure, F. (1916/1977), *Course in General Linguistics*, Glasgow: Fontana/ Collins.

Schein, E. (1991), 'The role of the founder in the creation of organizational culture', in P. Frost, L. Moore, M. Louis, C. Lundberg and J. Martin (eds), *Reframing Organizational Culture*, London: Sage.

Schollhammer, H. (1982), 'Internal corporate entrepreneurship', in C. Kent, D. Sexton and K. Vesper (eds), *Encyclopedia of Entrepreneneurship*, Englewood Cliffs, NJ: Prentice Hall.

Schulyer, G. (1998), 'Social entrepreneurship: profit as a means, not an end', Kauffman Center for Entrepreneurial Leadership Clearinghouse on Entrepreneurial Education (CELCEE), www.celcee.edu/products/ digest/Dig98-7html (accessed 30 January 2006).

Schumpeter, J. (1934/2000), *The Theory of Economic Development*, New Brunswick, NJ, USA and London, UK: Transaction Publishers.

Schumpeter, J.A. (1934/1968), *The Theory of Economic Development*, 2nd edn, Cambridge MA: Harvard University Press.

Schumpeter, J. (1939), *Business Cycles*, New York, Toronto, London: McGraw-Hill Book Company.

Schumpeter, J. (1942/1950), *Capitalism, Socialism and Democracy*, New York: Harper Publishing.

Schumpeter, J. (1947), 'The creative response in economic history', *Journal of Economic History*, **7**(2), 149–59.

Shane, S. (2003), *A General Theory of Entrepreneurship*, Cheltenham, UK and Northampton, MA, USA: Edward Elgar.

Shane, S. and S. Venkataraman, (2000), 'The promise of entrepreneurship as a field of research', *Academy of Management Review*, **25**(1), 217–26.

Shaw, E. and S. Conway (2000), 'Networking and the small firm', in S. Carter and D. Jones-Evans (eds), *Enterprise and Small Business: Principles, Practice and Policy*, Upper Saddle River, NJ: Prentice Hall.

Smith, R. and A.R. Anderson (2004), 'The devil is in the *e-tale*: forms and structures in the entrepreneurial narratives', in D. Hjorth and C. Steyaert (eds), *Narrative and Discursive Approaches in Entrepreneurship*, Cheltenham, UK and Northampton, MA, USA: Edward Elgar.

Smålandsposten (SMP) (2008a), 'Alla vill väl starta eget, eller?' ('Everybody wants to start a firm of their own, don't they?'), 30 May.

Smålandsposten (SMP) (200b), 'Kvinnliga ambassadörer är redo' ('Women ambassadors are ready'), 19 September.

Sørensen, B.M. (2008), '"Behold, I am making all things new": The entrepreneur as savior in the age of creativity', *Scandinavian Journal of Management*, **24**(2), 85–93.

Southern, A. (2000), 'The social and cultural world of enterprise', in S. Carter and D. Jones-Evans (eds), *Enterprise and Small Business. Principles, Practice and Policy*, Upper Saddle River, NJ: Prentice Hall.

Spinosa, C., F. Flores and H.L. Dreyfus (1997), *Disclosing New Worlds: Entrepreneurship, Democratic Action, and the Cultivation of Solidarity*, Cambridge, MA and London: MIT Press.

Stevenson, H.H. and J.C. Jarillo (1990), 'A paradigm of entrepreneurship: entrepreneurial management', *Strategic Management Journal*, **11**, 17–27.

Steyaert, C. (1997), 'A qualitative methodology for process studies of entrepreneurship', *International Studies of Management and Organisation*, **27**(3), 13–33.

Steyaert, C. (2004), 'The prosaics of entrepreneurship: certain local knowledge through stories', in D. Hjorth and C. Steyaert (eds), *Narrative and Discursive Approaches to Entrepreneurship*, Cheltenham, UK and Northampton, MA, USA: Edward Elgar.

Steyaert, C. (2007), '"Entrepreneuring" as a conceptual attractor? A review of process theories in 20 years of entrepreneurship studies', *Entrepreneurship and Regional Development*, **19**(6), 453–77.

Steyaert, C. and D. Hjorth, D. (eds) (2003), *New Movements in Entrepreneurship*, Cheltenham, UK and Northampton, MA, USA: Edward Elgar.

Steyaert, C. and D. Hjorth (eds) (2006), *Entrepreneurship as Social Change*, Cheltenham, UK and Northampton, MA, USA: Edward Elgar.

Steyaert, C. and J. Katz (2004), 'Reclaiming the space of entrepreneurship in society: geographical, discursive and social dimensions', *Entrepreneurship and Regional Development*, Special Issue, *Entrepreneurship in Society: Exploring and Theorizing New Forms and Practices of Entrepreneurship*, **16**(May), 179–96.

Stryjan, Y. (2004), 'Balancing central support and local embeddedness: the Swedish cooperative development system', paper presented at the ICA Research Committee Conference in Valencia/Segorbe, May.

Styhre, A. (2008a), 'Critical management studies and the agelaste ethos', *Journal of Organizational Change Management*, **21**(1), 92–106.

Styhre, A. (2008b), 'Transduction and entrepreneurship: a biophilosophical image of the entrepreneur', *Scandinavian Journal of Management*, **24**(2), 103–12.

Sundbo, J. (1998), *The Theory of Innovation: Entrepreneurs, Technology and Strategy*, Cheltenham, UK and Lyme, NH, USA: Edward Elgar.

Sunesson, S (1987/2003), *Inledning till Michel Foucault*, Övervakning och Straff (*Introduction to Michel Foucault*, Discipline and Punish), Lund: Arkiv förlag.

Swedish Ministry of Foreign Affairs (2008), 'Topphemligt besök av Carl Bildt när ambassaden i Kabul öppnafes' ('Top secret visit by Carl Bildt when the embassy in Kabul was opened'), available at: http://www.regeringen.se/sb/d/10036/a/114794 (accessed 3 November 2008).

Szarka, J. (1990), 'Networking and small firms', *International Small Business Journal*, **8**(2), 10–22.

Tarde, G. (1903), *The Laws of Imitation*, New York: Henry Holt & Company.

Thompson, J., G. Alvy and A. Lees (2000), 'Social entrepreneurship: a new look at the people and the potential', *Management Decision*, **38**(5), 328–38.

Thrift, N.J. (1996), *Spatial Formations*, London, UK and Thousand Oaks, CA: Sage.

Trädgårdh, L. (2000), 'Utopin om den sociala ekonomin' ('The utopia about the social economy'), in F. Wijkström and T. Ronstad (eds), *Om kooperation & social ekonomi. Röster i ett nordiskt samtal. Kooperativ Årsbok 2000 (About Cooperation and Social Economy. Voices in a Nordic Conversation. Kooperativ Annual 2000)*, Stockholm: Föreningen kooperativa studier.

Tuan, Y.-F. (1974), *Topophilia: A Study of Environmental Perception, Attitudes, and Values*, Englewood Cliffs, NJ: Prentice-Hall.

Tuan, Y.-F. (1977), *Space and Place: The Perspective of Experience*, Minneapolis, MN, USA and London, UK: University of Minnesota Press.

van de Ven, A. (1986), 'Central problems in the management of innovation', *Management Science*, 32, 590–607.

VA-rapport (2005), *Lärare om företagsamhet (Teachers on enterprise)*, Stockholm: Vetenskap & Allmänhet.

Venkataraman, S. (1997), 'The distinctive domain of entrepreneurship research', in J.A. Katz (ed.), *Advances in Entrepreneurship, Firm Emergence and Growth*, vol. 3, Greenwich, CT: JAI Press.

von Wright, G.M. (1971), *Explanation and Understanding*, London: Routledge & Kegan Paul.

Vygotskij, L.S. (1995), *Fantasi och kreativitet i barndomen (Imagination and Creativity in Childhood)* (original title: *Voobrazenie i tvorcestvo v detskom vozraste*), Göteborg: Daidalos.

Weick, K.E. (1989), 'Theory construction as disciplined imagination', *Academy of Management Review*, **14**(4), 516–31.

Weick, K.E. (1995), *Sensemaking in Organizations*, Thousand Oaks, CA: Sage.

Weiskopf, R. and C. Steyaert (2009), 'Metamorphoses in entrepreneurship studies: towards an affirmative politics of entrepreneuring', in D. Hjorth and C. Steyaert (eds), *The Politics and Aesthetics of Entrepreneurship*, Cheltenham, UK and Northampton, MA, USA: Edward Elgar.

West, C. and D.H. Zimmerman (1987), 'Doing gender', *Gender and Society*, **1**(2), June, 125–51.

Westerdahl, S. (2001), *Business and Community*, Gothenburg: Bokförlaget BAS.

Westlund, H. (2001), 'Social economy and employment: The case of Sweden', paper presented at the Uddevalla Symposium 2001: Regional Economies in Transition, 14–16 June, Vänersborg, Sweden.

Wigren, C. and L. Melin (2009), 'Fostering a regional innovation system: looking into the power of policy-making', in D. Hjorth and C. Steyaert (eds), *The Politics and Aesthetics*, Cheltenham, UK and Northampton, MA, USA: Edward Elgar.

Winnicott, D.W. (1971), *Playing and Reality*, Harmondsworth: Penguin Books.

Winter, S.G. (2006), 'Toward a neo-Schumpeterian theory of the firm', *Industrial and Corporate Change*, **15**(1), 125–41.

Wittgenstein, L. (1958), *Philosophical Investigations*, Oxford: Basil Blackwell.

Woolgar, S. (1991), 'Configuring the user: the case of usability trials', in J. Law (ed.), *A Sociology of Monsters: Essays on Power, Technology, and Domination*, New York: Routledge.

Ylinenpää, H. (2008), 'Entrepreneurship and innovation systems: towards a development of the ERIS/IRIS concept', in B. Johannisson and Å. Lindholm Dahlstrand (eds), *Bridging the Functional and Territorial Views on Regional Entrepreneurship and Development*, Örebro: Swedish Foundation for Small Business Research.

Yu, T. (1999), 'Bringing entrepreneurship back in: explaining the industrial dynamics of Hong Kong with special reference to the textile and garment industry', *International Journal of Entrepreneurial Behaviour and Research*, **5**(5), 235–50.

Yu, T. (2001), 'The Chinese family business as a strategic system: an evolutionary Perspective', *International Journal of Entrepreneurial Behaviour and Research*, **7**(1), 22–40.

Zan, L. (2006), *Managerial Rhetoric and Arts Organizations*, Basingstoke: Palgrave Macmillan.

Zelazo, P.D. and S.F. Lourenco (2002), 'Imitation and the dialectic of representation', *Developmental Review*, **23**, 55–78.

Zoller, H.M. and G.T. Fairhurst (2007), 'Resistance leadership: the overlooked potential in critical and leadership studies', *Human Relations*, **60**(9), 1331–60.

Index